Strategic Flexibility

A Management Guide for Changing Times

Kathryn Rudie Harrigan
Columbia University

Lexington Books
D.C. Heath and Company/Lexington, Massachusetts/Toronto

85780

Library of Congress Cataloging in Publication Data

Harrigan, Kathryn Rudie.
  Strategic flexibility.

  Bibliography: p.
  1. Organizational change.   2. Industrial management.
I. Title.
HD58.8.H367   1985   658.4'06   84–40815
ISBN 0–669–10222–9 (alk. paper)
ISBN 0–669–11033–7 (pbk.: alk. paper)

Second printing, December 1985

Published simultaneously in Canada
Printed in the United States of America on acid-free paper
Casebound International Standard Book Number: 0–669–10222–9
Paperbound International Standard Book Number: 0–669–11033–7
Library of Congress Catalog Card Number: 84–40815

Contents

Figures

Tables

Acknowledgments

This collection of essays was made possible through funding for travel, telephone interviews, research assistants, and typing by a grant from the Strategy Research Center, Columbia Business School. I am deeply grateful to the corporations that support the Strategy Research Center, for these funds greatly facilitate our scholarly investigations of strategic-management issues. Earlier funding was provided by grants from the Division of Research, Graduate School of Business Administration, Harvard University; S. Prakash Sethi, the Center for Research in Business and Social Policy; the Office of Sponsored Projects, University of Texas at Dallas; and the Board of Research, Babson College.

I am grateful for the support of my research assistants at Columbia Business School: Nida Backaitis and John Michel (Ph.D. candidates); Holly Wallace, M.B.A. 1983 (of Merrill, Lynch); Elizabeth J. Gordon, M.B.A. 1983 (of Time, Inc., Video Group); John Richardson Thomas, M.B.A. 1983 (of Topaz, Inc.); Mary Ellen Waller, M.B.A. 1982; Stanley Seth, M.B.A. 1983; Paul A. Gelburd, M.B.A. 1982 (of Booz-Allen & Hamilton); Kris Ishibashi, M.B.A. 1982 (of Metro-North Division, New York Metropolitan Transit Authority); and Kurt Feuerman (Bank of New York). Special thanks are due to Harold Hamman Martin, J.D.-M.B.A. 1982, of Shearman & Sterling, for legal research assistance, and to Carlos Garcia, M.B.A. 1984 (of Pfizer, Inc.) for computer programming.

My students at Columbia have helped me substantially to clarify my understanding of vertical integration and joint-venture strategies. In particular, I thank Dean Hoke Simpson and Dr. James Coakley of Executive Programs for their valuable assistance and research support. I thank the members of the 68th Executive Program in Business Administration and their faculty directors, William H. Newman and David Lewin, for allowing me to present my ideas in that program. My MBA classes have also provided helpful criticisms of these ideas.

The essays are based on two major studies that required vast typing efforts. I received enthusiastic assistance from Dr. Marianne Devanna, the most helpful administrator of the Strategy Research Center's funds, and from Gayle Lane, who managed the financial details of my research grant. Early typing assistance was given by Sally Markham of Harvard University, Jan Manter, Brenda Lumsen, and Victoria DelBono of Babson College; and Linda Chianese, Rhonda Tobin, and Wilma Oakes of the University of Texas at Dallas. Carol Landes and Linda Brodzinski in the Office of Support Services, Columbia University, provided extra helpers—additional typing, transcribing, and telephone assistance—for which I am grateful. Maxine Braiterman, Lisa Lowell, Joy Glazener, and especially Marta Torres typed endless versions of this manuscript while maintaining their sense of humor. Marta managed the herculean task of converting the articles into essays, and the continuity has benefited greatly by her careful attention to detail.

Many colleagues helped me by providing suggestions and comments on pieces of the manuscript at various stages of its development. The articles are reprinted by the generous permission of the journals where scholars of strategic management publish their works. I thank in particular John W. Slocum, Thomas Mahoney, and Janice Beyer *(Academy of Management Journal),* Dan Schendel *(Strategic Management Journal),* James Rozenzweig and Don Hellreigel *(Academy of Management Review),* Robert Lamb *(Journal of Business Strategy),* and their respective boards of anonymous reviewers who have given me many useful suggestions concerning how to improve each article. Thanks also to Ian MacMillan (New York University); John O'Shaughnessy (Columbia University); and Jesse Markham, Norm Berg, and Michael E. Porter (Harvard University). Many corporate executives (who must remain anonymous) commented on the background papers, interview notes, chapters, and supporting materials to provide very useful feedback.

My greatest intellectual debt in this book is owed to William H. Newman, the Samuel H. Bronfman Professor and director of the Strategy Research Center, Emeritus, and Donald C. Hambrick, director of the Strategy Research Center. In addition to supporting my research, Bill and Don have commented extensively on the vertical-integration materials, and have offered thoughtful suggestions on their development. Don has commented on almost every article from which these essays were taken and has shaped them significantly. They have been most enthusiastic in the support of my research projects by virtue of their willingness to read manuscripts, offer ideas, and improve their presentation. The shortcomings in the manuscript are mine alone, but the merits must be shared with my supportive and brilliant colleagues at Columbia.

Foreword

Donald C. Hambrick
Director
Strategy Research Center
Graduate School of Business
Columbia University

T he essence of strategy is in the balancing of focused, concerted commitments on the one hand and resource flexibility on the other. It is a difficult balance to achieve, and one in which flexibility is probably the more often slighted. In part, this imbalance is due to inevitable asset rigidities. But in greater part, the problem is due to mental rigidities: managers do not sufficiently rethink their resource deployments. They too often view their present commitments as an adequate blueprint for the future. Even when they think anew about their businesses, they often lose sight of the immense array of strategic options they have.

In this book, Kathryn Harrigan provides a host of insights for managers who want to view their businesses more flexibly. Among the many ways that managers can rethink their firms, Professor Harrigan has focused on those that can make a major difference: entering markets, exiting markets, vertical integration, and joint ventures. In discussing each, she provides the reader two things: conceptual frameworks and hard data.

Professor Harrigan's conceptual frameworks bring order to otherwise intractable strategic issues. Not only is she able to identify a limited number of key variables that affect each type of strategic choice, but she also discusses a rich array of subchoices. For example, in discussing vertical integration, she goes well beyond a simplistic make-or-buy view. She considers the "breadth" of integrated activities, the "length" of the integrated chain, the degree of product transfers within the chain, and the forms of ownership used to control various links in the chain. In short, Professor Harrigan brings a subtlety to her frameworks which is of great benefit to students of strategy as well as to practicing strategists.

But this is not just a book of frameworks and models. It presents data. Professor Harrigan is an empirical researcher who carefully gathers unique blends of qualitative and quantitative information. This means that the reader is given a rich, clinical view along with more measurable and generalizable patterns.

This book is essential reading for managers who are intent on being analytically and strategically flexible. For scholars, the book represents a compilation of some of the most significant research done on strategy in the first half of the 1980s.

Part I
Strategic Flexibility

T his book is about *strategic flexibility*. It examines firms' abilities to reposition themselves in a market, change their game plans, or dismantle their current strategies when the customers they serve are no longer as attractive as they once were. It is a collection of essays about how competitive strategies often ignore questions of strategic flexibility, with the distasteful result that firms get stuck in an obsolete strategic posture while competitors move on.

What Is Strategic Flexibility?

The barriers to flexibility can be asset-specific, but they are more likely to be mental. Too many managers refuse to face the ugly reality that they are in a sick business or that their firm's strategic posture is simply wrong. Even when it comes to phasing out their no-longer-profitable products or product lines, many otherwise well managed companies hang on for too long. The worst offenders are plant or brand managers who recognize the trouble but cannot face giving up their own positions or laying off loyal workers. Thus bad news is kept from top management for as long as possible.

More than half of all U.S. businesses have to run hard today just to stay in place in terms of return on investment, profit margins, and market share. Consequently, there are now a great many managers who must find ways to run a troubled business successfully. For some, the problem is short run, the result of a tough and lingering recession that has increased competition and slowed sales. For many other companies, however, recession only heightens a long-term fact of life for the business: slow or no growth because of foreign competition, technological changes, or resource scarcities. Many of the chapters contained herein should be of interest to managers of such businesses.

The chapters provide both conceptual frameworks and statistical tests of their propositions. This structure permits managers to skip over the

Adapted from an article that originally appeared in *Academy of Management Review*, July 1983, by permission of the publisher, the Academy of Management.

scientific tests that support each chapter's arguments. (Strategic-planning professionals will find the data sources and models in the technical appendixes of interest.) The topics are developed in a way that builds toward a discussion of how to overcome *exit barriers*, those forces that hamper strategic flexibility. To prepare for that discussion, a foundation is laid by introducing some misnomers; prevailing wisdoms are reviewed and refuted in light of evidence to be presented in a later section.

Getting into the Game

In chapter 1, the old concept of *entry barriers* is updated to take into account changing structural traits and competitive dynamics. Although it may be true that within some older industries, where products have become increasingly commoditylike and no firms can find an effective way to differentiate their products in the minds of consumers (if not physically), traditional entry barriers may still apply. Nevertheless, the question of strategic self-renewal still looms: "What will you do for an encore? After the firm has paid the price of admission, then what?"

Entry barriers are merely the price of admission. There are timing questions concerning entry to address as well. For example, in some industries, there is an advantage to early entry *(first-mover advantages)* due to the standard-setting opportunities of pioneering. But there may be greater benefits to entering later (piggybacking) after others have taken the risks and developed primary demand for the firms that follow.

If a game moves so quickly that there is less tolerance for error, then perhaps the *true* barriers to entry are in the systems, management, and people. If a wrong control system emphasizes wrong targets, then firms will have the wrong means of mobilizing resources.

New measures of entry barriers are proposed and tested in chapter 1 because traditional ones seemed inadequate in a sample of mature industries. Entry opportunities are found to be most attractive for fringe firms where labor-to-capital ratios are high and excess capacity is low.

Occupying a Niche

Chapter 2 discusses how firms place themselves into *strategic groups* in terms of which customers they will serve and how they will compete. Special emphasis is given to the notion of *guerrilla strategies*—the competitive approach of the underdog—because there can be only one leader per industry.

The guerrilla-warfare framework is illustrated using examples of underdog competitors from industries of varying maturities. Guerrilla strategies are found to be most effective where products can be differentiated and markets can be segmented. The keys to effective guerrilla strategies lie in recognizing the depth of competitors' commitments to various products (and markets) and moving their attentions to an arena where underdog firms are better prepared to compete.

A methodology for analyzing strategies groups appears in appendix 2A. Readers seeking only an understanding of the conceptual framework without the statistical evidence can skip the discussion of clustering techniques in this appendix.

Remaining Flexible

Barriers to entry (and exit) represent mental baggage that managers carry with them into problem solving. These barriers are the established way of looking for solutions to a problem. They are the traditional excuses for why actions are not undertaken. They are a mind-set that inhibits firms' strategic flexibility.

Managers must ponder questions of greater importance than mere entry if they are to sustain strategic flexibility, especially given the rapidly changing arenas in which firms compete. Confusion concerning competitive responses is exacerbated by rapidly changing customer attributes, including changes in buyer knowledge and hence in customers' switching-cost barriers. Changing technology results in increasing interdependencies between industries that were previously conceptualized as being separate. Changing factor costs, coupled with the information-technology revolution, have made more industries global. Changes of this magnitude require firms to embrace a new way of remaining flexible.

It is difficult to overcome inertia barriers by fostering a new way of thinking in the midst of so much turmoil. The do-nothing solution that seemed so right in the past is a difficult life preserver to sacrifice when one is afloat in the vast, cold ocean. But it is necessary to overcome these mental barriers in order to reposition the firm with ease.

The barriers that permeate firms' cultures, creating a no-can-do atmosphere, prevent people from taking risks and abandoning the mediocre. They exist in managers' outlooks, their way of conceptualizing market and means of competing, their way of giving service. Flexible firms must be willing to hang loose. Being flexible means being willing to create flexible systems wherein people (the differentiating factor) are given autonomy to change their organization and its focus.

For many firms, however, time is running out. Shorter product lives, which blur industry boundaries, must be translated into new ways of doing things, new ways of conceptualizing markets, and new performance standards. This must happen sooner rather than later because the timing advantage to be gained is substantial. Chapter 3 considers the use of joint ventures as one means of coping with the uncertainties created by erratic sales growth and by the globalization of competition. Chapter 3 is also a reminder that innovation within industries characterized by rapid change no longer occurs only in centralized laboratories. The organizations that compete in the 1980s are polycentric in their orientation. To cope with the many sources of new ideas and directions in which firms might advance, a new, flexible approach to organization is needed.

Chapter 3 introduces the temporary organization concept of *transformational teams*. The tasks that strategic transformational teams perform are nonroutine and unlike other project team tasks. Relatively drastic changes in the organization are often required to change direction. Knowledge of how to design and administrate a highly dynamic, professional cadre of task-force integrators and participants will be a desirable managerial skill when industries grow more volatile.

Make-or-Buy Decisions

Chapters 4 and 5 make up the section on strategic inflexibility, as exemplified in intrafirm business unit relationships. The example used is firms' vertical-integration strategies, and the two chapters ponder the reasons that managers are often wed so firmly to a concept that may be inappropriate for their businesses.

It is hard to imagine a better way for a company to grow than by having people work for it as if they were part of the company without having expensive capital investments committed to the work they do. More managers should consider contracting out many tasks performed in house right now.

Vertical integration, the drive to do more and more in house, can lead to frozen assets and illiquidity—both dangerous situations in today's economy. Managers are often lured into making it in house in order to reduce the firm's exposure to risk and uncertainty, but they wind up increasing both because once assets are in place, managers often become inflexible about changing buyer-seller relationships.

Somehow, managers tolerate poor service from sister units that they would never accept from outsiders. Moreover, their businesses become cut off from the stimulus of outside ideas. As the company becomes more of a supplier of its own parts, outside suppliers grow wary of sharing ideas. As a result, managers lose opportunities to cut costs or develop new processes, while their firms' competitors pick up these opportunities.

Contracting out is also helpful in bringing the firm through fast-paced changes in technology by letting the contractors try out new technologies for production while avoiding committing the firm to major investments in making products that change rapidly. IBM has become a master at this strategy in its personal-computers strategy. It lets other companies all over the world help build its computers rather than committing only its own resources to current designs. What a transformation for a firm that once made almost everything in house!

Chapter 4 takes a new look at vertical integration and develops a framework for better make-or-buy decisions. Because the environments in which firms use vertical integration differ, it suggests, many different strategies could be appropriate for coping with firms' needs for a ready supply of raw materials and a ready market for their outputs. The trick lies in matching the best strategy to the competitive (and internal) situation.

For consultants and other interested readers, tests of these propositions are presented in chapter 5. When tested, effective strategic business units (SBUs) were found to make less in house (and firms were engaged in fewer stages of processing) when demand was highly uncertain. Internal transfers—from upstream or to downstream business units—were greater when synergies with adjacent SBUs were substantial. Results suggest that managers must disabuse themselves of misguided ideas concerning vertical integration, lest they sacrifice their firms' strategic flexibility on this dimension, as well.

Results suggest ineffective firms transfer goods and services internally more often under adverse industry conditions. Ineffective firms also perform more tasks in house and engage in longer chains of processing from ultraraw materials to finished goods. Often the firms that owned the vertical business units in question possessed the bargaining power needed to contract advantageously for the goods or services needed, but accepted an overly risky ownership position by producing them instead.

Strategic Exit

When a market has gone sour, managers should not hang on too long. Doing so creates extreme price volatility as companies fight to maintain volume; highly uneven financial results, as well as a waste of precious management time and talent; the sterilization of assets that could be used productively; and a technology lag from which the company may never recover.

Even when managers know a business unit is in trouble, however, too many hang on, electing to keep a bleeding operation going until the hemorrhage weakens the entire company. Usually their reasons include heavy previous investments (perhaps not yet fully depreciated); big differences between book value and liquidation value; fear of image loss in the business community; emotional attachment to the line of business; feelings of responsibility to employees, suppliers, and customers; and fears of customer reprisals against *other* company products. All these are forms of *exit barriers*.

Chapters 6 and 7 introduce the strong statistical evidence concerning strategic flexibility. The effects of exit barriers on firms' strategic flexibility are detailed within diverse settings, and a managerial tool is introduced to aid resource-allocation decisions. Chapter 6 explains how exit-barrier heights are raised and suggests how managers might cope with high exit barriers. Chapter 7 provides empirical tests of these arguments. Chapter 8 provides managerial guidelines for managing decline.

Results suggest resource immobility can be overcome by helping marginal competitors to exit from volatile businesses. Tactics for doing so can be adapted to the firm's own strategic commitment and to the nature of the business in question, although results indicate that firms that purchase the physical and intangible assets of competitors in order to help them to scale high exit barriers must themselves perceive the business in question to be of sufficiently high strategic importance to justify doing so.

A Comment on Scholarly Research in Strategic Management

Scholars of strategic management follow rules of science in their research, and the care they exert in their research methodologies ensures objectivity in their results. This section of the introduction discusses the research approach embodied in the chapters that follow.

Strategy research needs sophisticated research methodologies because it treats a complex topic. *Business strategy* is a difficult-to-measure construct that can differ from competitor to competitor within the same industry. One approach to understanding business strategy is to investigate why firms within the same industry pursue different strategies to attain similar objectives. Understanding a particular firm's business strategy requires knowledge of its history and corporate strategy, its management team, and its competitive environment. The essence of these relationships can be captured in the results of large-sample studies, but statistical analyses lose (in their error terms) the unexplained variances that could offer richer insights concerning business strategies. For this type of research a hybrid methodology is needed.

Shortcomings of Previous Methodologies

In much existing research, insights gained using fine-grained methodologies (such as case studies) lack generalizability and statistical rigor, but coarse-grained methodologies, such as the Profit Impact of Market Strategies (PIMS) studies, lose the nuances and insights concerning individual firms' strategies that a contingency approach seeks to capture. The finest texture is attained with cases treating individual firms, an expensive methodology (usually based on field studies) that may be difficult to replicate. They have great potential as illuminating vehicles for studying questions of corporate strategy if coupled with *other* data-gathering methodologies and integrative analysis.

The major advantages of such studies include meticulous attention to detail, relevance to business practice, and access to multiple viewpoints. Case studies, if they are done well, capture the complexities of corporate strategy, competition, and uncontrollable environmental factors surrounding strategy formulation. Access to these data depends on corporate interest, however. Because managers seek timely information, their interest (hence cooperation) is likely to be greater if *they* perceive a study to be relevant. Consequently, researchers are denied access if no immediate payoff is apparent.

Field studies are important, for they permit multiple administrative viewpoints within a firm (or diverse competitors' outlooks within an industry) to be represented. But their value alone as research methodologies is limited (as a result of shortcomings in hypothesis generation, replicability, and statistical summaries—all features that are the hallmark of careful and objective research).

Because of the hypotheses tested in the contingency approach to strategic management are complex, and because relationships among industry structure, competitive conduct, and firms' performance are dynamic, researchers that have relied on either single-site case studies or large-database methodologies have missed important aspects of the construct they studied. Contingency approaches to strategy formulation require hybrid designs, incorporating attributes of both fine- and coarse-grained research methodologies. Coarse-textured studies alone do not incorporate intraindustry competitive nuances well; and fine-textured, single-site studies may not be externally valid, particularly if they rely on a maverick firm's strategy and industry aberrations for their generalizations.

By merging these streams of investigation, however, strategy researchers can benefit from the general laws of science regarding validity and statistical inference. They also can isolate the forces salient to an industry that might permit its competitors to attain different performance levels (or the same performance using different strategies).

One could straddle the gulf between these extremes in strategy research by devising a medium-grained methodology wherein the generalizability of case studies is combined with the detail of large-sample methodologies. Because of the exploratory nature of much medium-grained research, however, few studies have exploited opportunities to impose greater rigor on their analyses by incorporating testable hypotheses in their sample designs. The chapters that follow represent the exception.

Hybrid methodologies are characterized by multiple sites, multiple data sources, and intricate sample designs. Such research methodologies need a carefully structured sample design—for example, one permitting the investigator to hold key dimensions of industry settings constant while varying others in order to scrutinize how various firms in each of several types of industries handle the problems of change.

Research designs that sample multiple sites are expensive in time and travel costs. They require robust data-collection designs that could include published materials, field interviews and archival materials, Delphi panels, databases, and researchers' inferences, among others (including survey data). Using several data sources and measures of phenomena provides cross-checks on data accuracy and enrichment of the conclusions researchers might present. Juxtaposing multiple data sources increases the likelihood that convergence will be reached between the subject's perceived environment and competitive position and its actual (or measured) position. Also, using better measures or descriptions of the phenomena studied increases the replicability of researchers' findings concerning them.

In summary, strategy research needs many sources of information to reconstruct firms' business strategies and comprehend their strategy choices. Hypothesis generation and testing benefit from tightly defines research designs and numerous perspectives regarding the variables under study.

For students of corporate strategy, the cross-sectional, time-series nature of multiple research sites and the opportunity to use intricate sample designs suggest that new vistas of intellectual inquiry can be opened by implementing these types of methodologies. Hybrid methodologies can be used to verify academic hypotheses concerning the appropriateness of various strategic responses to industrywide challenges. This avenue of research should be of interest to corporate strategists. The monitoring of competitive histories is an additional tool, which belongs beside scenario analysis in the corporate arsenal of planning tools.

Strategy can be formulated using the seat-of-the-pants, direction-of-the-wind-is-blowing, and other time-honored methods of decision making. Or a methodology can be embraced to generate rigorous criteria for evaluating strategy alternatives. The frameworks presented herein have been tested using the scientific tools of scholarship. Results have been interpreted to suggest managerial implications. Space constraints necessitated abridgement of these chapters. Interested readers are encouraged to consult the original articles.

1
Barriers to Entry Determine Competitive Strategies

E ntering a mature industry is seldom expected to be easy because early entrants have already defined competitive norms. Moreover, *entry barriers,* a key determinant of the attractiveness of an industry, may be relatively high (Porter 1980). Knowledge of the nature of entry barriers can be helpful in suggesting whether the strategic window of market opportunity is open (Abell 1978). (When the window of opportunity closes, an industry loses its attractiveness as a candidate for entry.) The costs of overcoming some entry barriers are so high that they exceed the benefits of successful market penetration (Bain 1956; Bass, Cattin, and Wittink 1978; Ornstein, Weston, and Intriligator 1973; Scherer 1980). Yet firms, if they understand how entry barriers work, may not only pay the price of entry but also invest further to insulate themselves from subsequent penetration by new and sizable firms.

What is needed is a framework for evaluating markets that firms might enter, particularly to avoid wasting resources by trying to overcome a lethal combination of high entry barriers and competitors' resistance. Preentry analysis of these barriers might prevent firms from committing resources to battles that cannot be won cheaply.

This chapter reviews the theory and evidence supporting the existence of entry barriers. It proposes a new way of thinking about them in the context of mature manufacturing industries. Studying entry barriers in mature industries is particularly interesting because these environments are widely assumed to be inhospitable to enter. Yet entry does occur, and firms have prospered by entering the right mature industries. Thus it seems that a discussion of entry barriers would be of interest to outsiders looking in as well as to ongoing firms that seek to keep outsiders out.

Adapted from articles that originally appeared in the *Strategic Management Journal,* December 1981, by permission of the copyright holder and publisher, John Wiley & Sons, Ltd.; and in *Advances in Strategic Management,* Volume 2, 1984, by permission of the publisher, JAI Press Inc.

Entry Barriers Defined

Entry barriers are forces that discourage firms from investing in a particular industry (or niche of an industry) that appears attractive. Because entry barriers can represent substantial disadvantages for many types of potential entrants, they suggest that higher-than-average profits may be difficult to attain, not only as a result of size or timing advantages enjoyed by existing firms but also as a consequence of the willingness of these firms to lower prices to the *limit price* (that is, to the price level that will limit new entry) in order to discourage other firms from trying to enter (Collins and Preston 1969; Gaskin 1971; Spence 1977, 1979). Industries characterized by such high entry barriers have generally been considered to be more profitable in the long run (Bain 1956, 1972; Modigliani 1958; Stingler 1958) and increasingly have become the targets of those large domestic firms or foreign entrants that can afford to overcome such entry deterrents (Gorecki 1976).

High entry barriers are a necessary *but not sufficient* condition for long-term industry profitability. The steel industry, for example, possesses extremely high capital barriers, yet is only marginally profitable. High entry barriers are necessary because without them, plant expansions (a strategic investment that is difficult to reverse) could rapidly outpace demand. The pressures created by underutilized plant capacities precipitate price wars, which may drive out some firms (provided the exit barriers they face are low; see chapters 6, 7, and 8) but will surely ruin profit margins for all (Chamberlain 1962; Fellner 1949; Vernon 1972). The presence of one or more other unattractive traits—high exit barriers, a fragmented structure of nonhomogeneous firms, commoditylike product traits, or other unfavorable characteristics—all reduce an industry's profitability potential, as in the case of steel.

Mature Industries

Mature industries are those that generally grow slowly (less than 10 percent annually in real terms), where demand is frequently inexpansible, and where product traits are generally familiar to consumers or users. Although technology may have been stable within mature industries, process innovations and new technological configurations could compete alongside the relatively aged (and frequently capital-intensive) assets that populate such industries (Utterback & Abernathy 1975). Although competitive structures usually remain stable in mature industries, there have been cases where a newcomer's entry changes the old structure, as in the example of Hanes's pantyhose strategy.

Market Niches

There may be several market segments within an industry where a potential competitor might gain entry. The abilities of some industries to sustain different competitive profiles as a result of the needs of these customers provides the foundations of the notion of *strategic groups* (Caves and Porter 1977; Hunt 1972; Newman 1978; Porter, 1979b; see chapter 2). Note that these various market segments will not be equally desirable to serve because they are not equally profitable, and that they will not constitute a market *niche* unless the firms serving them are *protected* by entry barriers from invasions by outsiders. Thus the market segments that are easiest to enter will be the least attractive. They will offer an initial entry point for firms that cannot afford to invade the *oligopolistic core* (that is, the market niches often dominated by the top four firms).

Strategic Groups

Strategic groups are firms that embrace the same strategies for serving customers; their competitive postures are similar. Although the number of strategic groups is probably fewer in maturity than when the rules for successful competition were yet unestablished, differences among competitors exist and are relevant when evaluating opportunities for entry. (Chapter 2 expands on this idea. It is developed here briefly because it is germane to assessing entry-barrier heights.) The most successful strategic groups are sometimes called *core competitors* because they serve the most attractive core of customers.

Core competitors are generally believed to possess substantial market power as a result of their relatively large market shares. Acting collectively, core competitors can influence prices and behaviors in their markets. Frequently their rate of return is higher than that of *fringe competitors* who are not protected by niche boundaries. Because new entrants are less likely to enjoy scale economies or advantages of experience initially, they are most likely to hover on the less profitable fringes or periphery of industry influence until they can penetrate the core successfully.

Although new firms more frequently occupy the fringes of a competitive landscape, some late entrants do eventually make significant inroads to the core of competition. Among these firms, process innovations are particularly likely to be their ticket to capturing substantial market share. Because firms operating the conventional technologies of a mature industry are more likely to be far down existing experience curves and would have exhausted the cost-saving benefits of many easy operating innovations, new firms seeking entry would be more likely to introduce *radical* process innovations.

The theory of entry barriers (and their implications for managers) is reviewed next. Construction of variables approximating these forces is presented in appendix 1A. These techniques for assessing industry attractiveness may be helpful in identifying acquisition candidates or in assessing whether an industry appears attractive to outsiders.

Entry Barriers in Mature Industries

In mature industries, the most important influences on entry behavior are (1) technical factors and (2) competitive conduct variables. Technological factors include: (1) capital requirements; (2) scale economies; (3) the age of an industry's productive capital (physical plant and equipment); and (4) the balance of labor intensity to capital intensity predominant in an industry's technology. Competitive behavior variables include: (1) previous entries; (2) changes in the dispersion of market shares; (3) industry advertising and research and development (R&D) outlays; and (4) average levels of excess productive capacity.

Firms can influence the heights and natures of some entry barriers, but they cannot affect others (those relating to demand and other exogenous factors such as technological scale) except indirectly by their investments. This distinction is useful in noting how managers could use their knowledge of entry barriers as a competitive weapon.

Technological Factors

Mature industries can be penetrated if entrants obtain superior operating economies through improved technologies. Changes in capital-to-labor ratios and minimum-efficient-scale (MES) factors could provide the necessary edge. Alternatively, the key technological advantages needed for entry may be newer physical plant and equipment, or meeting large capital requirements.

Capital-to-Labor Ratios. Industries where existing firms' technologies are already relatively capital-intensive offer fewer opportunities for fringe firms to enter than those that are labor-intensive. The introduction of labor-saving technologies offers opportunities for fringe firms to attain lower operating costs, as well as licensing revenues for their technological innovations.

Capital Requirements and Technological Scale. Capital requirements have long been identified as entry barriers (Bain 1956), and they were expected to act as entry barriers for fringe firms in the study. The technologies used to produce the goods of various industries each possess scale economies—that is, plant sizes where, if fully utilized, average unit costs of production will be lowest. Potential entrants would be obliged to enter at this large scale in order to avoid incurring significant diseconomies (Scherer 1980). (Moreover, demand would be satisfied by existing plants in a mature industry unless the market is growing rapidly.) Erecting a new plant would be tantamount to challenging the ongoing firms to a price war in a slow growth environment. Accordingly, the potential entrant must assess its willingness and ability to absorb losses from such warfare until its new plant has been established in the industry. Firms with ample capital could afford to buy their way in. Other fringe entrants could not.

Age of Physical Plant. The presence of new physical assets can indicate a recent change in an industry's technologies, or several recent entries. If the vintage capital of an industry is relatively new, it may indicate that an unsettled market opportunity exists. Thus relatively new physical assets may indicate an environment where entry may be more successful.

Although the cost of acquiring assets for manufacturing products that are subject to frequent style changes may be high, the most specialized—hence inflexible—forms of these assets will quickly become vulnerable to obsolescence (Menge 1962). This means some industries characterized by increases in the newness of physical plant (a seemingly attractive attribute) would also be subject to high exit barriers, an unattractive industry trait covered in chapters 6, 7, and 8 (Porter 1976b; Caves and Porter 1977; Harrigan 1981b; 1982; 1983a).

Absolute Cost Strategies. Fringe competitors (or potential entrants) seeking sizable shares of their market are most likely to attain success through process or product innovations. Both are strategies that require fringe firms to overcome entry barriers based on *absolute cost advantages,* a strength originating from access to scarce resources that new entrants cannot develop as inexpensively as earlier entrants did, if at all. Examples include access to distribution channels, ownership of a uranium mine, or other factors that would be more costly to replicate when entering late. This cost advantage would be due in part to inflation and in part to the limited nature of the resources possessed. New entrants would be obliged to spend heavily in order to match the access to scarce raw materials, vertical relationships, or patents that constituted these advantages. Although some experience-curve advantages can be replicated through accelerated spending programs, a few cannot be copied by late entrants, except by acquiring existing firms.

Competitive Behavior Variables

Study of an industry's history often suggests patterns of competitive behavior that act as entry barriers to outsiders. Most prominent among these is evidence that demand is satisfied adequately by ongoing firms.

Previous Entries. Most studies of competition have found that industrywide profitability rises with concentration (Weiss 1963; Qualls 1972; Lustgarten 1975; Wright 1978). Fewer firms, each operating fully utilized plants, earn higher profits than many firms, each with underutilized plants. When there are many recent entries into a mature industry, it means the window of opportunity has closed (not opened) for most firms. Although favorable expectations might encourage entry by firms seeking to pursue a me-too business strategy, the net economic effect of multiple entries into mature industries in previous periods will be a more fragmented market structure. (Fragmented market structures are generally unattractive because they are subject to a greater likelihood of price warfare, especially in industry maturity.)

Thus mature industries where total U.S. demand can be served by only three fully utilized plants, for example, are relatively concentrated and characterized by large capital requirements for entry. New plants in such settings were more likely to be prevalent during early phases of products' evolutions than at industry maturity. If they do appear in maturity, it suggests that scale barriers were not substantial and that recent entrants invested superior high-scale production technologies, thereby raising entry barriers behind them. (Again, the window closes.)

Changes in Market Shares. High variability in market-share changes indicate firms are jostling for position. An outsider should expect competitive conditions to be volatile where market shares change frequently *and substantially.*

Sizable changes in share (relative to average industry market-share changes) suggests that some competitors are pursuing growth objectives. Since market-share points are quite difficult to gain in mature industries, the presence of large relative changes should signal a volatile environment, which discourages entry. Moreover, firms possessing high market shares enjoy relative cost advantages (as a result of the distances they have traveled down the industry's experience curve). New firms entering this type of environment would be less likely to succeed unless they can insulate themselves from these cost pressures by exploiting a technological innovation.

Excess Capacity. Firms that already hold a stake in the health of an industry will erect protective barriers around their markets. If they are highly determined to do so, they may even hold a portion of their own plant capacity *idle* as a warning against entry, thereby signaling their willingness to fight a war of attrition to prevent entry (Esposito and Esposito 1974; MacMillan 1980). Although evidence of recent successful entry by other firms might encourage potential entrants, the presence of several underutilized plants should deter yet another firm from entering. Building capacity in anticipation of demand has been a particularly effective method of shutting out new entrants—as antitrust courts have noted since the ALCOA decision of 1947—and this tactic is still attractive in mature industries. High levels of excess capacity should discourage new entry, especially if history suggests existing firms cut prices to fill their underutilized plants (to lessen the substantial cost disadvantages of excess capacity). Market share will be difficult to capture in such settings, and losses will be high if outsiders try to enter when excess capacity is high.

Advertising Expenditures. Firms can make investments in entry barriers through physical plant, R&D, advertising and other assets to discourage new firms from following them into an industry. They can hold outsiders at bay, largely by dint of pricing pressures but also by virtue of absolute cost advantages. Entry barriers erected through advertising and R&D can be ephemeral, however. Outsiders that possess ample cash reserves could hurdle many such barriers to reap the benefits of early entrants' missionary advertising, product introductions, or engineering breakthroughs. In short, successful performances may attract well-endowed entrants who can scoff at these forms of entry barriers.

Outsiders could enter a mature industry by creating demand for a branded product. If products are not yet commodities but their markets are mature, however, it is likely that buyer loyalties favor incumbent firms. The product is older, consumers are better informed of its attributes, and many ways of differentiating existing products have already been employed. Product innovations could permit entrants to challenge the core of industry competition (and seize large market shares) if their product is truly something new.

Measurement of product differentiation is a problem, however. A useful measure of this critical phenomenon has not yet been developed in industrial economics. Yet the implications for competition within environments where products can be differentiated (as compared with environments where products are commoditylike) are critical when evaluating whether entry should be attempted. Tactics such as branding, advertising, quality variations, and other differentiating maneuvers might be employed effectively to dominate a desirable market segment within noncommodity businesses. But the cost of building a niche is substantial. Firms desiring to do so must be able to withstand the several years of losses required to erode the barriers that successful firms have erected to gain entry. In this context, the advertising expenditures fringe firms must make to overcome the customer loyalties attained by ongoing firms (a variable that *is* measurable, although it is scarcely a global estimate of product differentiation) may approximate the product-differentiation entry barrier.

If high advertising expenditures are indicative of an environment where many different configurations of a product could satisfy customers' needs, they also suggest that some competitors (representing a particular strategic group) have been supported in these expenditures by the market's response. High advertising outlays could indicate a market opportunity for firms that can afford the cost of advertising campaigns. This argument parallels that in Menge (1962), which says that, although the high cost of frequent style changes should reduce the absolute number of competitors and deter entry, the opportunity to satisfy diverse consumers' preferences could permit several firms to occupy modest but specialized market niches.

R&D Expenditures. Research and development outlays offer the first path to penetrating the established market positions of earlier entrants. In order to match patents or licensing advantages enjoyed by leading firms, potential entrants must spend heavily on R&D to obtain new skills or draw on research skills developed for other industries (Kamien and Schwartz 1975; Mueller and Tilton 1969).

Enticements to Enter

Despite formidable entry barriers, firms will try to penetrate mature industries if demand appears attractive or leading firms are enjoying high levels of return on investment (ROI). Rapid growth in demand within otherwise mature markets will attract new entrants.

New firms will be attracted to industries where there appear to be opportunities to enter easily and earn acceptable profits. The more attractive candidates for entry would be those industries where growth in demand is outpacing ongoing competitors' abilities to satisfy it (for example, where excess capacity is low).

If leader firms have enjoyed high rates of productivity and have made effective use of their assets, some spillover or halo effect might be shared by follower firms, given an environment where lead firms' technological improvements and other innovations can be emulated (after a lag) by follower firms. This form of success attracts new entrants.

In summary, high levels of ROI and growth in demand encourage potential entrants to invest, as would high levels of industrywide advertising. Firms could discourage tentative entrants by building additional plants before ongoing plants are fully utilized.

Firms evaluate entry decisions within the context of a national economy as well as in light of competitive dynamics with an industry. Entry is more likely to occur during periods of increasing incorporations and less likely (after a lag) during periods when high numbers of business failures occurred. Rapid increases in economic price levels (signaling higher costs) depress profitability, particularly within those markets where severe price competition makes increasing operating costs more difficult to pass on to customers.

Results of Tests of Entry-Barrier Heights

Tests of the relationships between entry-barrier heights, rates of entry and performance are described in appendix 1A. Results will be discussed.

In table A–1 in the appendix, negative signs indicate forces that acted as entry barriers; the raised letters indicate their levels of statistical significance. These included excess capacity, high technological scale, and entry by other firms (for detailed discussion of these and other results, see Harrigan 1981a). Advertising and R&D expenditures have positive signs, suggesting that differentiable products offer more attractive environments for investment than industries with commoditylike products. These conditions encourage entry by outsiders. The ROI variable turned positive when it was lagged an additional year, suggesting that outsiders cannot respond quickly to favorable signs within mature industries.

Results concerning the excess-capacity variable suggests an interesting dilemma. Failure to operate plants at engineered capacity within industries where scale economies are significant will incur costly diseconomies. Yet the decision to operate those plants near their engineered capacities appears to encourage potential entrants to construct additional plants, which they will then, predictably, set out to fill through price cutting. Depending on expectations concerning future demand for the products of the line of business in question, ongoing firms must elect whether to act in a manner that reduces their own short-term or long-term profitabilities. If the industry in question is a mature one, it would appear that some reduction in attainable profits would be necessary to reduce the potential volatility that could occur if severe excess capacity were allowed to develop through the entry of a new firm.

In table A–2 in the appendix negative signs indicate conditions that *reduce* ROI, and the asterisks indicate levels of statistical significance. Excess capacity and high R&D expenditures are among the forces that reduce an industry's attractiveness to outsiders.

ROI performance appears to be higher where concentration is high and firms' past performances seem to be fair indicators of future ROI, a finding that would be expected within professionally managed firms whose executives are well aware of the importance of well-managed financial statements. Exits by competitors do not appear to help remaining firms' ROIs in this sample. As chapters 6, 7, and 8 suggest, exit is a complex factor, whose effect depends on industry traits as well as on the behavior of the other firms within that industry.

Interpreting Results

Results tend to suggest that technological variables are the more difficult to overcome by firms contemplating entry. All potential entrants must invent a means of hurdling technological barriers when pursuing a new line of business; hence all face similar needs for the capital required to inaugurate productive or distributive assets.

The common aspects of the entry-barrier problem have been illuminated in the results presented. No attention was devoted to the important differences among competitors within an industry after these commonalities have been overcome, however. The common entry barriers may be likened to the α term in the equations of portfolio-valuation models. The risks of assuming a specific strategic posture that may be strongly correlated with the strategic postures of ongoing competitors may be compared with the β coefficient, much as capital-asset pricing models consider covariance among securities.

Following this analogy, results suggest that the *value* or long-term performance of the firm (which is the embodiment of its strategy) reflects the investment decisions the firm has made there in common structural assets, plus investments in unique strategic-posture assets that may (or may not) overlap the strategic postures of competitors.

Entry barriers are of different heights as they protect the strategic postures of firms occupying diverse niches of the market (or serving the same customers using differing postures). If, as results suggest, capital requirements alone are not adequate entry barriers, then ongoing firms might aggressively shift their capital-to-labor ratios in favor of more efficient, technologically innovative assets. Results also suggest frequent improvements in manufacturing technologies (new assets).

Results indicate that conditions of excess capacity and a history of price cutting to fill that capacity are formidable deterrents to entry by outsiders. Thus the generally held theory that price wars and excessive idle capacity offer strong negative signals for potential entrance has been confirmed. Results also suggest that firms could further barricade their portals by investing in R&D effective (1) to increase technological scale economies within their respective industries or (2) to force their industry's structure to evolve in a manner that would make subsequent attempts at entry even more ineffectual.

Adherence to alternative (2) poses an interesting public-policy dilemma. Firms whose R&D efforts force industry standards to be redefined and drive the progress of innovating behaviors will improve the general level of consumer welfare at the cost of ever-steepening entry barriers. Such behavior suggests scenarios of increasing concentration (as marginal entrants are rebuffed by towering entry barriers) where entry can be successfully undertaken by affluent, diversified firms possessing (1) the staying power to survive a protracted war and (2) the perspicacity to offer innovations of sufficient value to force the industry's structure to evolve in a manner that favors them.

Results suggest that potential entrants are less likely to attempt entry where they expect little chance for success. If a market is already suffering excess capacity, firms may be discouraged from entering. This finding suggests that defending firms might adopt a policy of keeping some level of capacity idle by always building first and in the most appropriate locations to preempt would-be competitors (see Dixit 1980; Rao and Rutenberg 1980).

Finally, if, as results suggest, the recent entries by competitors act as high barriers against subsequent entry, then defending firms should give some thought to the selection of those firms they might permit to enter. Some competitors are preferable to others for their different competitive styles (which can be observed by studying their behaviors in other industries). Ongoing firms might control the profitability of their industries by making entry especially difficult for the types of firms they would prefer not to admit.

Excess capacity is a malevolent type of barrier that could explode into price warfare (and create an unpleasant exit barrier later) if it is not controlled properly. A policy of raising customers' expectations for service, variety, and quality may be more appropriate than creating excess capacity as a way to discriminate among candidates for entry. Raising customer expectations moves products further away from commoditylike status. Results suggest this type of defense is more effective in deterring entry than is merely raising capital requirements. Forcing innovation could lead to patented process improvements (cost leadership), savings from scale economies, and other types of entry barriers that are more controllable than those created by excess capacity.

For aspiring entrants, results suggest that firms that are determined to keep new firms out would be more effective in focusing their competitive responses, rather than emphasizing the structural traits of their particular industry. Devoting substantial budgets to maintaining trade relations, improving delivery and customer service, or other forms of marketing may be a more effective means of shielding market niches from entry than others—for example, where industry marketing expenditures have been generally low. If ongoing competitors focus defensive actions on structural traits, informed entrants that recognize this discrepancy and exploit it may ease into an industry without setting off price wars or incurring other significant forms of resistance.

In summary, results suggest firms could use excess capacity (created internally or by admitting new competitors) to discourage potential entrants. Given the difficulties excess capacity might create, however, other factors might do instead. If there are outsiders that possess the needed capital and can afford to make the appropriate investments to enter, ongoing firms would do well to monitor fluctuations in scale economies, capital-to-labor relationships and other competitive investments in order to assess whether the strategic window of opportunity is open too wide.

Appendix 1A
Entry Barriers Determine
Competitive Strategies

Variable Construction

Measures of entry barriers are difficult to construct in a manner that will be useful to strategists contemplating entry. Yet such estimates are crucial in assessing the relative attractiveness of those lines of business strategists hope for their firms might undertake successfully. The *entry* decision in this study considered the likelihood of successfully entering into an industry de novo—that is, as a new competitor, *not* by acquiring an existing industry participant. The dependent variable denotes whether entry occurred within a particular industry in a given year. Entry was deduced by counting the firms listed in Dun & Bradstreet indexes and corroborating that count with *Census of Manufacturers* reports of firms in operation. Entry was indicated as a binary code (where "1" indicated entry occurred).

Table A–3 in the appendix summarizes the traits that approximated entry barrier heights and enticements to enter. Details concerning their construction appear in Harrigan (1981a). These tests develop variables by drawing on a number of data sources to improve on the foundations of the economic theory. The early studies of entry barriers were inconclusive, yielding ambiguous results. An example of these models is presented in table A–4 in the appendix using the same dependent variable and data of table A–3, and independent variables suggested by these earlier economic studies. Its results are poor. The R^2 (coefficient of multiple determination) is quite low (.0200), and the value of the intercept term (.494) in table A–4 approximates closely the actual mean value of the dependent variable (.500), suggesting the independent variables add relatively insubstantial information to predictive power of this model. More meaningful models were needed when the precepts of this topic were translated into questions of interest to scholars of strategic management.

The construction of independent variables that indicate influences on the likelihood that fringe firms will enter requires special commentary as well. The financial data (from COMPUSTAT®) used to construct the independent variables exemplified the market postures of firms that may be considered to be the *core* competitors. Entry, by contrast, was expected to occur on the *fringes* of an industry. Therefore, information about the core firms (and the environment they created) are used to infer patterns of entry behavior among fringe firms. By standardizing the available information describing leading firms, measures describing the environmental variables new entrants would face were constructed. (Industry-average information was available from *Census of Manufacturers,* the National Science Foundation, and *Leading National Advertisers* studies. The industries in the sample were meat packing, distilled liquors, tobacco products, hydraulic cement, and aircraft manufacture. The COMPUSTAT® industries examined were relatively undiversified, thus offering information about firms that approximated that of the single business firm.)

Transformations were made for corrections of the heteroscedacity, serial correlation, and lagged structure. The observations used to test the models that follow spanned a decade (the differences of nine intervals). These were pooled (and corrections made) to yield a total of 540 data points.

In time-series specifications that are pooled with cross sections, the residual is assumed to be composed of a time-series error, a cross-section error, and an interaction effect. Transformations are required to correct for autocorrelation, and special interpretation of the error term is needed. Moreover, the pooling of data describing heterogeneous-sized firms required generalized differencing corrections using weighted least-squares estimates to obtain the appropriate error term (see Bass, Cattin, and Wittink 1978; Hatten 1974). Complete explanations of these procedures appear in Harrigan (1981a).

After corrections, there was relatively little serial correlation in the models estimated (as indicated by the Durbin-Watson d-statistic); and the correlation coefficients of the absolute values of the observed residuals to the predicted values of the dependent variable were quite low, which suggests that the variance of the residuals generated by this process does not depend on the values of the independent variables (see Balestra and Nerlove 1966).

Models

A lagged structure (of one year in most cases) was imposed on the models tested to reflect the assumed reaction time necessary before firms could convert liquid assets to capital goods and production capacity following industry-performance stimuli. The lag structure is a fundamental element of this model because specifications that allow entry to occur during the same period as the impetus encouraging entry violate the basic assumptions of a nonfrictionless environment, where assets are not completely flexible and not immediately available.

The models that explained the greatest amounts of variance in entry behavior and firms' performance are of the general form presented for the entry model that follows. In each, the error term of first-stage analysis provided ρ_i, the correction term.

$$P_t = \alpha_i + \beta_i x_{it} + \epsilon_{it}$$

where P_t was the probability of entry at time t (where 1 designates entry occurred, 0 otherwise); x_{it} corresponds to the variables of table A–3 as they are numbered therein; and

$$\epsilon_{it} = \rho_i \epsilon_{i,t-1} + u_{it}$$

where ρ_i is the correction used in generalized differencing. The error term is corrected for the three components of bias such that

$$E(\epsilon_{it}^2) = \sigma^2$$
$$E(\epsilon_{it}\epsilon_{jt}) = 0, \quad i = j$$
$$E(\epsilon_{i,t-1}u_{jt}) = 0, \quad i = j$$
$$u_{it} \sim N(0,\sigma_u^2)$$

2
Strategic Commitment

Product-market matrixes have been popular strategic planning tools since their introduction in the late 1960s. Known by names such as the BCG or General Electric Strategic Matrix, among others, they juxtaposed managers' assessments of an industry's (or market segment's) attractiveness with their firm's (or business unit's) ability to compete effectively. The key to their effective use has always been in managers' skills in operationalizing the axes of the two-by-two (or three-by-three, etc.) grid.

This chapter suggests a refinement of those tools, a *correction term* in two-dimensional graphics, which incorporates the effects of competitors' strategic commitments to a product or market on the firm's (or business unit's) ultimate positioning within strategic matrixes. In doing so, it draws on literature concerning *strategic groups* and *guerrilla tactics* and demonstrates how managers might incorporate these concepts into their arsenal of strategic planning tools. The last section of this chapter offers an empirical test for strategic groups, using cluster analysis.

The Strategic Groups–Mobility Barriers Paradigm

Observation of competitive activities within an industry suggests that firms may elect to specialize in serving narrowly defined niches of customers and thereby not compete head to head with other firms that appear to be in the same industry. Alternatively, firms may serve the same markets using a variety of approaches to doing so. Thus firms that may not appear to be similar may in fact be competing for the same customers.

In the first example just given—where firms define narrow, nonintersecting niches of customers as target markets—the analytical problem is one of merely identifying market segments. The second example—

Adapted from an article that originally appeared in the *Strategic Management Journal*, January–March 1985, by permission of the copyright holder and publisher, John Wiley & Sons, Ltd.

where firms using diverse strategies pursue the same customers—is the more complex analytical problem of isolating strategic groups, identifying the relevant dimensions along which they differ, and assessing the ease with which these mobility barriers (factors that provide one strategic group of firms with relative competitive advantages over another) can be hurdled.

Niches, Strategic Groups, and Mobility Barriers Defined

Market Niches. *Niches* are pockets of demand that possess a unique willingness to pay premium prices for certain product attributes (such as high quality, rapid delivery, or customized designs, for example), and which cannot be served by all comers. Thus niches are *defensible* (at least temporarily) from incursions by competitors from other strategic groups who do not offer the mix of attributes these customers value. Defensible niches are served by firms within a strategic group that is protected from outsiders by mobility barriers; but, as will be explained, the heights of mobility barriers can be reduced (or new firms can hurdle them) through changes in the nature of demand, product attributes, or other competitive forces.

Strategic Groups. *Strategic groups* comprise firms that may compete for the same customers' patronage in diverse ways. In an idealized industry, one strategic group would serve a niche of demand. In reality, strategic groups need not correspond in a one-to-one fashion with market niches (although the concept is often confused with that of market segments). Different strategic groups approach competition dissimilarly. A particular market segment could be served by more than one type of strategic group, and groups' products may sometimes be substitutable for the products of another group as far as a particular customer is concerned.

One danger inherent in bringing dissimilar strategic groups into competition for the same customers is their inexperience in sending and receiving competitive signals and their differing orientations concerning conduct. Firms with many years of experience in battles against each other often find it easier to compete obliquely, thereby avoiding head-to-head warfare. Firms, rather like continuing opponents in a weekly poker game, need experience to test each other out before they learn which maneuvers signal detente and which moves mean war. Thus the convergence of markets that were formerly separated by significant mobility barriers may throw together firms that misread each other's willingness to coexist. Destructive battles may result. Since strategic groups are separated by mobility barriers that may eventually become irrelevant as boundaries, investments and competitive expenditures made by firms within adjacent strategic groups could easily affect each others' behaviors, either directly or indirectly. Prior empirical studies of strategic groups were operationalized using cross-sectional data (Newman 1978; Porter 1979), but the first postulations of this concept (Hunt 1972; Newman 1973) examined the behaviors of firms within single industries—the home-applicance and chemical-process industries, respectively. The example in the appendix also examines a single industry—retailing—and thus conforms to the original spirit of strategic group analysis that was also exemplified by Hatten, Schendel, and Cooper's (1978) study of the brewing industry.

Mobility Barriers. *Mobility barriers* are structural factors that protect successful firms from invasions by adjacent competitors (Caves and Porter 1977). They are internal (to the industry) barriers that delineate boundaries between different strategic groups, and they may be contrasted with the external entry barriers discussed in traditional economic theory, which deter outside firms from entering any part of the industry. The distinction is a fine one, which recognizes the outsider's perspective. Ongoing competitors scan the heights of mobility barriers for strategic postures they might wish to emulate; potential industry entrants scan the height of barriers germane to the entire industry *as well as* those particular to the way in which they might desire to enter (those of the target strategic group).

The height of each strategic group's mobility barriers will be determined by the type of competitive investments its firms have made in the past. Successful strategic postures can emanate from differences in the attributes of firms' products or variations in their means of distributing them, and successful firms often preserve their advantages by developing steep mobility barriers. Thus analyses of the identities of strategic groups and of the nature of mobility barriers that separate them can provide important clues to understanding profitability differences and other performance variations among these firms. It can also help to predict where entry may occur and thus provide assessments concerning the future defensibility of market niches.

Asymmetry. *Strategic group asymmetry* refers to intergroup differences, and the distances between strategic groups are indicated in part by dissimilar mobility barrier heights. Asymmetries determine whether firms' strategic postures can be emulated easily. If their competitive advantages arise from attributes that rivals could appropriate easily, strategic groups may be more vulnerable to copying by outsiders. Thus their mobility barriers would offer little protection in these areas. This concern becomes relevant within industries where competitive conduct changes frequently, where customer segments are converging, or where firms seek new ideas for serving existing customers.

Overlapping Maps of Strategic Groups on Market Segments

Firms within the same strategic groups can serve the special needs of a particular market niche because they have chosen the same approaches to competition and developed their postures accordingly. All market segments are not *niches,* however, in the jargon of strategic planners, because they cannot be protected from easy invasions by competitors. When firms are prospecting for new opportunities to exploit (Hambrick 1979), they would do well to compare their topographic maps of market segments with those of strategic groups. An overlay of these schema may suggest opportunities that can be developed because they are ill served by current suppliers. The key to finding these opportunities will lie in uncovering asymmetries between customer needs and competitors' responses.

The value of studying strategic groups and mobility barriers for strategists, then, is to isolate significant asymmetries among firms' strategies and performances in order to generate estimates regarding the nature of important mobility barriers. This information can suggest which desirable strategic groups' positions might be most vulnerable to entry. The next section discusses a limiting force in discovering new market opportunities. It explains why managers should give highly committed firms that use guerrilla warfare tactics heavier weightings in assessing the firm's ability to compete effectively within some market segments.

Guerrilla Warfare and Underdog Competitors

Guerrilla tactics often succeed because of the new way of ordering priorities they suggest. Guerrilla warfare uses the tools of organization, education, and explanation to spur troops onward to achieve remarkable results. More ominously, guerrilla warfare succeeds because leading firms are not willing to pay the price an underdog competitor might accept. Like kamikaze fighters, guerrilla fighters possess different values and fight for different objectives. Thus they are the most dangerous type of nontraditional (or maverick) competitor (Schelling 1960; Harrigan 1979, 1980). Therein lies the danger of ignoring or underestimating the hungry competitors who might embrace these tactics. As the example of American Revolutionary War hero Francis T. Marion (the Swamp Fox) will attest, guerrilla fighters will endure harsh competitive conditions, subsist on a shoestring, and fight to the death if necessary. More frequently, however, the guerrilla fighter is an irritant who harasses larger opponents until they abandon their efforts and retreat in disgust. These tactics have often been used to make weakness a strength (Sun Tzu 1961).

Underdog firms often divide their resources and efforts among activities of varying strategic importance, which require differing competitive strengths. They do so to achieve narrowly defined (or niche) successes by diverting competitors' attentions from the true product (or market niche) these weaker firms hoped to serve. This strategic approach has been called by other names, such as a *going-for-the-crumbs* or *ragpicker* strategy (MacMillan 1980). Whatever name is given to guerrilla warfare, however, a basic assumption of this philosophy of competition is the weakness of the firm that will employ it. Guerrilla strategies are very timely ideas for firms possessing low market shares, especially within industries that face stagnant (or declining) demand or import competition. Guerrilla tactics can help firms limit their activities to relatively few alternatives and conserve resources for crucial battles.

Guerrilla Strategies and Military Tactics

In guerrilla warfare, the battlefield and combat resources are divided between *guerrilla bases* and *guerrilla fronts*. A direct analogy can be made to competitive strategies. Delineation of these theaters of warfare explicitly recognizes the weakness of the forces commanded by the revolutionaries. The allocation scheme it espouses seeks to turn the enemy's strengths into weaknesses. When Mao Tse-Tung used guerrilla tactics, he advised his troops to consolidate their resources in areas of relative strength where they were militarily secure. (These are the guerrilla bases.) When there were slack resources available, an offensive could be launched against the enemy on the turf of Mao's choosing. (These are the guerrilla fronts.) In short, guerrillas defend their bases when necessary but prefer to fight on their fronts, where losses are less meaningful. Mao was prepared to fall back in retreat within these guerrilla fronts all the way to his guerrilla bases, if necessary. The objective was to exhaust the enemy by making him fight under conditions that were more favorable to Mao and his army. Thus when Mao ran away, it was to lead the enemy to a baited trap (Mao 1961, 1966).

Underdog competitors often behave like guerrilla fighters. They tire out the big players within their strategic group by engaging in skirmishes where market leaders cannot respond without shooting themselves in the foot. Mao would not fight unless he saw an opportunity to seize an advantage. When the enemy was strong, his troops hid. When the enemy was in retreat, Mao's troops harassed them. When the enemy was tired, Mao turned to fight; his troops were prepared to surrender their lives if it were necessary to defend their guerrilla bases. Mao's first law of war was to preserve oneself and destroy the enemy. In doing this, his troops sought to fix the enemy's attentions on a less meaningful battle (distraction), but strike where and when the enemy least anticipated the blow (concentration of effort). Minimal losses were incurred where the battlefront was chosen well. Often the battlefront provided symbolic victories if not military success.

In summary, Mao's strategy was intended to minimize the carnage of his troops by fighting only when the chances of success were high, thereby avoiding battles he could not hope to win. Mao saved his scarce resources and used them wisely in battle. As the world has witnessed, the devotion of Mao's troops to this battle plan and their willingness to make both the Long March and the ultimate sacrifice enabled Mao's ragtag army of five thousand to conquer the vastness of China. (Also, Mao outsmarted his less adept enemy many times.) Their triumph represents an extreme ideological success, which could be extended to the corporate battlefield.

Using Guerrilla Principles

Resource-constrained firms can use guerrilla principles for success if they will make painful introspections and accept harsh realities (MacMillan 1980). The key to success is preemptive striking capability. Avoid wars of attrition (those where resources would be wasted needlessly), and make efforts to fortify those defensible niches where firms enjoy strength. If no *defensible* strengths are enjoyed, firms should either devote their efforts to making a base strong enough to withstand competitive onslaughts or move on to a base that can be defended successfully. Timing is the key to preempting competitors and building the ideology needed for commitment to the task at hand. Effective guerrilla strategies enable corporate armies to excel even where market share would be difficult to capture.

Guerrilla bases are market niches where competitors are unlikely or unable to enter. If not immediately profitable, guerrilla bases must ultimately generate surplus resources to be used elsewhere in the firm, or at least provide enough resources for survival, because effective guerrilla warfare involves a timetable of resource allocations that allows future guerrilla bases to be funded by current guerrilla bases. To build these bases, some firms have even been willing to operate below break-even for several years. Where their commitment is very high, entire firms may not break even in order to fund these future guerrilla bases now.

Guerrilla fronts are the arenas where underdogs take on the goliaths; they are arenas for drawing out opponents and wasting their resources. Again, the key to using Mao's tactical framework effectively is to choose those guerrilla fronts that will be most favorable to the firm, *not* to the firm's competitors. Much of MacMillan's (1980) definition concerning which products or markets could serve as guerrilla fronts depended on the ability of guerrilla firms to create coalitions with suppliers, distributors, customers, and other forces in the firm's environment, just as Mao's guerrilla fighters won the support of the local populace. In brief, a hospitable setting makes a better guerrilla front than a hostile neighborhood, for a guerrilla army thrives on the support and sustenance provided by its environment and on the ideology it holds dear.

Using the Framework

This philosophy of guerrilla warfare can be applied to the task of identifying niches where firms with weak competitive positions might thrive, and to the creation of investment priorities to attain long-term strategic objectives. Note that guerrilla strategies differ by competitive environments, just as guerrilla fighters' neighborhoods differ. When this framework is applied to the challenges faced by mature businesses, the strategic objectives guerrilla fighters seek will differ from those sought by underdog competitors within new industries. For example, the use of Mao's guerrilla tactics for those businesses that are fulfilling a so-called harvest mission for their corporate parents requires refinements that recognize how cash-flow performance criteria differ from guerrilla tactics applied to emerging industries where many years of prosperity could be enjoyed.

In drawing parallels, the concepts of guerrilla base and guerrilla front must be modified to include products and markets that could satisfy the business units' cash generation mission while keeping long-term strategy objectives firmly in mind. Since a firm comprises people with skills they could adapt to new products and markets, the process or style of execution will be at least as important as which arenas serve as bases, fronts, or buffer zones (explained later).

When offensives receive priorities, some products (and customer groups) will be judged to be so important to the long-term character of firms that they will merit being treated as guerrilla bases. These are the niches of present (or future) profitability for which the troops would sacrifice all to defend and nurture product attributes or market identities. Other arenas will be treated as guerrilla fronts because, although these products or markets will seem attractive to guerrilla fighters, they are also highly attractive to their competitors. If opponents are highly committed to these arenas, they will be excellent fronts for guerrillas to engage their enemy because it will hurt rivals more to waste resources fighting off guerrilla fighters than it will cost them to harass the enemy. Finally, the remaining products and markets that are less important than guerrilla bases and fronts are *buffers*. They are like pawns in a chess game. Buffer zones may be less profitable products or customers. They may face limited futures. Perhaps they are highly attractive to competitors, but the guerrilla firm cannot hope to serve them as well as its larger, more skillful opponents. Under a guerrilla-warfare approach to competition, buffers are surrendered to the enemy with a great flourish in order to distract their attention from guerrilla bases.

Defining Guerrilla Bases. In order to deploy scarce resources effectively, firms that use guerrilla tactics must identify their guerrilla bases, for these are the activities they will protect above all others. Within mature, cash-generating industries, guerrilla bases could be those products (or customer segments) where the firm expects demand to endure and be viable for the longest time into the future. Many mature businesses face technological obsolescence from dramatically different product forms, yet their customers will still have a generic need for some version of the product. Even within declining businesses, there may be pockets of enduring demand that would rather pay higher prices for the older product than be inconvenienced by changing to new ones (Harrigan 1979, 1980c), for example, stainless steel percolator coffeemakers or wringer washing machines. Savvy firms can preempt their less astute (and ill-prepared) competitors in an endgame situation by analyzing their markets early and repositioning themselves to serve the best niches. By the time endgame occurs, few firms have the desire to press onward in competition, so it is relatively easy to discourage many opponents. But successful positioning in such settings depends on development of those guerrilla bases while industries are still mature. Little cash is expended on buffer businesses (exceptions are noted later) because they are expected to fund battles on guerrilla fronts and to nurture the next generation of guerrilla bases.

The key to turning products or a group of customers into a guerrilla base is timing. Firms must mobilize resources to lock up the loyalties of those customers that will endure the longest, and they must do so *quickly*—before competitors reach the same conclusions. (This point is particularly important if competitors could dominate any market or product application they elected to serve by dint of their superior resource expenditures. These are battles fought for the hearts and minds of the customers as well as those of the firm's employees.)

Be Realistic about Success Criteria. Firms must have strengths in the niches they choose as their guerrilla bases because these bases are intended to be the safe haven they could always retreat to if competition became too bloody. Customer bases should be those with relatively low bargaining power and high product loyalty. They could be a base of customers that current competitors do not service adequately—for example, farmers in the personal computer market, or the military in leather boots. Product bases should be differentiable in a manner that is difficult to emulate—for example, those protected by patents, trade secrets, deep customer loyalties, or secret ingredients.

Kamikazelike Devotion. The last criterion for choosing guerrilla bases is a prospective one. If there are new products, new technologies, or new activities that are still embryonic, some of these could be included as bases *if their successful commercialization and capture is judged to be absolutely vital to the long-term survival of the firm.* If these embryonic businesses are truly of strategic importance, they will necessarily have to be defended with a *kamikazelike* devotion.

Avoid Losing Battles in Base Businesses. Firms face a difficult choice when products (or customers) they wish to treat as guerrilla bases are also being treated as bases by competitors. Whether they take actions to displace the position of competitors or relegate the business in question to the status of a guerrilla front, instead, depends on their diversification strategies and their own strengths. Wars of attrition could be avoided if firms have other guerrilla bases to nurture, and they should certainly be avoided if competitors are the stronger. But if the two rivals are evenly matched (and equally determined), decisions regarding how much emphasis to place on this fight may turn on how important the guerrilla base is for future activities and for the attainment of rivals' missions. A clash between mature businesses will sap firms' cash-generating potentials; a conflict between embryonic businesses will inhibit firms' futures if the base is easily abandoned. Thus a semiconductor firm such as Texas Instruments has to compete in some consumer electronics businesses to protect its true core of activity in microelectronic research.

Note that there are many differences between the guerrilla-base concept and that of the stars and question marks of portfolio strategies. Given their smaller size, guerrilla fighters are often seeking objectives other than market share (Woo 1979; Woo and Cooper 1980, 1982). They do not spread resources haphazardly to attain a balanced portfolio of products (or customer groups). Instead, they may be cream-skimmers and cherry-pickers early in an industry's development. They will probably be ragpickers in mature settings. Finally, the responses of guerrilla fighters to incursions on their inner-sanctum businesses are draconian, thus making the way firms conceive of competition dramatically different from that of market-share maximizers.

Defining Guerrilla Fronts. It is important (but often painful) for firms to face the essence of guerrilla fronts. Underdogs cannot do everything; they must choose their arena for retaliation carefully. Guerrilla fronts may have to be sacrificed under adverse competition to prevent damage from occurring to guerrilla-base businesses. Guerrilla fronts feed the bases at times, just as the mature guerrilla bases feed the guerrilla fronts during expansionary campaigns. That means products (and customer groups) are ordered according to their long-term strategic importance to firms. If a plethora of products (or customer groups) is available, the first action of many firms when initiating guerrilla tactics will be to slough off the least important products (or customers) in a manner that will distract their enemy while an aggressive campaign is launched on a front opponents have left unguarded. The purpose of this maneuver will be to waste the enemy's resources at minimal cost to guerrilla firms on turf that is less important to their long-term plans, but may be very important to their opponents. Thus guerrilla fronts are competitive cross-parries designed to harass other firms, such as Seagram's "fighting brands" in whiskey or video-cassette cameras introduced by Kodak.

Defining Buffer Zones. Buffer products (or customer groups) have the lowest strategic importance to guerrilla fighters. They are ongoing products (or customers) that firms assess to have poor future demand, unfavorable economics, or other bleak attributes that make them expendable. Buffers are stepchildren, produced in facilities to absorb excess capacity or make an easier transition until that plant is shut down. Buffers for guerrilla fighters are often bases for their stronger opponents, and it should be clearly understood (given these distinctions) that no rational firm would *ever* fight a war of attrition over a product (or customer group) it considered to be a buffer zone.

Illustrations of the Framework

This section discusses some problems and cautions associated with using guerrilla warfare to carve out a prosperous position as an underdog. In using these tactics, it will be necessary to find defensible niches to serve as guerrilla bases or fronts. Competitor intelligence systems must be adjusted to guerrilla fighters' needs to distract their enemies. Reward systems must reflect counterculture trade-offs, and managers who use this strategic philosophy must often develop a new procedure for competitive signaling, as well.

Guerrilla warfare offers a different perspective from other treatments of how low-market-share firms (Woo 1979; Woo and Cooper 1982) might prosper, particularly within hostile or unpromising environments (Hamermesh, Anderson, and Harris 1978; Hall 1980). It is a perspective that some managers will find difficult to implement because the mindset it embraces is alien to their way of doing things. But where firms' markets are besieged and their organizations suffer from a malaise that cripples their resourcefulness (Hayes and Abernathy 1980), this radical philosophy might revitalize their viability by suggesting new competitive options.

Finding Defensible Niches

Guerrilla strategies seek attractive niches that larger competitors do not serve adequately. They use fighting brands to engage their opponents on other battlefronts. Sometimes a small firm could fill in the gaps left by firms that pioneer new technologies. For example, Key Pharmaceuticals develops a variety of novel application forms for administering drugs formulated by others—for example, nitroglycerine osmosized through adhesive pads on cardiac patients' chests. Or the guerrilla fighter may have to pioneer a new idea in order to attain credibility in a mature industry—for example, Archer-Daniels-Midland in high-fructose corn sweeteners. In declining businesses, guerrilla fighters could revive discarded products to serve loyal customers; for example, Beaunit makes cupramonium-process rayon, which is preferred for casket velvets. (The advantage of this last example is that demand is frequently too small to accommodate two firms, and customers are somewhat more loyal after previous suppliers have relegated them to the dustbin.)

The key in choosing niches to serve as guerrilla bases will be *differentiation*. The niche must be defensible, yet not so attractive that rivals would spend their way into the niche. Advantages based on cost reductions (those usually associated with commoditylike products) are more easily surpassed by large competitors, particularly by global firms producing at world-scale volumes (Hout, Porter, and Rudden 1982). Guerrilla fighters would be well advised to turn their commoditylike products into specialties and cater to a specialized group of customers. Limiting their bases to a size that is large enough to sustain the guerrilla firm but not large enough to attract outsiders is another way to preserve their competitive niches.

Competitor Intelligence

Timely intelligence will be a decisive factor in the success of guerrilla operations, and members of the firm's guerrilla intelligence network must be tightly organized and pervasive. In a military guerrilla network, every person was considered a potential source of information to be cultivated, and access to intelligence was obtained with relative ease by guerrilla fighters because they were perceived by the populace as being the good guys. When using guerrilla tactics in corporate battles, customers, distributors, and suppliers must be persuaded to join with the firm's employees in contributing information concerning their environment, competitors, and other useful topics because the firm is a good guy, such as Apple Computer.

As an important contrast, however, successful guerrilla fighters will devise ways of denying all information about themselves to the enemy. They will throw up smokescreens and persuade their grass-roots information network not to help the enemy. As a corollary to this principle, noncooperating outsiders often must be cut off to prevent intelligence leaks. Here is where guerrilla fighters must identify and develop those unique capabilities that will give them bargaining power over outsiders. Patient efforts at persuasion—the velvet glove—must be backed by the will and capability to punish—the iron fist. In order to elicit grass-roots support, guerrilla fighters who are seeking intelligence must offer the values their sources will esteem. Ultimately, guerrilla fighters, if they are to survive, must link up with customers who will not abandon them in their old products while they develop new ones.

Managing Guerrilla Cultures

Effective management of these tactics requires the firm to recognize that it is a guerrilla fighter and to act accordingly. The key to successful guerrilla strategies is strong commitment by the organization and management that will sustain its morale. Communications must be managed carefully lest misunderstandings occur. (Consider, for example, how the same competitive tactic used by patriots to free the American colonies from Great Britain became a highly misunderstood communist tool two centuries later.) Taken out of context, discussions of guerrilla tactics should not be disseminated far within the firm because they have the potential to be even more devastating to the morale of managers than the pejorative mandate of managing a "dog" business. The logical conclusion of this philosophy is that some troops will be lost, and, in order to get cooperation, the concept of a *cadre* of comrades must be developed. In this manner, a spirit of teamwork can encourage useful ideas to percolate up to those managers who possess the power to fund radical tactical suggestions. Moreover, this type of camaraderie reinforces the need to think and behave like a guerrilla fighter.

Guerrilla warriors are sustained by the support of their environment. This support network must be managed both within and outside of the firm. Top management should be seen to support the guerrilla unit *visibly*. Warriors need maximum autonomy to do their jobs given the unorthodox approach guerrilla tactics often embrace. Guerrilla business units need the types of swashbuckling heroes as leaders who embody corporate myths concerning success. The reward system must be adjusted to honor the guerrilla battle that was fought well; that means different measures of success will be needed, given the objectives of the competitive cross-parry inherent in the concept of guerrilla fronts. If the firm has had a tradition of taking care of its family, that policy helps implementation because corporatewide policies regarding continued employment can be invoked to cushion the fall of those loyal soldiers who gave their all for the protection of the guerrilla bases.

Extending Guerrilla Controls

Guerrilla warriors are also sustained by support from parties outside the firm. Often they will try to align outsiders with their cause (MacMillan 1980). Using sympathetic outsiders to achieve one's objectives in a guerrilla-warfare context is not without peril, however, although the guerrilla fighter often must rely on the assistance of suppliers, customers, distributors, or employees to survive.

Achieving control can be a problem, for autonomy is an important part of guerrilla warfare. Strategists have sometimes delegated responsibility and authority for geographically remote targets to so-called warlords who achieve their guerrilla-strategy objectives in manner left to their unique discretions. Moreover, guerrilla tactics are often serendipitous (to the extent that uniform campaigns need not be mounted for all offensives). Yet control over outsiders is desirable because quasi-autonomous warlords could follow instructions while acting in a manner that is not consistent with policies that are of long-term importance to the guerrillas. If these warlords are not reined in, they could rage out of control (in pursuit of their own objectives) by misinterpreting their missions.

Thus guerrilla fighters who delegate power (or control) to independent agents must ensure that their signals will communicate to them the need to make those trade-offs deemed appropriate by the firm. Although warlord agents may use whichever tactics are appropriate to attain the guerrilla fighter's objectives, a careful system of coordination (backed by a strong communications system) will be needed to avoid short-term myopia during the battle.

Mapping Guerrilla Bases, Fronts, and Buffer Zones

Guerrilla warfare suggests that an analysis of competitors' strategic commitments to various products (or customer groups) should accompany other analyses used to asssess firms' opportunities. In addition to evaluations of the relative attractiveness of markets served (or products sold) and of the firm's relative strengths in serving them, an evaluation of relative strategic importance will be appropriate for each product (or market). By mapping out the relative importance of business units to their corporate missions, firms can identify where they will encounter the strongest competition from larger and more powerful firms. With this assessment, they can devise priorities for resource allocation. Recognizing which products (or markets) are those worthy of asking the troops to die for (rather than surrender) helps the firm realign its objectives and muster its energies to the battle before it. Moreover, identification of businesses that are embryonic but crucial to the firm's future prevents misallocations of resources to less important activities by mistake.

Figure 2–1 illustrates a mapping of guerrilla bases, fronts, and buffer zones as rings of concentric circles. In this diagram, the farther businesses are mapped from the center of the circles, the less their strategic importance to the long-term mission of the firm. If many layers of guerrilla-front businesses protect the heart of the business unit (its guerrilla base), then only those businesses in the outermost rings (the buffer zones) will be surrendered at the first sign of adversity, and they will be abandoned in a smooth and timely fashion because their strategic mission is cash generation for guerrilla bases and fronts. To do otherwise would be to waste precious resources on battles that cannot be won.

Figure 2–2 illustrates guerrilla-warfare dynamics using the example of fiber-optic networks. In the development of this industry, Corning Glass Works (a glass firm) offered a full range of fiber-optic components, materials, and services. Its core interest was glass fibers, but larger firms such as Western Electric, Northern Telecom, and ITT were also making optical cables. Their core interests were telecommunications services (and electronic components), however. By competing in the arenas they valued highly, Corning could take advantage of their vulnerabilities. By teaming up with Siemens to form Siecor, Corning let a stronger firm fight its opponents with the result of lower internal expenditures in electronics for Corning.

Analysis of competitors' strategic commitments provides additional evidence to corporate finance committees (or other controllers of stra-

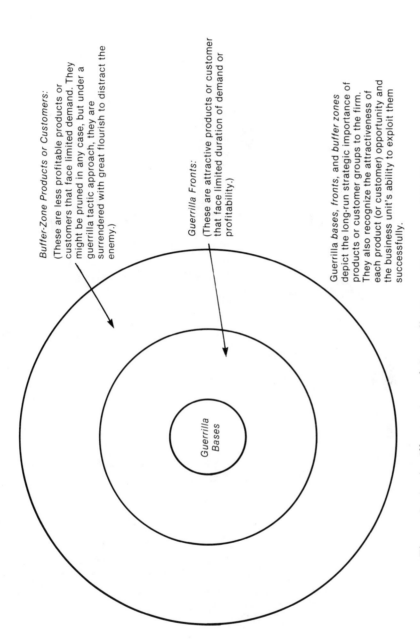

Buffer-Zone Products or Customers:

(These are less profitable products or customers that face limited demand. They might be pruned in any case, but under a guerrilla tactic approach, they are surrendered with great flourish to distract the enemy.)

Guerrilla Fronts:

(These are attractive products or customer that face limited duration of demand or profitability.)

Guerrilla *bases, fronts,* and *buffer* zones depict the long-run strategic importance of products or customer groups to the firm. They also recognize the attractiveness of each product (or customer) opportunity and the business unit's ability to exploit them successfully.

Guerrilla Bases

Figure 2–1. An Illustration of Guerrilla Bases, Fronts, and Buffers

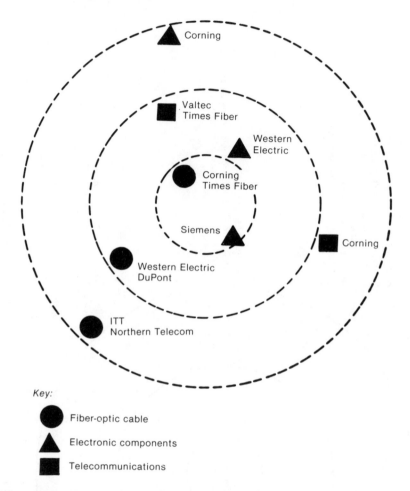

Figure 2–2. Comparison of Firms' Strategic Commitments to Components of Fiber-Optic Networks

tegic funding) that resources requested by guerrilla fighters would be astutely deployed. The mappings of guerrilla terrains suggest that the firm has made difficult but necessary decisions to preserve the cash-generating potential of its bases and fronts.

Translating Guerrilla Topology to the Strategy Matrix

Application of guerrilla strategy concepts to the traditional strategic-planning matrix assumes that managers have assessed the near-term attractiveness of each product line and each market segment where re-source-allocation decisions are in question, and that they have positioned their firm (or business unit) within the matrix relative to competitors. The next step makes a horizontal adjustment in their ultimate placement in order to reflect the responses of highly determined competitors and their resource-draining effects upon the firm, as figure 2–3 indicates. In this hypothetical strategy matrix, the nine cells represent climates of varying attractiveness for resource allocation. The diagonal line represents the boundary between cells that will be funded ("cash customers") and those that will remit cash to the firm for uses elsewhere ("cash generators"). The diagonal line is a qualitative "hurdle rate" for resource allocation within firm B. The dotted circles indicate where SBU D would be placed on the matrix without considering whether the turf in question is a competitor's guerrilla base (for example, glass optical fiber is a guerrilla base for Corning Glass Works in figure 2–2). The horizontal adjustment (to the right), in the form of a solid SBU D, reflects the predicted response of Corning to firm B's attempts to increase market position there. If the implications of the diagonal line are accepted, adjusting for competitors' strategic commitment to a product line or market segment (as in this example, adjusting for Corning Glass Works) moved SBU D from an ambiguous funding category into a clear candidate for no more funding.

Cautions

The guerrilla-warfare framework proposed herein is a superior analytical tool for underdog firms because it recognizes the limitations of such firms when taking on the giants of the industry. The prescriptions of most product-market matrixes reward large market-share positions. The guerrilla-warfare framework does not suggest that underdogs should stretch themselves to achieve ephemeral market-share objectives that may not advance their corporate missions. Instead, it suggests that underdog firms should limit the number of products (or markets) they treat as guerrilla bases. Weak firms should not attempt to do too much. Rather, underdog firms should be prudent in their selection of which businesses to protect, which businesses to nurture, and which businesses to use as lures to dissipate the energies of their competitors.

Above all, firms must keep in mind their ultimate aims. Small but narrowly focused resources can be very powerful against well-chosen targets. A realistic matching of strengths and opportunities (a rifle approach) is preferable to a buckshot approach; and weaker forces must be wary of trying to push their mammoth opponents too far. Guerrilla warfare is a realistic approach for small firms to use in maximizing their potential. They need to draw out competitors on terrains of their own

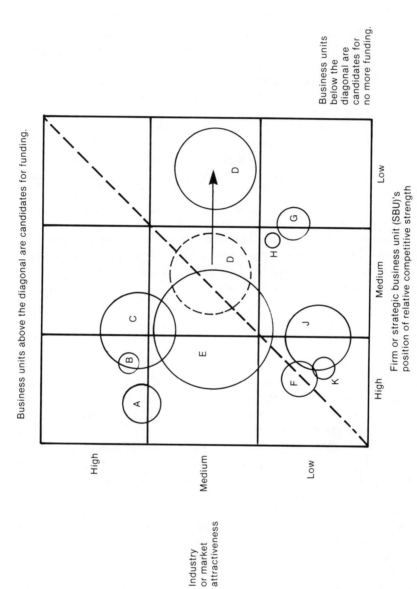

Figure 2–3. Firm B's Resource-Allocation-Strategy Matrix

choosing. Then they can hope for victory in their niches by reaching a truce with potential invaders.

Conclusions

Exploration of the differences among strategic groups (as they might be measured using cluster analysis as in the next section) can suggest which strategic groups are most likely to converge when industry growth slows or shrinks. Recognizing these diversities could improve the chances that firms might avoid volatile competition when they expand their horizons to enter each other's markets. Evaluating the importance of what appears to be key differences between converging strategic groups in advance may prompt managers to reduce those differences most likely to set off warfare. The best candidates for change are those attributes (strategic postures) that seem less efficacious than those of onrushing rivals. It is hoped that mobility barriers can be hurdled with ease in the areas where attribute changes are desirable. By revising significant attribute differences as diverse strategic groups converge on the same customers, strategists may reduce the likelihood of friction, misunderstandings, poor signaling, and bloody battles.

Empirical Tests for Strategic Groups

Statistical tools such as clustering techniques may be used to identify potential guerrilla competitors. They are the other firms within one's strategic group, and strategic groups can be mapped. Strategic-group mapping is a useful way of tracking industry dynamics as firms become more similar to or different from each other. Matching market-segment changes with strategic-group evolutions provides a useful means of predicting the nature of competition. Such analysis investigates the strategy and operating differences among firms within an industry and, by doing so, focuses managers' attentions on salient differences in how competitors approach the marketplace. Such analysis is useful because it could help managers to assess (1) the attractiveness of market opportunities for their firm (and for their competitors), (2) their abilities to exploit industry changes, and hence (3) their long-term opportunities for profitability within the industry in question.

Operationalizing Estimates of Strategic Groups

There have been a variety of techniques used to classify competitors in strategic management research, ranging from a priori groupings to those generated by computer algorithms. In each case, selection of the dimensions used to segregate firms has been a crucial step in thinking about industry competition.

Newman (1978) challenged the then-prevailing assumption of intra-industry homogeneity by examining the structures of 34 producer-goods industries. His measure of variations in strategic postures among industries was a Herfindahl index, and he compared differences in the performances of his groups based upon these criteria. Porter (1979) bifurcated his cross-sectional sample of PIMS-defined, consumer-goods SBUs into "leader" firms and "follower" firms. Hunt (1972), Newman (1973), Harrigan (1979), and Hambrick (1979, 1983a, b, and c), used prior analysis of the industries' structural contexts and theoretical constructs to suggest which factors would prove most fruitful as criteria for grouping competitors. Such a priori analyses can reduce the number of control variables needed in generating strategic groups (parsimony) while yielding more powerful models of industry competition. Alternatively, a large number of factors could be tested both individually and in combination with each other to ascertain which variables possess the greatest discriminatory power for grouping competitors.

Cluster Analysis. The term *cluster analysis* collectively refers to several different algorithms used to group similar entities. Each entity is usually described by its position on a set of attributes (dimensions) and the boundaries of the groups are *not* prespecified (Joyce and Channon 1966; Ball and Hall 1967; Green, Frank, and Robinson 1967). Rather, these boundaries are derived according to patterns found in the attribute measurements, making this tool suitable for estimating the heights of mobility barriers that segregate strategic groups, assuming that managers can isolate dimensions that describe the key differences among competitors. Then the distances generated by clustering algorithms can approximate mobility-barrier heights and generate descriptions of the boundaries segregating strategic groups.

Multiple Dimensions. The advantage of using a cluster analysis is the inclusion of more than two dimensions for sorting competitors into strategic groups. Unfortunately, the mobility barriers protecting diverse strategic groups within an industry may be asymmetrical. (Different barriers may define their strategic cores, making standard measures of their differences of unequal efficacy for diverse groups.) Thus an optimal number of dimensions probably cannot be created for *all* groups when using clustering algorithms. A compromise solution would be to select a few dimensions that seem to be theoretically appropriate for the greatest possible number of relevant strategic groups.

Managerial Interpretations of Clustering

The tightness of a strategic group's structure (within-group variance) suggests its relative homogeneity and stability concerning competitive outlooks. (Information concerning stability is useful in charting the dynamics of strategic-group migrations over time.) Between-group variance suggests mobility barrier heights; the distances separating asymmetric strategic groups from a convergence that could result in volatile competition. Useful scalings of this information depend on algorithm choices and dimension selections.

Assuming that an acceptable scale has been selected for clustering and that some range of the appropriate number of clusters can be estimated, managers who use cluster analysis must still choose the dimensions for clustering and appropriate measures of those variables. If managers seek a parsimonious solution (one that uses the fewest variables to enhance clarity of interpretation), then selecting the *right* dimensions becomes the most crucial part of this analysis.

Discussion of Clustering Analysis

This section refers to an empirical test of clustering, described in Harrigan (1985a), to map retailing establishments. Space constraints require the technical details to be deleted herein. The discussion is offered to suggest how one might interpret cluster analysis results. Interested readers are encouraged to consult the original article.

When interpreting the clustering output which generated strategic groups information concerning both the within- and between-group distances is useful. Briefly, the tightness of the group's structure suggests the relative homogeneity within the group. Loose groups—those with large distances among members—are more likely to face intra-group discord because their outlooks toward competition would be less homogeneous than a tight group. Intra-group discord could signal group instability. (See appendix table A–5 for a sample interdifference matrix. The analysis presents a mere snapshot of industry dynamics. Depending on the fineness of data employed, the analysis could be repeated frequently enough to track significant intragroup migrations toward boundaries with other groups.)

The distances between strategic groups—represented by the distance between clusters in table A–5—suggest the relative heights of mobility barriers separating groups from emulation by potential entrants. Where there are great distances between the strategic groups—where the mobility barriers between the strategic groups are high—the likelihood of convergence by firms with dissimilar outlooks is lower—hence the dangers of volatile competition erupting between members of different strategic groups is lower.

But where the interdifference matrix in table A–5 indicates that the distance between the strategic groups is not great—where the mobility barriers are not high—but where the groups are asymmetric on key dimensions, the likelihood that volatile rivalry will erupt as market growth slows becomes *greater*. Thus clustering output can suggest a mapping of the structure within an industry as well as its dynamics.

Managers with an intuitive feel for their industry and many years of experience in competing with other firms would find this expository tool of lesser value for them than for an analyst that lacked these insights and needed a first-cut approach to understanding the industry's population. Successive iterations of cluster analysis, using different dimensions as criteria, could be helpful in developing a sense of competition within fragmented industries or where there are many factors to consider.

A very heavy element of managerial judgment is needed in developing the cluster dimensions and interpreting the results. To the extent that each industry may require different strategies to attain competitive advantage (because their structures differ and evolve dissimilarly over time), managerial discretion is needed in assessing how competitors differ most significantly. Whether strategic groupings are accomplished by using statistical algorithms or hand-sorted categorizations, the dimensions used in grouping firms can best be developed *after* studying differences in competitive conduct to identify significant but overlooked ways of attaining strategic success.

The strategic-groups and mobility-barriers concepts are theoretical in nature. Clustering algorithms are essentially *atheoretic,* and caution must be used in applying this tool to generate estimates of mobility barriers and members of strategic groups. The dimensions employed must be consistent with those theorized as being most important in distinguishing competitors' approaches to their market.

3
The Changing Locus of Competition

T his chapter is devoted to disabusing managers of the notion that good ideas are created only (1) at headquarters research facilities and (2) in house. The chapter presents evidence concerning where innovation has been occurring and why new approaches to maturing innovation may be necessary. In particular, suggestions are offered concerning the need for joint ventures as a part of firms' global strategies and for temporary management teams as a transition agent in moving to a new policy on innovation. First, however, to set the stage for those ideas, the old model of international innovation must be contrasted with the new realities.

The International Product Cycle and the Diffusion of Innovation

The international product-cycle model (Vernon 1966) assumed that as products evolve through their life cycle (Kotler 1972), their marketing and production needs change. It suggested that international trade and investment patterns of these products evolved over time as well. Thus it explained why products were manufactured at one location and sold at another. One important premise of the international product-cycle model was that innovations usually occurred close to home (Hirsh 1965; Vernon 1966).

Support for this proposition came from both supply and demand factors in the mid-1960s. On the supply side, innovators were believed to be more likely to recognize the preferences and needs of local markets, and accordingly would direct their energies toward fulfilling these needs.

Adapted from articles that originally appeared in *Advances in Strategic Management,* Volume 1, 1983, by permission of the publisher, JAI Press Inc.; in the *Journal of Business Strategy,* Spring 1984, by permission of the publisher, Warren, Gorham & Lamont, Inc.; and in the *Columbia Journal of World Business,* Summer 1984, by permission of the publisher, Columbia University.

(Risk-averse innovators focused their attentions close to home because they perceived the exploitation of local markets to be less risky than the attempted exploitation of geographically remote ones.) On the demand side, the price elasticity of demand for new products was generally low (Rogers 1971). Thus cost considerations were held to be less important than the need to persuade consumers to adopt new products at this early stage. The need for frequent and effective communication between the producer and the market was considered paramount at this embryonic phase of development.

The international product-cycle model held that product traits evolved toward those attributes that best represented the trade-offs between cost and differentiation as time passed. Under this model, a ten-year-old product was rarely a replica of its prototype, as a result of experience-curve factors, changing tastes, and the nature of competition. It also argued that firms' domestic corporate bases would be the locus of primary innovation and manufacturing for those labor-saving products that appealed to consumers in the home markets with high disposable incomes. (Note the ethnocentric assumption that only domestic markets are comprised of consumers with high disposable incomes.)

The international product-cycle model was used to explain U.S. patterns of innovation for over a decade. In 1984, however, this model no longer reflects behaviors within U.S. firms adequately. It misses questions concerning product and process innovation that have become key to effective strategy formulation. It misrepresents reality in several ways.

First, the traditional model suggested that as products matured, many forces would push cost reduction closer to the foreground of competitive needs because, as more information about market needs became available, more opportunities for standardization became feasible (although concessions to the stylistic preferences of each nonstandardizable market were also made). Second, it argued that competitive pressures would force firms to seek ways of increasing consumer value by lowering costs. Finally, it suggested that the bulk of purchases would be made by the early majority rather than the innovators as consumer price elasticities increased (Rogers 1971). As the maturing process occurred, knowledge would be diffused overseas.

The international product cycle suggested that few exports from firms' domestic bases would occur early in the life of products. As time progressed, however, and as experience levels increased and their export volume grew, decisions to expand their scope of manufacturing operations would occur. Often production facilities would be set up in key foreign markets after marketing facilities there had proved successful. Thus the decision to operate abroad progressed in stages, as did the diffusion of innovation.

Competitive forces leading innovating firms to set up production facilities overseas were quite predictable. Growing export volume in firms' domestic markets eventually reached levels where production operations (at volumes respresented by minimum efficient scale) could take place at another plant site. Even where the opportunity to produce at minimum efficient plant scale *alone* was not attractive enough to induce firms to locate manufacturing sites overseas, the desire to preempt potential competitors was a strong motivation (MacMillan 1983). Moreover, the desire to hurdle tariff barriers (or other barriers to protect local employment goals, balance of payments, economic growth, or other economic objectives from import competition served as an added inducement for timely investments in overseas markets. Soon after innovating firms decided to produce abroad, rivals followed in short order (Knickerbocker 1973b).

Changes in the Logic of International Competition

Global strategies are those that recognize that competition can no longer be confined to a single nation's boundaries. Industries become global for many reasons, and firms need an approach designed to meet the new challenges of this change (Hout, Porter, and Rudden 1982). When this occurs, firms must reexamine their assumptions concerning how competitive advantage can be gained by integrating the operations of diverse geographic locations.

The international product cycle discussed earlier has described the logic U.S. firms once used in forging international strategies. These old ways of thinking about international competition must be revised in light of the effects of resource scarcity, changing demographics concerning affluence, and local governments' industrial policies. Also, firms must cope with the effects of technological change on minimum efficient scale, shorter product lives, and highly appropriate knowledge in their core businesses. The effects of these forces on the locus of innovation and competitive dynamics are considered in this section.

Innovation and Scarcity

The international product-cycle model suggests that innovation is a response to relative scarcity or abundance of factor endowments in particular locations (Vernon 1966). In essence, "necessity is the mother of invention" (Ewing 1981; Gilpin 1975; Franko 1976). There is abundant historical evidence to support this contention. If one reads the popular economic literature of England during the 1890s, including the writings of Jevons, one realizes that the entire Industrial Revolution was threatened by the coal shortage (Rostow 1977). The British feared they had come close to exhausting all the deposits of coal close to the surface. Their redeeming innovation was new mining technology that permitted the recovery of deeper coal deposits. During the Napoleonic Wars, when France was cut off from Spanish alkalis, the French invented the Leblanc process for creating synthetic alkalis. When the Germans were cut off from Chilean nitrates during World War II, they developed the Haber process for making nitrates (Vernon 1977). U.S. firms developed synthetic rubber in response to wartime threats to natural rubber supplies, and began intensive research and development efforts (which resulted in sulfa drugs and other miraculous cures), respectively, only after being severed from German parent firms (Harrigan 1983c).

The relative scarcity of labor in the United States once made it a fertile ground for the innovation of labor-saving devices (Vernon 1966). During the 1970s the demand for energy-saving devices and processes stimulated innovation activity in the area of alternative forms of energy, including biomass, solar, and photovoltaic processes. (For some innovators, the energy glut of 1984 is merely a temporary aberration in the consumption of a finite resource whose reserves are clearly declining.)

The implications of energy scarcities for the geographical pattern of innovation and for future movements through the international product cycle are particularly noteworthy. The Japanese, who are heavily dependent on outsiders for energy supplies, have undertaken innovative business arrangements to supplement their weaknesses (Yoshino 1976; Tsurumi 1976). The ramifications of their willingness to accommodate the desires of local partners in order to achieve their objectives will have far-reaching effects on the structure of other global industries and on the locus of innovative activity. Given their historical experiences, it is likely that the infrastructures of Japanese (and European) R&D facilities will be conducive to the development of energy-saving products and processes. One would expect to see energy-saving innovations developed in Europe or Japan and then moved to the United States initially via export and subsequently through local manufacture via foreign direct investment by these innovators. This pattern of geographical development and diffusion has already been witnessed in small automobiles, consumer electronics, and other industries where local manufacturers ignored these sizes or product configurations in their product lines (Orski 1980). In summary, there is good reason to believe that a new pattern in trade and investment will emerge for a significant range of products. Innovation will occur in Europe or Japan. At first, the new products will be exported to the United States, and later they will be manufactured in the United States under license, through joint ventures, or by the subsidiaries of innovating European and Japanese multinationals, as well as by the *overseas affiliates* of U.S. firms (Hughey and Kanabayashi 1983; Mariti and Smiley 1983; Vitorovich 1983).

Innovation and Affluence

The presence of a large high-income market is also significant in shaping innovative behavior and patterns of trade. By 1984 median income levels for the Japanese and for many European markets had been level with those of the United States for a good length of time, with the result that the portfolio of consumer goods in many Japanese and European households is far more similar to that of U.S. households than was the case fifteen years earlier. In some consumer electronics products, in fact, maturity and market saturation occurred in Japan earlier than in the United States (thus spurring exports of those products from Japan to the United States).

There is ample reason to believe that the United States is no longer the primary site of innovations designed to appeal to a mass high-income market. For example, the Michelin radial tire was developed in France but is now manufactured and widely used in the United States. Videotape recorders (VTRs) were invented for professional use by Ampex but were developed for the consumer electronics market in Japan (by Sony and Matsushita). Videotape machines are manufactured by U.S. and European firms under licenses from the innovators (or the innovators act as sources for private-brand labeling if a U.S. firm's sales volume is too low to manufacture the VTRs in house). To be sure, U.S. firms will continue to have a share of the innovations aimed at high-income consumers, but the key point is that the almost exclusive U.S. dominance in this sector of innovation (Vernon 1966) has eroded substantially (and will continue to erode).

Innovation and Industrial Policy

Having discussed how changes in factor scarcity and income patterns may alter the geographical pattern of product innovation and diffusion, it is necessary to explain herein how changes in the role of government could substantially modify the international product-cycle model's predictions. Changes in U.S. industrial policy, such as support for local R&D efforts, relaxation of antitrust laws to facilitate joint ventures, legislation of local-content quotas, and other efforts designed to stimulate local innovation, could modify the pattern Vernon (1966) had predicted (Baldridge 1983; Brodley 1979; Merrifield 1983; Rowe 1980). Government-guided emphasis on research signals an increasing role for federal policies in shaping future technologies where leadership is desired (Ewing 1981). As U.S. firms develop strategies for sharing ideas, technological innovations, and other assets that could give them competitive advantages, federal industrial policies could have significant effect on the structures of many domestic industries that are becoming global (Banks 1981; Beamish and Lane 1982; Davies 1977; Duncan 1980; Ferguson 1981; Flaim 1977; Gullander 1975; Hlavacek and Thompson 1976; Killing 1980, 1982).

Shorter Product Lives

The time frame in which products pass through the product cycle is shortening as a result of changes in the strategies and structures of modern business enterprise, particularly within the multinational corporation due to the development of global industries (Porter 1980). Competitive strategy has become more concerned with experience-curve and appropriability concepts, and these concepts limit the applications of the international product-cycle model. Finally, the way in which multinational enterprises develop innovations and diffuse them across national boundaries is affected by their organizational structures.

The experience-curve concept, which relates how unit costs of production decrease from the first prototype to present-day volumes, suggests that firms that pioneer promising products subject to steep experience curves should seize large market shares by pricing low and expanding production facilities rapidly. Low-cost producers who preempt potential entrants by racing quickly down experience curves will export their products or manufacture overseas more rapidly than firms that are skimming their markets or exploiting a niche. Their need for large-volume markets means the former group of firms will develop foreign markets more rapidly to sizes that make foreign manufacturing economic.

It is not surprising that new products have become more important in firms' portfolios recently. If innovations are difficult, time-consuming, and costly to copy, they offer an enduring competitive advantage. If innovations are easily, quickly or cheaply copied, innovators must move preemptively to exploit their competitive advantage before rivals copy their ideas.

New products have played an increasingly important role in the strategies of many firms as their industries became subject to shorter product lives. The percentage of sales accounted for by the new products (those less than four years old) of machinery firms, for example, virtually doubled between 1960 and 1970 (Scherer 1980), and in the consumer sector the percentage of sales attributed to new products similarly doubled during this period. Table A–6 in the appendix shows the increasingly important role of new products in international arenas. One strategic response global firms could use to cope with these technological pressures is to focus their innovative efforts on those products that offer an enduring competitive advantage. Some global firms are still involved, to a substantial degree, in product lines whose innovations can be copied easily as a result of exit barriers or in order to hold these products in their full-line portfolio to block potential entrants.

How could such firms exploit their transitory competitive advantage? Assuming that innovators seek to maximize sales revenue during their short-run advantage while minimizing investment exposure (and maximizing scale economies) basic research efforts could be combined in a skillful mixture of timely export, licensing, or joint-venture agreements to maximize market penetration and short-run profits. By moving quickly in using these proceeds, they could later develop products that offer more enduring advantages before emulators can reduce their margins.

The implications of this example for the international product-cycle model are similar to those for an aggressive experience-curve strategy. One would expect firms with transitory competitive advantages to pass quickly to a strategy of global transshipments from low-cost manufacturing sites. Thus corporate strategy creates a temporal compression in the rate of innovation needed to succeed. As table A–6 indicates, the international product cycle has been compressed with respect to time. From 1971 to 1975, almost 40 percent of all U.S. innovations included in the sample were produced overseas within one year of their U.S. introduction. This statistic stands in sharp contrast to a 10 percent rate from 1956 to 1960.

By starting with these corporate strategies—racing down the experience curve and quick exploitation of transitory competitive advantage—and incorporating other contemporary realities, a more powerful application of the product cycle may be developed. The key variable that best seems to explain the time compression of the product-cycle model is multinational organizational structure. The next section explains how skillful use of organizational arrangements have enabled firms to manipulate their global strategies more effectively.

Corporate Strategy and Organization Structure

All these changes to accommodate the changing locus of competition cannot occur overnight. Several researchers have substantiated that changes in organizational structure are painful and complex, but inevitable once strategy changes have been realized (Bartlett 1983; Chandler 1962; Davies 1976; Rumelt 1974). Thus, as firms become more involved in foreign markets, their organizations (and ways of conceptualizing the coordination of international activities) necessarily undergo changes. Whether international operations are centralized in a division that administers export sales, licensing arrangements, and facilities overseas or are integrated into product-line responsibility, the changes sketched earlier in the international product-cycle model suggest a need for new ways of thinking about introducing new products and organizing this process.

Global Organizations

In an emerging multinational organization, innovations developed in domestic markets are exploited there first, and international units are often given second priority. As foreign operations assume a greater role in overall corporate activities, and the focus of corporate strategy becomes global, firms have the opportunity to match product innovations with market opportunities almost immediately *wherever they may occur*. Effective global systems would permit a rapid matching of local product needs with innovations; and, where the specific products needed are not immediately available, centralized resource allocators could hire the innovating unit within the corporate family that is best suited to develop products to be its supplier. (Priorities would be established according to market-attractiveness measures, experience-curve and appropriability criteria, and other dimensions deemed crucial to global strategies in order to ration scarce research monies.)

Table A–7 suggests a general trend toward faster responses for firms using globalized organizational structures. Thus firms with international divisions manufacture new products abroad more rapidly than do similar firms without divisions of commensurate status. In the case of functionally organized firms, 40 percent of the innovations from firms with some form of international division were manufactured overseas within two years or less, but only 6 percent for those without international divisions. For firms organized along product lines, the analogous figures were 33 percent for firms with international divisions, 18 percent for firms without. About 80 percent of all products innovated within globally integrated organizations were manufactured abroad within two years or less, and every innovation for that subgroup was diffused globally within five years or less.

As the structures of multinational firms evolve (in response to their global strategies), the time frame in which the international product cycle progresses is compressed substantially. Briefly, in a world populated by global firms with globalized matrix structures, questions of the geographical location of innovation have virtually *no* place in explaining patterns of trade. As global systems become crucial as a means of competing for competitive advantage, innovations must be developed in multiple locations, refined in other sites where value can be added, and adapted to local markets where opportunities seem most attractive. Rapid product lives and rapid technological change will exacerbate firms' needs for coordinating mechanisms to accelerate information exchange and facilitate innovative activity.

In some settings, these mandates will be achieved by forming coalitions with a variety of domestic industry participants (Harrigan 1985c). In other settings, firms will have to break down insular viewpoints and parochial loyalties to surmount national boundaries and a not-invented-here syndrome that can taint innovative organizations. Greater autonomy and status equalization may also be necessary to incubate the type of corporate setting where overseas subsidiaries receive commensurate attention and opportunities to innovate in the interests of their global family. Although the precise balance of these trade-offs will differ from firm to firm, it is no longer safe to rely on a unidimensional innovation strategy within global industries.

Joint Ventures

As business risks soar and competition grows fiercer, firms will embrace joint ventures with increasing frequency. This should not be surprising. Joint ventures have long been used by entrepeneurial firms to expand into new markets, particularly within newly industrializing nations. Operating joint ventures represent a significant change in industry structures and in competitive behavior. They can be a more versatile competitive tool than earlier studies have indicated (Berg, Duncan, and Friedman 1982).

Operating Joint Ventures Defined. *Operating joint ventures* are partnerships by which two or more firms create an entity to carry out a productive economic activity. Each partner takes an active role in decision making, if not also in the child's operations. Operating joint ventures do not include passive financial investments made by parties who are not involved in the new entity's strategic business decisions. They are the type of arrangements Killing (1983) suggested firms avoid.

Parent firms embrace joint ventures because they are ways to implement changes in their strategic postures or to defend current strategic postures against forces too strong for one firm to withstand (Edström 1975a and b). They allow each partner to concentrate their resources in those areas where they possess the greatest relative competence, while diversifying into attractive but unfamiliar business areas. Firms could use joint ventures to coordinate their activities within a global system. This is a novel suggestion. Although firms will often think of production scale economies, technological innovation, and new sourcing arrangements as a means of meeting the global challenge, fewer firms may recognize the advantages of joint ventures. Yet operating joint ventures offer a means of leveraging firms' advantages to succeed within global industries.

Managers have often disparaged joint ventures in the past, believing them to be too complex, too ambiguous, or too inflexible (Killing 1983). But as the challenges of global competition increase, as projects grow larger and more risky, and as technologies become too expensive for one firm to afford, managers must learn how to use joint ventures, even in their firms' home economics. As an intermediate option (between acquisition or internal development and dependence on outsiders) joint ventures represent a special, highly flexible means of facilitating innovation or achieving other strategic goals that managers should not overlook as their industries become global (Gullander 1976). Joint ventures offer firms a window or promising new technologies such as genetic engineering, videotext, and synfuels. They can be a means of utilizing a new manufacturing process (such as continuous casting in the steel industry), a by-product (as in many chemical processes), or a new capability (such as transmitting services over existing communications lines).

Joint ventures offer salvation for firms within older global industries (such as automotive, farm equipment, and petrochemicals) as well. Given the political realities of offsets and coproduction requirements in order to conduct international trade, joint ventures among partners of different nationalities are becoming imperative (Vernon 1977). Joint economies, coproduction, common procurement, and other aspects of joint ventures are being used to ward off competitors that are making inroads into firms' key markets (Harrigan 1985c).

In brief, joint ventures offer many internal, competitive and strategic benefits. They provide firms with resources for which there are no equally efficient and available substitutes (Bachman 1965). Some projects would never be undertaken without this means of spreading costs and risks (Ballon 1967). Some firms could not retain their positions, given the rapid pace of change in global competition, without joint ventures (Bivens and Lovell 1966).

The Decision to Form Joint Ventures. Firms will cooperate in forming joint ventures only if the needs of each partner are great enough and if they can add resources that are complementary to the other's attributes. The resources firms possess will give them the basis for bargaining power when entering joint ventures, but if their needs for cooperation are great enough, this potential power will be mitigated (Fouraker and Siegel 1963). The balance between these opposing forces will be realized in the form the joint venture (JV) takes. It will be apparent in the control mechanisms partners use to control thĕir interests in the JV, in the vertical relationships they maintain with the JV, and with its stability.

Successful joint ventures serve their purpose without disrupting their parents' strategic well-being. The key to successful joint ventures will be a meeting of minds (Riker 1962). Effective joint ventures depend on trust, but they are often forged as a compromise between two or more parent firms who would rather own the child wholly (Schermerhorn 1976). Like a marriage, they tolerate their wayward partners to attain some advantage that satisfies their needs.

Barriers to Joint-Venture Formation. Joint ventures can be used to fortify parent firms' weaknesses in the face of global competition, but recognition of weaknesses does not come easily to complacent firms (Harrigan 1985c). Their unwillingness to see that their industries have become global creates barriers to firms' uses of joint ventures or other adaptive strategies.

The principal barriers to forming joint ventures are strategic in nature. Uncertainties regarding their abilities to manage operating joint ventures also erect barriers to joint-venture formation. Briefly, strategic costs are valued more highly than the benefits firms believe they can attain. The high entry barriers that would normally deter a single firm from penetrating a new market or learning about a new technology are reasons to band together in forming joint ventures in the face of global competition.

Externally imposed barriers to joint ventures include political restrictions on ownership, patent restrictions, competitor retaliation, and other conditions. These may be easier to overcome than firms' own attitudinal barriers because the comparative costs of off-shore manufacturing would inevitably drive domestic firms to relocate unless governments permitted them to join forces with efficient world-scale firms.

Joint ventures are transitory organizational forms. In environments of scarce resources, rapid rates of technological change, and massive capital requirements, however, joint ventures may be the best way for some underdog firms to attain better positions in global industries that they consider important.

Temporary Management Organizations

Stress will plague firms' management systems unless accommodations are made for new ways of transferring some information across shared facilities rather than along functional lines. Furthermore, new product responsibilities (encompassing the *make* and *sell* tasks) must be delineated to accommodate changing markets and ways of competing across geographical boundaries, and control systems must parallel these new realities. Finally, the divergent time and goal orientations of managers must be reconciled in firms' planning systems.

As technological life cycles grow increasingly shorter, organizations that make up a firm's major mix of businesses will be threatened unless they can facilitate transformational planning activities (Steiner 1969). *Transformational strategies* are those that lead the firm into a more desirable strategic posture. The transformation pursued may be a modification of the firm's existing posture within the same business, or a change of status such as entry into new businesses or exit from existing ones. Transformational strategies, if they are effective, surmount the mobility (or exit) barriers that inhibit change. The facile execution of such repositionings often requires the creation of specially trained temporary management teams during these periods of transition because the firm must proceed with ongoing operations while facilitating relatively major changes in its outlook and operations.

When demand for a mature product declines, for example, competitive pressures intensify until excess capacity can be eased out of the industry. Previous studies have indicated that the firm must commit its assets quickly if it hopes to implement certain types of strategies successfully (Harrigan 1980c). The firm chooses its best strategic response— to remain in that business or to depart—but its *means of implementing* the decision may be unclear as a result of (1) uncertainty concerning resource allocations and (2) competitors' actions. Implementation of its strategy will be incremental because each subsequent step is dependent upon the actions of competitors, and coordination of the many tasks within the business unit will be needed. The strategic transformation team's task will also be delicate because they must engineer a program to achieve a specific outcome, not fully understanding what pitfalls may be encountered as they grope to attain the company's goals and to learn to work with each other.

Creating Strategic Transformation Teams. Temporary management organizations (TMOs) comprising professional managers and supported by technicians offer a facility that can position the firm to initiate strategic changes in its industry context, or can make the firm more adaptable to structural changes initiated by others. However, it may be difficult to institutionalize the facility to create this type of temporary team despite the benefits that could accrue to the firm as a result of organizational resistance. Such attitudes constitute *mobility barriers* that managers must strive to overcome.

Classical organization theory has not developed an adequate approach to the dynamics of strategic task groups because it does not resolve the difficulties of creating a program where none existed before. However, organizations do adapt their structures to handle new constraints and contingencies somehow (Thompson 1967). The process by which this occurs is determined by the purposeful manipulation of the planning and controls system, the measurement and evaluation system, the formal reporting relationships and information flows, and the use of standardized procedures (Bower 1970; Lawrence and Lorsch 1972).

Changes would be required in the firm's organizational context to foster a culture where these teams could be created and disbanded. The measurement and evaluation of performance would have to change, and rewards would be needed to elicit the desired behaviors from managers in the pool considered for TMO formation. Promotions and career-path planning would have to incorporate the new behavioral expectations implicit in team membership. Special prestige would have to be accorded to participation in the team or in past service to such teams. As with Jelinek's R&D-intensive firm (1977), the "particularized culture" of traditional work groups would have to be replaced by a "common culture." Implementation of this strategic tactic would necessarily mean that the perception of the management task would be different from that prevalent in U.S. society, except perhaps in military societies. This change would mean that innovation no longer would come gradually from fragmented groups who were mildly unsatisfied with procedures or performance. Rather, *all* managers would be expected to function effectively within temporary task groups that would be dedicated to intense periods of analysis, innovation, and integration.

Remaining Flexible. Designing complex organizations for transformational planning implies that in the process of institutionalization, as described by Selznick (1957), one of the values that is incorporated into the firm's operating system is *flexibility*. Designing an organization to remain flexible—that is, to shift easily into the appropriate design mode—in this case, task forces—and out again, raises issues of self-interest of organization members, as well as issues concerning whether and how to institutionalize the transformation process. There seems to be a contradiction in this concept.

If an organization has used a particular strategy successfully in a past problem-solving context, it is likely to try to apply the same strategy for solution of a similar problem. In addition to this attempt to repeat past successes, March and Simon (1958) note that an institutionalized innovative group loses some of its problem-solving enthusiasm. Previously, when a task was managed by a project team, the organization members put in a great deal of overtime and took pride and pleasure in their work;

but as programmed activity replaced innovation, excitement waned and feelings of anticlimax were expressed.

It seems likely that future managerial challenges will be less routine and more complex, and will require a longer time orientation for responses. If this change endures, management and its strategic staff would require a better understanding of the use of task forces and other temporary management organizations to form the bridge between strategic positionings. Where management faces shorter response times and increasingly diverse task orientations in the future, as in the example of increasing globalization of their industries, an understanding of contingency plans to manage strategic transformational teams would seem to be desirable. Similar skills will be needed to enter (and exit) joint ventures without friction and to nurture innovation more effectively.

Part II
Intrafirm Business-Unit Relationships

T he chapters in part II explore vertical-integration strategies to study questions concerning synergy and strategic flexibility. These are *make-or-buy* decisions involving sister business units in buyer-seller relationships. Firms can often increase their strategic flexibility by deintegrating operations and contracting out instead.

Managers appear to like vertical integration. Why else would their firms do so much of it when so little is warranted? Fast-growing companies in brand-new industries often move too quickly toward making their own materials. They do so because they understand the technology and hope to dominate the industry as they mature. In most cases, embryonic industries are volatile. Markets and technology change so swiftly that the firms do better if they concentrate production on the highest-margined niches and wait to expand operations either into suppliers' areas or into end-user markets later.

Well-run companies in established industries usually integrate vertically to increase margins. The shrewdest of established companies, however, integrate vertically only when they are certain that a market is enduring. Prudent managers can recognize when their business units are becoming trapped by vertical integration. For example, when industries start to decline, managers often weaken their companies by integrating vertically without realizing what they are doing. When they give special terms and financing to struggling customers, this is a de facto form of forward integration. Instead, managers should be asking whether it is time to cut losses and get out of the business.

When companies operate at low capacity, they often bring back work they previously contracted out. This makes sense if it does not require more investment in fixed assets; but even then, companies should resist vertical integration if their industry is sharply cyclical, if they have strong bargaining power with distributors and suppliers, or if their strategy is geared to market niches.

The Reagan administration's looser antitrust policy is providing an opportunity for companies to work more closely with suppliers and competitors. Two firms in the same business, for instance, might try to work out an informal arrangement where one firm concentrates production on building components for the other firm, which acts as a supplier to the end-user market. Firms might move toward joint ventures as an alternative to vertical integration where possible. Joint ventures spread risks and open the company to new technologies and markets.

A sharp increase in demand for the company's products offers a great opportunity to try contracting out, especially in mature industries. By doing so, managers hedge their companies' risks. Better yet, managers do not have to add plant capacity or new equipment until they are certain that demand will endure. Contracting out is also a way to stop the erosion of the company's rate to return on products that may be very important to their customers (because they encourage them to buy other, higher-margined products that the firm also makes). What better time to use outsiders as sources of supply? A low-margined product could be a winner for another company with less overhead even though it is a loss leader to the firm that pioneered it.

Even when management is certain that vertical integration is wise, they could keep an eye on the company's production costs by contracting out some part of the work on an experimental basis. (Such comparisons are not costly or difficult to make.) Other sourcing opportunities include: parts of the production process that require new, expensive equipment; distribution for a new product; design work and R&D; and company financial services.

The greatest barrier to contracting out is management's fear that it may lose control. The way to get around that fear is to enter the process *slowly*. Ask questions before contracting out any work, and then go slowly. Discuss specifications in great detail. Get prospective suppliers to suggest changes in design or in ways the work is done. Let suppliers bid for the work with tight quality-control specifications and delivery requirements. But be tough about contractors' performances, and do not build inventories up too high because of fear that the contractors cannot deliver on time. To win the advantages of contracting out, firms may have to raise their tolerance for stockouts for some products. Be careful, however, about contracting out to firms that may go under if the contract is withdrawn. (That situation will encourage companies to *stay* with inadequate suppliers longer than they should.)

The prime candidates to shed in-house production now are in basic industries: autos, farm machinery, food processors, industrial equipment, organic chemicals, and steel. Industries that have already improved profits by discarding a great deal of their in-house production include textile producers that at one point were integrated from producing fibers to making clothes, and whiskey distillers that used to make their own bottles and barrels.

Managers of companies that are forward-integrated (into distribution and marketing of their product lines in company-owned retail establishments, for instance) or backward-integrated (making all their own parts and components) must take a hard look at the cost-effectiveness of those operations right now. That is hard to do. In-house sources seem so comfortable, and therein lies the danger. Many companies outgrow the reasons for vertical integration—but fail to question them. Managers should take an especially hard look if companies are producing more of a part than they need for their own use. This often leads to inefficiencies. If the facilities that produce parts are running at low capacity, the cost of each unit may be much higher than it should be. Also, companies have to sell excess parts, using scarce management talent that should be put to use selling higher-margined final products. Finally, there is danger in making parts whose prices are more volatile than in the past. This could be a good time to move the risk out of the company and into the hands of suppliers.

From this overview, it should be clear that the approach taken in chapters 4 and 5 differs substantially in its outlook from that of earlier studies of vertical integration. Briefly, it argues that business units may be vertically related to each other in the chain of processing (from ultraraw materials to finished products) yet not buy from or sell to each other. Intrafirm transfers of goods and services are discrete strategic decisions separate from the investment decisions of diversification. Synergies from sharing resources or capabilities must be consciously managed in order to make them occur.

The issues of intrafirm business-unit relationships are developed in the following sequence. A framework for using the dimensions of vertical integration strategy is developed in chapter 4. Empirical tests of the relationships follow in chapter 5. Although readers may skip the empirical results of these tests without damage to their understanding of these concepts, examinations of them will provide a more robust understanding of the limitations of arguments concerning the appropriate uses of vertical integration. (Tests of vertical integration strategies as exit barriers are presented in part III. Many forces that create impediments to strategic flexibility, in addition to vertical integration, are covered therein.)

4
Strategies for Vertical Integration

Make or buy? This simple phrase masks the complexities of firms' *vertical-integration strategies,* decisions that include whether to engage in the production of goods and services that could be sold to (or purchased from) other strategic business units (SBUs) of the firm, among others.

Vertical integration describes a variety of make-or-buy arrangements firms might use to obtain a ready supply of raw materials (and services) and a ready market for their outputs. It encompasses the coordination of vertical relationships between SBUs. Vertical integration is often necessary where markets cannot allocate resources in a manner that alleviates uncertainty (Williamson 1971, 1975), and it can be a means of avoiding search, negotiation, and regulatory costs (Coase 1937; Wiek 1969), especially where firms are highly dependent on stable supplies of resources (Pfeffer and Salancik 1978). Vertical integration could propel firms into businesses very different from their strategic core, as in the example of a motion picture studio entering the pay-cable television business.

Although vertical integration is one of the first diversification strategies firms consider as they progress from being single-business companies, it is not clear that vertical strategies that have worked well in the past will work as well as certain competitive factors change. Many business-unit managers resent a corporate policy requiring them to deal with a sister unit. Vertical-integration strategies involve decisions regarding the autonomy of these business units in trading with each other. Most research concerning it has assumed that the transaction cost savings of integration supersede the autonomy needs of SBUs. Accordingly, integrated firms have been expected to transfer all their relevant goods and services to adjacent, in-house business units.

This chapter offers a dynamic concept of vertical integration in which

Adapted from articles that originally appeared in the *Journal of Business Strategy,* Winter 1982, by permission of the publisher, Warren, Gorham & Lamont, Inc.; and in the *Academy of Management Journal,* October 1984 and June 1985, by permission of the publisher, the Academy of Management.

the key to effective management will be understanding when corporate needs for intrafirm cooperation might take precedence over the concerns of autonomous business units, and when the opposite might be true. It argues that the key to successful use of vertical integration is determining how broadly integrated the firm should be at a particular time, how much of each task should be done internally, and what form the venture should take. In developing this strategy framework, several new dimensions that characterize *all* vertical integration strategies are introduced. The new theoretical framework seeks to bridge the gap between economic treatments of vertical integration and activities observed in the histories of several industries. The nature of this gap is sketched in the following section.

The Phenomenon of Vertical Inegration

Although vertical integration has been recognized as one of the oldest and most frequently embraced growth strategies (Chandler 1977), strategy researchers have just begun to understand its complexities. It has long been a key force in the development of high productivity and managerial sophistication in U.S. business, and vertically integrated corporations have been key engines of change in the past and have increased shareholder wealth (Lubatkin 1982). There has been a significant diversity of findings concerning whether it is a profitable strategy or not (Buzzell 1983; Hawks 1984). Earlier findings that "dominant verticals" (Rumelt 1974), and vertical mergers were least successful as diversifications (Baker, Miller, and Ramsperger 1981) may have soured managers and academic researchers on the usefulness of this strategy unnecessarily. Often researchers took an overly aggregated view of vertical integration and did not recognize that it could be an effective strategy, provided it was used prudently.

There have also been a variety of opinions concerning how to use vertical integration effectively. Porter (1980), for example, has cautioned firms that backward (or forward) integration is a strategic decision that firms can make but once. This chapter, by contrast, argues that the several *dimensions* that characterize vertical integration can provide firms with substantially greater opportunities to fine-tune this strategy than had been recognized previously.

Because critics have not discerned how the important dimensions of vertical integration might be adapted over time (as industries change), they have not recognized how to make this a more durable and keen competitive weapon. Because successful vertical-integration strategies require the cooperation of several strategic business units (SBUs), the formulation of such strategies is in the province of the chief executive officer (CEO). In some cases, effective vertical integration may even require temporary subsidization of one business unit at the expense of another. Decisions regarding such SBU coordination (and resource allocation among them) must be made by the chief strategist, and thus effective vertical-integration strategies need to reflect both business-unit and corporate-level strategy requirements.

The issue of vertical integration deserves additional analysis because it has been misunderstood in the past, and because the development of a more rigorous means of analyzing this strategy (and the performance it promises) could result in the formulation of more effective industry linkages, more rapid technological improvements, stronger global strategies, and better use of vertical integration.

Benefits of Integration

As table A–8 in the appendix suggests, vertical integration should be considered from two viewpoints: (1) internal benefits (and costs), and (2) effects on competitive posture. Internal benefits affect the profitability of the strategy, and strengths in competitive posture enable firms to be more responsive to changes in market needs and less vulnerable to competitors' maneuvers. Firms sometimes knowingly undertake a more costly degree of integration than may be required to cut expenses. The principal competitive advantages of integration include:

Improved marketing and technological intelligence.

Superior control of the firms's economic environment.

Product differentiation advantages.

The last factor—irreplicable differentiation advantages—explains much of the costly integration observed in many industries.

Vertical integration has been an important managerial innovation and a necessary technological step in developing certain industries, but it may not be appropriate in the same form at all times. For example, ownership of ore mines, ships, foundries, rolling mills, and fabricating plants was necessary for steel companies to lower costs and improve productivity *in the 1890s*. In its early years, Ford Motor Company owned and operated every stage of processing, from iron ore to finish-and-trim operations (except tires and glass), because suppliers were not as willing to share Ford's gamble in "horseless carriages." Ford had to develop components to its specifications for itself. This is the type of vertical-integration behavior one might expect within emerging economies, where firms must provide their own infrastructures and other supplies.

By 1983, however, the U.S. economy and the automobile industry had matured such that uncertainties regarding generic product demand were reduced. Ford's outside suppliers were willing to invest in tooling and other assets to supply the automakers and high degrees of internal transfers were no longer necessary, if uneconomic. (Moreover, the throughput of U.S. automakers was not large enough for vertical integration to remain as economic as it once was.) The challenge from Japanese automakers was difficult to meet when firms such as Ford were so strategically inflexible. Moreover, vertical integration had lost some of its attraction because firms did not have the supporting mechanisms needed to reap the maximum synergies that might be available from vertically integrated linkages.

Costs of Integration

Being broadly or highly integrated is not risk-free, and it may be more costly. The technologies of some plants require large volumes of throughput to be efficient (suggesting a low-price, high-market-share goal). Yet during periods of depressed demand, when diseconomies (from excess capacity) are incurred, firms need customers who will pay premium prices for differentiations they value (suggesting a multilevel market approach is desirable). Firms must be wary lest their vertically integrated posture impede their strategic flexibility. Some firms, such as Robert Hall or Botany Industries, have suffered notable failures from vertical integration of the wrong type and/or used at the wrong time. But if managers better understood the many dimensions of vertical integration and the key forces that affect their abilities to execute vertical strategies well, they could better avoid fundamental errors associated with vertical integration and could maximize the benefits available in joining dissimilar but related businesses. The effects of these forces (and how firms could adjust them) are developed in this chapter's framework.

Vertical Integration as Diversification

Acquired firms are bundles of assets rather than single business units, as Occidental Petroleum discovered when courting Cities Service (and as duPont learned while absorbing Conoco). Acquisitions can offer vertical linkages as well as nonvertical diversifications. Corporate strategists must decide whether to retain the business units acquired incidentally in this fashion; and, if they are vertically related, strategists must decide whether to encourage intrafirm commerce (subsidy) or demand arm's-length transactions between vertical sister units. Thus more seemingly unrelated mergers have vertical elements to them than is generally recognized, but often strategists see no advantage to encouraging vertical relationships between in-house units. As explained later, this may occur because the opportunities for vertical competitive advantage have passed in some industries. In other cases, however, this occurs because managers did not recognize how to exploit the advantages of vertical integration effectively.

Definitions

Vertical integration is a complex strategy, and past economic treatments of it have not recognized the many ways to use make-or-buy decisions effectively. Vertical integration could involve *upstream* linkages, whereby sister business units provide raw or semiprocessed materials, components, or services to the business unit in question. Vertical integration could also involve *downstream* relationships, whereby sister business units purchase outputs from or act as distributors for the business unit under analysis. If corporate policies permit business units to make market-related decisions regarding intrafirm transfers of goods and services, each autonomous business unit could elect to trade (or not do business) with its sister. But sometimes corporate management intervenes in the make-or-buy decision to encourage integration between vertically related business units for reasons explained later.

Scholarly treatments of diversification have often skimped on discussions of vertical integration, and trade-offs in using it as a strategy have not been articulated adequately for managers. Vertical expansions should be screened with performance criteria as fine as those for firms' other diversification investments. To do so, this strategy option must be understood more clearly. The new approach is presented herein. The shortcomings of earlier concepts and measures of vertical integration are discussed in Harrigan (1985d).

Resource scarcities suggest that low rates of return can no longer be as acceptable as they once were. Thus, when managers realize that they have been *subsidizing* business activites for the sake of an advantage *whose time has passed,* they will have to divest unrenumerative activities and deintegrate disadvantageous relationships (Babcock 1970; Pearce 1984; Strebel 1983; Bowman 1980, 1984; Branch 1984; Montgomery 1984; Strategic Planning Associates 1984; and Woo 1984). In brief, the high-returns firms seek will not necessarily be found in high degrees or numerous stages of vertical integration. The problem is that some managers have not recognized these inefficiencies.

A New Look at Vertical Integration

The terminology introduced in this chapter explicitly recognizes that firms may enjoy the benefits of vertical relationships without owning upstream (or downstream) units entirely, and without transferring all their output internally. Firms may perform a variety of integrated activities in house (or not), and they may engage in many (or few) stages of processing in the chain of production from ultraraw materials to the final consumer. Most important, firms may adjust the dimensions of their vertical-integration strategies to suit competitive or corporate strategy needs. Vertical integration will not be the same under all circumstances in order to be effective; rather, it will be fine-tuned in accordance with changes in the forces to be outlined herein.

The economists' concept of vertical integration as involving only operations that are 100 percent owned and are physically interconnected to supply 100 percent of a firm's needs is outmoded. Under appropriate circumstances, quality control and access to stable supplies can be obtained through *quasi-integration* arrangements (explained later). Firms could contract for R&D services, for example, to use the technology of genetic engineering in product development. Or they could form joint ventures to obtain this capability. Firms could have components engineered to their tight and highly specific instructions by outsiders—as do Japanese automobile manufacturers, for example. And if their bargaining power is sufficient, firms can use a *kanban* or just-in-time system of inventory control that shifts the burden of holding costs to their suppliers (Ohmae 1982).

If firms prefer not to use outsiders as extensions of their corporate entity, a variety of other vertical arrangements are possible. Some firms may conclude they need not undertake certain activities at all. Eli Lilly, for example, uses outsiders exclusively with success to merchandise its ethical pharmaceuticals. Tandy/Radio Shack, by contrast, uses primarily its own retail outlets to distribute personal computers, but it has been increasing its use of outsiders. In other situations, firms may find they can enjoy the same integration economies, uncertainty reduction, competitive intelligence, and other benefits vertical linkages might provide through outsiders. Effective vertical-integration strategies mean recognizing *which* activities to perform in house, *how to relate* these activities to each other, *how much* of its needs the firm should satisfy in house, *how much ownership* equity needs to be risked in doing so, and *when* these dimensions should be adjusted to accommodate new competitive conditions.

The Dimensions of Vertical Strategy

In any vertical-integration strategy, conscious (or unconscious) decisions are made regarding (1) the breadth of integrated activities undertaken, (2) the number of stages of integrated activities, (3) the degree of internal transfers for each vertical linkage, and (4) the form of ownership used to control the vertical relationship. These dimensions will be explained in this section.

Number of Stages of Integrated Activity

The number of *stages* undertaken is the dimension of vertical integration many traditional views have embraced. The number of steps in the chain of processing in which the firm is engaged—from ultraraw materials to the final consumer—determines the number of *stages* of integration, as figure 4–1 illustrates. In it, firms A and B are both engaged in seven integrated stages. SBU 4 is the unit under study, and firms A and B are each engaged in three stages that are *upstream* of SBU 4 as well as three stages that are *downstream*. Also in figure 4–1, firm C is engaged in four integrated stages; two stages are upstream from SBU 4, and one stage is downstream.

Although figure 4–1 depicts the transformation process as an extension of adjacent stages' activities, it is possible for firms to skip a stage in the chain (by using outsiders for an intermediate processing step) in order to better monitor costs, to save an asset investments for facilities that would be underutilized if brought in house, or for other reasons. For example, within the electronics industry, some firms are engaged in several integrated stages connected to the microcomputers business; these firms produce not only microcomputers, but also microprocessor chips and semiconducter memories, photo-masks for etching electronic circuits, silicon wafers on which the circuits are inscribed, and other substrate materials. Other firms are engaged only in microcomputer assembly operations; they participate in one stage of processing. Within the oil industry, for example, some firms are engaged in many sequentially adjacent stages of operations, such as seismic exploration, land leasing, pipeline services, and refining, as well as production and wholesale (retail) distribution of gasoline, heating oil, and petrochemical products. Other firms only refine crude oil and ship it to wholesalers or other processors.

The number of integrated stages matters if firms do not manage complexity well. Thus firms must address decisions of *stages and breadth*

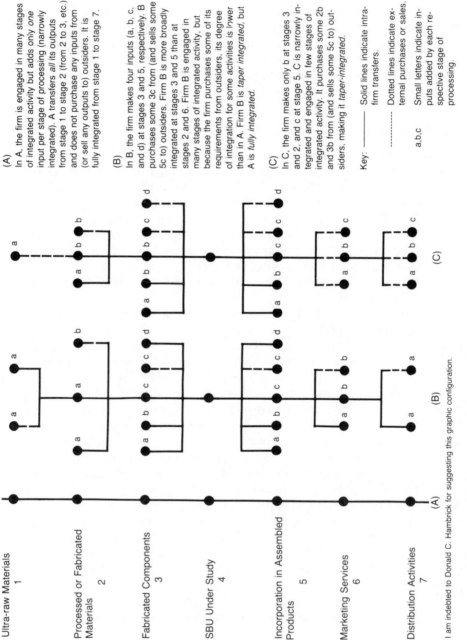

(A)
In A, the firm is engaged in many stages of integrated activity but adds only *one* input per stage of processing (narrowly integrated). A transfers *all* its outputs from stage 1 to stage 2 (from 2 to 3, etc.) and does not purchase any inputs from (or sell any outputs to) outsiders. It is fully integrated from stage 1 to stage 7.

(B)
In B, the firm makes four inputs (a, b, c, and d) at stages 3 and 5, respectively. B purchases some 3c from (and sells some 5c to) outsiders. Firm B is more broadly integrated at stages 3 and 5 than at stages 2 and 6. Firm B is engaged in many stages of integrated activity, but because the firm purchases some of its requirements from outsiders, its degree of integration for some activities is lower than in A. Firm B is *taper integrated*, but A is *fully integrated*.

(C)
In C, the firm makes only b at stages 3 and 2, and c at stage 5. C is narrowly integrated and engaged in few stages of integrated activity. It purchases some 2b and 3b from (and sells some 5c to) outsiders, making it *taper-integrated*.

Key: ———— Solid lines indicate intra-firm transfers.

.... Dotted lines indicate external purchases or sales.

a,b,c   Small letters indicate inputs added by each respective stage of processing.

Ultra-raw Materials
1

Processed or Fabricated Materials
2

Fabricated Components
3

SBU Under Study
4

Incorporation in Assembled Products
5

Marketing Services
6

Distribution Activities
7

I am indebted to Donald C. Hambrick for suggesting this graphic configuration.

Figure 4–1. Diagram of the Dimensions Characterizing Vertical-Integration Strategies

when they contemplate vertically linked strategies. For each technologically distinct activity, several stages of processing may be involved. Firms' SBUs may elect to perform some activites in house, but corporate strategists must decide whether upstream or downstream investments are warranted. The boundaries defining an SBU from its sisters are defined by top management and called *breadth* herein.

Breadth of Integrated Activities per SBU

The way in which firms define their SBUs' boundaries vary. The number of activities firms perform in house at any particular level of the vertical chain determines that SBU's *breadth* of integration, as figure 4–1 indicates, and broadly integrated SBUs (such as B3, B5, C3, and C5) perform more activities in house than others do. Broadly integrated SBUs could increase the firm's value-added margin substantially at their stage of processing because they make more goods and services in house, and vertically integrated firms could be broadly integrated at several stages of processing. Yet under the old image of vertical integration, no distinction would have been made between strategies involving broad (firms B and C) versus narrow (firm A) integration. No distinction would have been made, for example, between oil refineries that made a multitude of petrochemical products and those that made one product from petroleum feedstocks.

The breadth of integration matters because plants that engage in trying to produce too many components for a product line may lose opportunities to enjoy scale economies if their components are too diverse. Overly broad manufacturing policies could also mean that SBUs lose the cost advantages of purchasing components (or services) from more efficient outsiders. Sometimes, corporate strategy needs will impinge on SBUs' freedoms to adjust their breadth or degree of integration. The managers of an SBU often try to reduce its degree of internal transfers from sisters units and enlarge its sphere of responsibility by making many components the SBU could purchase from others.

Degree of Internal Transfers

Degree of integration determines the proportion of total output (of a particular component or service) an SBU purchases from (or sells to) its sister SBUs. *Fully integrated* SBUs transfer 95 percent (or more) of their requirements for a particular resource in house. *Taper-integrated* firms purchase more than 5 percent of their requirements for that resource from outsiders (Crandall 1968a, b). The degree of internal transfers matters because (as economic studies have noted) the minimum efficient plant sizes of upstream and downstream activities are rarely the same. Excess capacity is costly; yet some firms have concluded that the costs of allowing some portion of one SBU's plant capacity to be idle are justified by the advantages they perceive from fully integrated strategies.

Some portion of firms' vertically integrated chains are likely to be out of balance as a result of scale differences. Thus one SBU will either have to engage in transactions with outsiders or let its sister SBUs' excess capacity lie fallow. Corporate reward systems encourage (or discourage) efforts to dispose of excess outputs; and there could be several reasons for corporate strategy to prefer taper integration over more fully integrated arrangements, particularly where questions of technology are involved. Depending on the outside sources available, strategists could encourage the transfer of some, all, or none of the services and materials a business unit might provide its sister, and they can change the degree of integration upstream or downstream to suit their changing needs to control uncertainty over time.

Form of Integrated Ownership

The *form* of integrated ownership indicates the proportion of a firm's equity invested in a vertically linked venture; often carefully specified contracts, franchise, joint ventures, or other forms of quasi-integration can be good alternatives to wholly owned ventures. Figure 4–1 does not illustrate different forms of ownership, but these alternatives could be identified by the percentage of total equity firms risked in a particular vertical relationship.

Although many firms prefer to own vertically integrated units entirely, they need not own a business unit to control it and enjoy the benefits of vertical relationships. A variety of other control arrangements are possible. Quasi-integrated firms, for example, share ownership with others, underwrite part of the vertically related firm's capital structure, or possess other stakes in the business unit short of full ownership (Blois 1972). Hayes and Abernathy (1980) note that Japanese firms successfully use nonequity forms of controlling adjacent firms through long-term contracts (*kanban*), for example.

In many environments, firms can obtain leverage over other's assets without owning them fully. Often firms can secure knowledge, services, and materials in this manner with only a small ownership stake. For example, fledgling or undercapitalized firms can hurdle entry barriers by forming joint ventures with established firms. In brief, firms that exercise control over adjacent business units but do not own them are practicing a form of vertical integration as surely as firms that do not own their adjacent units because both firms can treat the outputs or services of these adjacent firms as though they were their own.

In summary, *all* vertical-integration strategies are comprised of degree, stages, breadth, and form; and some combinations of these dimensions occur more frequently than others. The decision to alter one dimension of this strategy will affect the values of the other dimensions, just as all pieces of a mobile will jiggle when one piece is moved.

Vertical-Integration Strategy Alternatives

How can firms best manage their needs for secure supplies or access to distribution channels (or other needed services)? There are several alternative vertical-integration strategies, but some are particularly tricky to manage because they require the firm to assume much of the responsibility for upstream or downstream services (or supplies) that would otherwise have been purchased. Unless strategic requirements (or competitive weaknesses) make full integration a necessity, the firm should transfer some of the risk of vertical integration to outside parties. These alternatives are: nonintegration, quasi-integration, taper integration, and full integration.

Nonintegration

Strategies for attaining materials and markets with *no* internal transfers and *no* ownership are like contracts. They are especially attractive when firms are reluctant to buy specialized assets, need to lower break-even points resulting from underdeveloped demand, or can arrange delivery schedules with suppliers (or distributors) as though they were extensions of the firm's assets. Koppers and Monsanto both used this approach to vertical integration successfully in genetic engineering, where demand was highly uncertain and technological change occurred rapidly, when synergies were low with ongoing businesses in 1981 and where they had high bargaining power with respect to upstream and downstream markets. Firms risk the lowest proportion of their assets when they contract for their needs.

Contracting out requires careful drafting of documents delineating responsibilities but no internal integration. Because virtually every function that firms perform internally could also be provided by outside suppliers, fabricators, wholesalers, and marketing representatives, a knowledge of how to use this network could be crucial when the firm must deintegrate or go to the external market. Contracting is best used in highly volatile industries. If the firm possesses great bargaining power, it may write contracts wherein outsiders perform R&D, promotion, or other services for the firm at preferential prices.

Quasi-Integration

Quasi-integrated firms need not own 100 percent of the adjacent business units in the vertical chain in order to enjoy the benefits of bonding their interests to other firms' interests. The bond between firms could take the form of cooperative ventures, minority equity agreements, loans or land guarantees, prepurchase credits, specialized logistical facilities, or understandings concerning customary arrangements (Blois 1972; Porter 1980). Downstream quasi-integration arrangements enable firms to retain a network of qualified distributors to maintain quality images. Upstream take-or-pay contracts and *kanban* arrangements enable firms to enjoy the advantages of vertical integration without assuming the risks of it. Whiskey distillers used quasi-integration successfully to penetrate diverse geographical markets, and microcomputer producers used it to obtain software and distribution of their products. The competitive scanning advantages of quasi-integration can be especially effective if firms using it devise intelligence-gathering mechanisms to use the information adjacent firms and competitors might provide.

Quasi-integrated arrangements place greater proportions of ownership equity at risk than contracting out does, but they also provide greater flexibility in responding to changing conditions than full ownership may provide. The third ownership alternative, full ownership, is not developed herein because it is most frequently observed. It assumes the firm exerts complete ownership control over the activities of the vertically linked business units. Full ownership risks the greatest proportion of equity, but many managers prefer it because they believe it is easier to control than contractual or quasi-integrated relationships.

Taper Integration

When firms have backward- or forward-integrated SBUs but rely on outsiders for a portion of their supplies or distribution as well, they are *taper integrated*. Such firms can monitor the R&D developments of outsiders, reduce vulnerability to strikes and shortages within their systems, and examine the products of competitors while enjoying the lower costs and greater advantages (and profit margins) of vertical integration. Their ability to buy from outsiders increases firms' bargaining power. Whenever physical interconnection is not necessary and firms can add substantial value through upstream or downstream activities, taper integration can be used effectively, as American Cyanamid did in ethical pharmaceuticals by supplying basic and finished chemicals to its Lederle Laboratories subsidiary when it was convenient to do so, but relying on outsiders to supply chemicals in other cases. Similarly, Amoco (Standard Oil of Indiana) and many other petroleum refiners found that upstream taper-integration arrangements provided them with access to enough crude oil to keep their plants running economically, and that selling a portion of their primary petrochemicals to other firms allowed them to gain scale economies through specialization in processing downstream. Taper integration represents a useful compromise between the desire to control adjacent businesses and the ability to retain strategic flexibility. It works well where raw materials are abundant (or subcontractors are readily available) and underutilized capacity does not incur meaningful diseconomies.

Full Integration

Fully integrated firms buy (or sell) *all* their requirements for a particular material or service internally. They operate their plants to satisfy a large portion of input requirements or consume a large portion of their output internally. This relationship frequently makes them market-share leaders for the materials in question (particularly if minimum-efficient-scale plants are large). Where balance is not a problem, economies can be substantial when using full integration. Transferring all the firm's needs for a particular good or service in house exposes it to increased risks of excess capacity, competitive inflexibility, and loss of information concerning customer or competitive changes. Nevertheless, Courtaulds used its own rayon fiber in textiles, and PPG Industries used its own synthetic soda ash to make glass with success. They were fully integrated with respect to these materials without encountering the problems other firms have faced using strategy.

Full integration can be appropriate only for a brief period. It is desirable when firms can protect proprietary processes adequately from competitive espionage by integrating, and when interconnection (or coordination) yields cost advantages. So long as price competition is not fierce enough for diseconomies to matter, no significant disadvantages are incurred with the imbalances caused by full integration.

Forces Affecting the Choice of Vertical-Integration Strategies

Firms adopt different vertical-integration strategies because they compete within industries that differ in volatility, they have attained differing degrees of bargaining power with respect to upstream and downstream industries, and they possess dissimilar (but germane) competitive needs (and strengths to attain those objectives). Among the forces that influence firms' vertical-integration strategy choices at a particular time, there are two that affect the riskiness (or stability) of the environment firms face—phase of industry development and industry structure—and two that indicate firms' abilities (and needs) to undertake certain types of vertical strategies—their bargaining power and their strategy.

It is important to note that vertical-integration strategies should change over time as industry conditions, corporate strategy needs, and firms' capabilities change. The CEO must assess the relative worth of the strategy alternatives sketched here in light of these forces. The firm's corporate strategy objectives and the industry's phase of development will influence most significantly decisions concerning the number of *stages* to be engaged in. The volatility of competition and the SBU's bargaining power vis-à-vis suppliers or distributors (or customers) will influence most significantly decisions concerning the *degree* of internal transfers. The *form* of ownership used to join adjacent stages will be influenced most significantly by the firm's corporate objectives and the SBU's bargaining power over adjacent parties. *Breadth* of integration within an SBU will be influenced most significantly by the phase of an industry's development and by the nature of competition therein. Table A–9 in the appendix details the effects of these factors on the various dimensions of vertical strategy alternatives. From this diagram and the following discussion, certain combinations of these dimensions are shown to be more appropriate than others when the key factors occur together in certain ways.

Phase of Industry (and Demand) Evolution

Industries evolve in structure as firms make diverse investments in them and overcome customers' reluctance to adopt new products (or new generations of products). Technological innovation is a major cause of accelerated industry evolution and of increased demand uncertainty. Different vertical-integration strategies will be more appropriate where technology changes rapidly (or slowly), depending on whether firms would be technological leaders or followers. Pioneering firms find the need to integrate forward *greater* than technological followers do. With this exception, however, *less* vertical integration is appropriate early (and late) in an industry's evolution. This pattern is attributable to (1) the risks of demand uncertainty and (2) differing needs to prove a new product's worth. Therefore, the most likely pattern of integration behavior one might expect to see over time (holding other factors constant) is an inverted U shape.

Demand and Infrastructure Uncertainty. Demand and infrastructure (industry life cycle) uncertainty exacerbate the difficulties of choosing strategic posture. As industries evolve and their structures change, new buyer-seller relationships develop as old ones unravel. Resolution of these uncertainties makes vertical integration, decisions to build large-scale production facilities, and many other risky investments seem more economic.

Early in an industry's development, firms must decide whether they will be technology leaders or followers, and whether they will be pioneers or late-entrants. Strong firms may be able to enter late, as IBM did in personal computers, but weaker firms may have to stake out positions early in an industry's life if they hope to participate at all. Pioneering firms may have to integrate forward in order to reduce customer confusion by explaining products, servicing them, or creating distribution channels where none previously existed. Are they rewarded for doing so? Even technology leaders can undertake too much vertical integration if it is the wrong kind. If uncertainties are high or if technologies are expected to change rapidly, high *degrees* of vertical integration are riskier than where technologies change infrequently.

Creating Credibility for New Industries. Vertical-integration strategies within new industries today differs from those within established industries, and they differ from the vertical-integration strategies within embryonic industries when they began in the previous century. In the 1880s there were significant differences in the need for infrastructures—channels of distribution, standard means of assessing quality, and so on—supporting the development of the embryonic steel, automobile, and tobacco industries as compared with the infrastructure needs surrounding the embryonic industries of the 1980s. In newly developing countries and earlier in the development of U.S. industry, it was frequently necessary for firms to undertake many stages of integrated activities (and to provide the necessary infrastructures) in order to help an industry to develop. In the 1980s many new industries can use the same infrastructures developed in an earlier era by firms that once integrated vertically to build these structures.

The major reason for pioneering firms within embryonic industries to undertake many stages of integrated activity *now* is to create credibility for a radically new industry. This was once the case in persuading textile firms to use rayon as well as cotton and wool on their looms, and Celanese integrated forward from rayon to yarn, textiles, and garment manufacture to prove to consumers as well as textile firms that its new fiber (rayon acetate) was viable. Similarly, ALCOA once integrated forward beyond its current number of integrated stages to fabricate aluminum products to sell to consumers when other metals fabricators would not use its new metal. In the 1980s, however, there seem to be few new industries (except perhaps genetic engineering and a few others with temporary needs) for which this need to create new market conduits is as high as it was in earlier eras. More likely, firms encourage high degrees of internal transactions between vertically related stages of processing now only to launch (or underwrite) new products.

Uncertainty increases the riskiness of committing to many integrated stages and high degrees of internal transfers prematurely because highly integrated production processes require most of the outputs from each stage to be absorbed internally. If demand for an SBU's outputs is highly uncertain, the likelihood of insufficient sales volumes (resulting in costly excess capacity) is increased, and that uncertainty will discourage vertical integration. Variability in demand increases the riskiness of vertical integration, in particular, when two or more SBUs have become dependent on each other for product transfers. Erratic, dramatically deteriorating demand will prove especially costly for integrated firms, and only those firms whose corporate strategies provide for subsidization of multiple, integrated stages of production will support such investments in such settings.

Volatility of Competition

If they were not forced to trade with each other, individual business units would not favor vertically integrated strategies in settings where price warfare depressed industrywide profit margins. Because such conduct devastates long-term profitability and saps the innovative resourcefulness of firms, vertical integration should generally be avoided in volatile industries. Other things held constant, the greatest number of successful linked stages and greatest successful breadths of integrated activities can be undertaken within settings where competition is stable.

Product Traits. In choosing which components or services to produce in house, it is important to understand which attributes of a product create those qualities consumers are willing to pay a premium for. Noncritical components and services (and those offering poor economics) could be purchased from outsiders while sensitive components and services (and those offering the best economics) are produced in house, instead. By freeing plant space and resources formerly devoted to noncritical and uneconomic components and services, firms can undertake a more profitable mix of activities with their resources while tying up the assets of outsiders for low-profit activities.

Where trade secrets protect some aspect of a firm's products, higher degrees of integration are necessary—as in the case of Polaroid, which stopped purchasing its negative materials from Kodak when its instant-photography patent expired. (Too much proprietary information was contained there to let competitors produce it.) Similarly, Schlumberger acquired its own custom logic semiconductor house (Fairchild Camera & Instrument) to protect is proprietary knowledge concerning well-logging services, and Dow Chemical is often fully integrated to prevent other firms from learning too much about its processes and designs.

Supplier Traits. If competition is escalating on the basis of innovations, firms should be wary about embracing high degrees of internal transfers because they cut off their access to the benefits of outsiders' innovations in an environment where flexibility is crucial to competitive viability. In such settings, it may be desirable to help create another new supplier (through quasi-integration arrangements that allow the new entity to serve others as well as the sponsoring, taper-integrated firm) rather than fall into the trap of technological inflexibility by fully owning such suppliers and buying inputs only from them.

Consumer Traits. Complex products that require substantial demonstration or explanations and servicing (as microcomputers did in 1978) are strong candidates for downstream linkages. Firms must be cautious to ensure (1) that they are not overly dependent on in-house merchandise for resale and (2) that they do not stay forward-integrated after the advantages of such integration have expired.

Manufacturing Technology Traits. Since the minimum efficient scale of some technologies is so much larger than firms' needs for that component, firms that integrate such activities may be forced to enter merchant sales to dispose of their unused outputs from oversized plants (or to run their plants at uneconomic volumes). Instead, firms should use subcontractors to perform those tasks that require assets most firms would use infrequently at present operating scales. Thus producers of solar collector panels send out for chrome plating, and ethical pharmaceutical firms send out for the bromine chemistry step in production.

Competitor Traits. Efforts to diminish the pressures of other structural traits toward price warfare can be undone by competitors who (1) compete on the basis of price or (2) use vertical integration as a means of foreclosure. When many firms have integrated, all face similar pressures to keep their vertical chains utilized efficiently, and price competition becomes more likely than if nonintegrated firms were allowed to supply or purchase excess volumes of materials and services to alleviate imbalances in vertically related technologies. Thus it may be preferable for an industry to have some nonintegrated firms to absorb other firms' excess capacities, lest industry bloodshed result instead.

Volatile industries increase the riskiness of vertical integration because competitors are more likely to use price cutting to fill their plants' capacities in such settings. If competition is volatile, firms should be reluctant to let SBUs rely heavily on each other for purchases or sales.

Bargaining Power and Asset Exposure

If firms possess bargaining power they can: (1) dictate price, terms, and shipping schedules to suppliers and distributors; (2) force suppliers (or distributors) to pay freight on their shipments and finance their inventories; (3) influence styling and promotional policies of downstream firms; (4) obtain superior information concerning demand (including desired product traits, preferred product mix, trends in ultimate buyers' tastes, and competitors' actions) from distributors' sales representatives; and (5) urge distributors to perform expensive missionary selling tasks to help introduce new products or add quality to established products. Aside from the many services firms can induce their suppliers (or distributors) to perform, however, bargaining power is crucial because it increases firms' asset flexibility. Outsiders' assets are exposed to demand uncertainty instead of the firm's assets being exposed. The most important determinants of bargaining power are (1) product specificity to the industry in question, (2) the existence of alternative outlets or sources of supplies, (3) the ability to self-manufacture the good/service in question, and (4) the dependence of the supplier (or distributor) on the business unit (Porter 1976a).

Corporate Strategy Needs

The foregoing arguments that *less* integration is preferable to *more* have taken the perspective of a single SBU's competitive strategy needs. The argument must be moderated by considerations of corporate strategy needs when intrafirm policies are forged, because vertical integration may be part of a larger strategy involving shared resources and experience-curve economies. Corporate intervention may subsidize one SBU for the sake of another temporarily in using vertical integration to capture more value-added, to protect past strategic investments, to increase the attractiveness of current strategic postures, or to ameliorate the destructive activities of outsiders. Firms pursuing global strategies requiring coordinated facilities on several national fronts would sustain higher degrees and breadths of vertical integration, especially while a worldwide market position was being won. In summary, diversified firms may use vertical integration to achieve long-term corporate benefits even when competitive conditions within the industry of *one* of their vertically linked SBUs would argue against doing so.

Synergies. Some vertical-integration strategies promise to improve long-term synergies for the entire firm, although they may appear to penalize a particular business unit. Supply-side economies, for example, could be gained by sharing manufacturing facilities for components that could be used in several dissimilar products. The number of stages undertaken would be highest where significant synergies are gained or other corporate needs are served. The key determinants of whether or not a firm should skip a particular stage in its integrated chain of activities are (1) the task's importance to its corporate mission and (2) the quality of goods or services provided by outsiders. A firm's position within its industry also suggests how many integrated stages it would perform, and firms on the fringes of an industry would be more likely to purchase (rather than produce) materials or services from leader firms whose upstream plants produced in excess of their downstream plants' capacities.

Innovation Needs. Previous sections indicated that less vertical integration was anticipated within turbulent industry settings, particularly those where technological change occurs rapidly. Firms pursuing technological leadership strategies offer an important exception to this pattern, however, because they are often willing to endure the temporary imbalances of full integration when producing sensitive components, and they are willing to endure the temporary imbalances of full integration when producing sensitive components, and they are willing to absorb the risks of many integrated stages (as detailed in table A–9) in order to be poised to exploit the next generation of technological innovation.

The scarcest resource firms possess is their entrepreneurial ability. Rather than seeing their mix of businesses as streams of cash flows, chief executives should consider them as reservoirs of capabilities instead. Vertical integration permits firms to pursue activities and relationships where personnel with crucial skills (or other scarce capabilities) might otherwise not be retained.

Other Needs. Firms may be more vertically integrated to capture greater proportions of value-added, protect product quality, maintain proprietary knowledge, or ensure manufacturing integrity. But it is useful to recognize that any corporate scheme to force vertically related business units to deal with each other without the benefit of open-market equivalents (for the purposes of transfer pricing and maintaining competitive flexibility) is penalizing one party to the transaction for the sake of the other. Subsidization of uneconomic and noncompetitive business units for the sake of ephemeral corporate advantages is a strategic trap that should be scrutinized carefully, lest the advantages gained in such subsidization arrangements be outweighed by the impairments to competitive flexibility that result.

Using Vertical Integration as a Strategic Weapon

The generic strategies suggested here and detailed in table A–9 are not intended to be static suggestions to gain access to resources, capabilities, and knowledge. As competitive conditions change, so too must the firm's vertical-integration strategy. In particular, changes must reflect revisions in the strategic relationships managers envision between their business units. For example, GTE (a telecommunications firm that once had a significant electronics position but divested its semiconductors around 1969) purchased EMI Semi Inc. in 1979 because it recognized its need again for custom integrated-circuit designs. Similarly, Tandy/Radio Shack adjusted its distribution policies to reflect new market realities in 1982 by selling some of its microcomputers through outsiders; Hoffman-LaRoche reduced its wholesaling activities (switching exclusively to outsiders); and Exxon brought its U.S. crude-oil refining and production capacity back into balance with each other as competitive conditions changed.

If bargaining power is considered in conjunction with the volatility traits of competition and demand, it should become evident that because certain industries can become very risky for high degrees of vertical integration, successful performance for firms without bargaining power becomes very difficult to achieve. It should also be evident that different competitors within the same industry could each execute vertical-integration strategies that are appropriate for them but different from each other (with the exception that relatively little internal integration is recommended in the very early and very late stages of industry development). If a business were pursuing profitability goals using product quality, it might use more internal upstream and less downstream integration than others, for example. If it were seeking technological leadership, it might seek taper integration even in the embryonic phase of industry development.

There will be some advantage (in stable industries where the business unit possesses bargaining power and where the firm is willing to invest some resources in internal integration if appropriate) in being able to commit oneself to an intelligent strategy, in the face of uncertainty, before one's rivals sort out the problem of vertical integration. Although it may seem desirable for the firm to wait to see how the industry evolves before selecting an action plan, waiting could be suboptimal. If there are several healthy and creative suppliers (or distributors) with which the firm might forge some integration linkages, for example, results (in chapter 5) suggest that it should do so *early,* thereby foreclosing competitors from acquiring, franchising, or gaining supply contracts from the best participants in upstream or downstream industries. If the firm needs internal integration to control some aspect of its product policy, it should build a pilot plant and learn about its suppliers early, before competitors can match this advantage with their own experience.

When the strategic window that favored integration has closed (Abell 1980) and the cost of emulating competitors' integrated strategies is no longer justified, prudent firms will uncouple their integrated linkages in a timely fashion—before other firms reach similar conclusions about the merits of integration—to dispose of their assets in a healthy market. Firms attempting late dis-integrations will face greater exit barriers than early firms did and realize less value for their assets when they do finally locate a buyer for them (Porter 1976b; Harrigan 1980b, c). A key review point for deciding whether to reduce integration is when cash outlays would be required to upgrade vertically integrated technlogies. Strategists must recognize that business units that are viable only if they have a guaranteed market (or source of supply) can become cash traps if they are not cut off at that time.

Vertical integration can offer temporary state-of-the-art advantages that must be weighed against the advantages of being flexible to exploit the next technological innovation. Firms that commit early to vertical integration, thereby linking themselves in a highly inflexible fashion to a particular technology, risk being wrong. The cost of error could be substantial. If these pioneers are right, however, vertical integration can be a rationalizing device that forges order in chaotic environments, establishes industry standards, or lowers operating costs significantly. Then, the harm of late entry can be substantial. The problem is complex, but the framework proposed herein offers one way of analyzing firms' vertical-integration capabilities and improving their strategies. Interested readers should proceed to the tests of this framework, presented in chapter 5.

5
Tests of the Vertical-Integration Framework

This chapter tests the vertical-integration framework developed in chapter 4. Because the vertical-integration strategy dimensions of chapter 4 are central to that framework, new measures had to be created to test them. This chapter explains a program of research that tested the framework in several ways and presents results suggesting its effective use.

A New Concept of Vertical Integration

From chapter 4, *vertical integration* was defined to include arrangements whereby sister business units provide raw or semiprocessed materials, components, or services to the business unit in question (or purchase outputs from or act as distributors for it). Although corporate management often intervenes in free market decisions regarding intrafirm transfers of goods and services, autonomous business units can elect to trade (or not do business) with their sisters. Thus vertical integration is often more than a mere make-or-buy decision, because some decisions to integrate upstream (or downstream) require firms to acquire capabilities far beyond the basic strengths of their core businesses. It is a type of diversification strategy that requires conscious management of potential synergies.

Vertical-integration strategies comprise a combination of decisions *(dimensions)* regarding whether the firm should provide goods and services in house through its own business units, or purchase them from outsiders instead. These decisions include their *degree* of integration— that is, how much of a particular good or service to transfer in house (or sell to outsiders), and how far backward (or forward) in a vertical chain to integrate. For each step or *stage* in the chain of transformations they wish to engage in, from ultraraw materials to the ultimate customer,

Adapted from articles that originally appeared in the *Academy of Management Journal,* June and December 1985, by permission of the publisher, the Academy of Management.

firms must also decide on their *breadth* of activities and ownership *form*—
that is, how much equity to hold in each business unit.

Stages of Integration

The number of steps in the chain of processing, from ultraraw materials
to ultimate consumers, in which a particular firm engages determines
that firm's number of stages of integration. A comparison of firms' stages
of integrated activities may be constructed by summing the number of
steps multiplied by the value-added ratio per each respective stage. Business units that have high index values are typically those whose parents
have pushed the stages of corporate involvement much further than the
boundaries of a single business unit's missions. A firm engaged in few
stages of integration would have lower index values than do firms in
many stages of integrated activity.

In this analysis, each firm was scaled according to the relative number of steps in the transformaton process it undertook. (Scaling procedures and sample composition are explained in a later section.) If metals
fabricating firms mined ores, transported and smelted them, and drew
their ingots into wires or other products, for example, they were considered to be engaged in many stages of production, and their total value
added was expected to be higher than for nonintegrated firms. The value
of their in-house processing at each stage, however, depended on their
degree of internal transfers and the *breadth* of tasks performed at that
stage, because some tasks offered wider profit margins. The information
obtained by estimating contributions to value-added at each stage offers
a more robust picture of differences in firms' vertical-integration strategies than earlier aggregated measures.

Breadth of Activities per Integrated Stage

The relative *breadth* of an SBU's activities was estimated by comparing
the number of adjacent activities in which it was engaged—design, product, or process R&D; production; testing; distribution; and other activities—divided by the maximum number of activities in which SBUs in
that industry might reasonably engage. Breadth is measured within the
boundaries of the target SBUs.

If firms were engaged in many activities at each integrated stage of
processing, their breadth of integration was high. In the metals-process-
ing example, if firms allowed outsiders to supply some components or
services, they were less broadly integrated than if they provided all components and services at a processing stage in house. If firms are *broadly
integrated,* they could increase their SBU's value-added by that particular

stage of processing substantially, by doing many tasks in house, provided the tasks they choose to perform offered high margins. Integration breadth was measured in this chapter at the SBU level, using an index that is explained in table A–10 in the appendix.

Degree of Internal Transfers

The degree of internal transfers indicates how much of each input is obtained from in-house sources or how much of firms' outputs are sold to in-house customers. A firm's degree of internal transfers was estimated by the percentage of internal sales to (or purchases from) sister SBUs. Separate estimates were constructed for upstream purchases and downstream sales when evaluating vertical integration from the perspective of a particular industry. *Relative* measures of degree were obtained by comparing degrees of internal transfers with those of equivalent SBUs within competitors.

Form of Ownership Control

Ownership *form* is the percentage of equity invested in an SBU at a particular stage of processing. The Great Plains Associates, a coal gasification venture, is an example of a vertical joint venture where partners that were public utilities shared the plant's outputs. Although firms need not own business units entirely to control them, if the economics involved at a particular stage of processing are very favorable, firms will often want to own SBU at that stage wholly to get all of the profits available. The form of a particular integrated relationship may be estimated by the firm's percentage of ownership in units within the industries under study.

Tests of the Vertical-Integration Framework

From chapter 4, the relationships between dimensions of firms' vertical-integration strategies and environment (and internal) forces may be stated by the following set of structural equations:

Stages = f(Corporate strategy, phase of industry development).

Degree = f(Number of stages, volatility of competition, SBU's bargaining power vis-à-vis outsiders).

Form = f(Degree of internal transfers, SBU's bargaining power vis-à-vis outsiders, corporate strategy).

Breadth = *f*(Degree of internal transfers, phase of industry development, volatility of competition).

Note that some dimensions of firms' vertical integration strategies will be influenced *indirectly* by the values of other dimensions of their strategy. Moreover, the environmental (and internal forces) sketched in chapter 4 exert a stronger force on some dimensions than others.

Table A–11 in the appendix summarizes the relationships tested and suggests which forces embody the effects of demand (and industry structure) uncertainty, volatile industries, bargaining power, and corporate strategy needs on the mix of vertical-integration strategy dimensions firms embraced. The most favorable environments for vertical integration were those where, for example, demand was increasing steadily, few process innovations destroyed accrued cost advantages, but switching cost barriers prevented customers from deserting vendors, and competitors behaved as a symmetrical and stable oligopoly. In light of their corporate strategy concerns, however, some firms were vertically integrated *even in less favorable settings* because they could not control the quality of suppliers' imputs or distributors' presentations adequately through their intrinsic market power.

Methodology

Information concerning the relationships between the target SBUs and adjacent business units was obtained from a hybrid program comprising three stages: (1) construction of industry notes using archival data, (2) validation using field interviews, and (3) a three-round Delphi questionnaire. The framework sketched earlier concerning the dimensions of vertical-integration strategies was tested by studying the make-or-buy decisions of 192 firms that competed in sixteen industries during the years 1960–1981. The unit of analysis may properly be considered these SBUs operating within the target industries described in table A–12, although measures concerning upstream and downstream sister units were also gathered.

Sample Design

Table A–12 in the appendix identifies the industries of the target SBUs and the sample's total distribution among the sixteen industries. Table A–13 in the appendix provides summary statistics describing the vertical-integration strategy dimensions for the total sample, and table A–14 describes the *average* vertical-integration strategies per target industry.

Both consumer- and producer-goods industries (as well as businesses of varying ages) were used to examine what made industries relatively attractive or unattractive environments for vertical integration. The sample was also stratified to compare industries having low demand uncertainty with those having high uncertainty, and to compare industries characterized by stable competitive conditions with those characterized by volatile competition.

Data Collection

The field studies used in gathering data progressed in several stages and employed a variety of sources to corroborate findings. First, preliminary hypotheses were generated, based on a literature search concerning the use of vertical integration. Industry notes were constructed from archival sources, which included annual reports and other financial disclosure documents as well as trade journals and publications and government documents. The industry notes were refined through field interviews, telephone conversations, follow-up letters, and revisions suggested by managers who participated in the study.

The Delphi Questionnaire

Initial estimates of the variables described in table A–15 in the appendix were developed from materials in the public domain and were scaled *relative to competitors*. (They were refined through interviews, questionnaires, and iterative scalings in a Delphi-like procedure.) Initial interviews were primarily face to face because plant tours were often necessary to understand many issues concerning technology and its role in vertical integration. Interviews, telephone conversations, follow-up letters, transcripts, and comments on preliminary drafts of each industry vignette provided revised estimates of these factors until estimates for the 192 competitors' contexts were developed for the Delphi study. Firms also provided information concerning the strengths and flexibilities of suppliers and customers, technologies, and other competitive factors. Newspaper accounts of price wars, divestitures, and acquisitions documented the changes in vertical integration that occurred over time; interviews with industry participants corroborated interpretations of the meanings of these events and estimates of these forces. For further discussion of the Delphi questionnaire, see Harrigan (1985b and d). Limitations of this methodology are also discussed therein.

Independent-Variable Construction

Using the Delphi procedure, independent variables were constructed as shown in table A–15 in the appendix. Although many other measures of industry structure were constructed, high multicollinearity prevented their use together in the models specified below (Johnston 1972).

Models

A regression model was chosen to estimate the effects of the environmental and corporate forces outlined earlier because the individual contributions of each class of predictor variable was of interest and it seemed to be the most appropriate tool. Discussion of an alternative treatment of these data appears in Harrigan (1985d). As noted earlier, some dimensions of vertical integration are dependent in part on the values of other strategy dimensions, and these relationships are recursive. (That is, each of the endogenous variables can be determined sequentially.) Since the righthand endogenous variables need not be correlated with the error terms, ordinary least squares was an appropriate estimation procedure, and two-stage least-squares techniques were used to solve the models for stages, degree, breadth, and form of integration.

Regression Estimates

In the ordinary-least-squares specification of these relationships, the *standardized* coefficients of the independent variables (b_1) may be interpreted as their relative contributions to the corrected coefficent of multiple determination. The magnitude of the *regular* coefficients represent contributions to the relative likelihood that (1) a firm will engage in many integrated stages, (2) an SBU will transfer much of its output in house (upstream) or (3) downstream, (4) an SBU will undertake many activities in house, or (5) a firm will own a large proportion of its adjacent business units. The model could be stated in the following form:

$$y_1 = a_1 + b_1x_{11} + b_2x_{13} + e_1$$
$$y_2 = a_2 + b_1y_1 + b_2x_{25} + b_3x_{27} + e_2$$
$$y_3 = a_3 + b_1y_1 + b_2x_{36} + b_3x_{38} + e_3$$
$$y_4 = a_4 + b_1y_2 + b_2y_3 + b_3x_{42} + b_4x_{46} + e_4$$
$$y_5 = a_5 + b_1y_2 + b_2y_3 + b_3x_{54} + b_4x_{59} + e_5$$

where y_1 equals the dependent variables—the stages, upstream degree, downstream degree, breadth, and form, respectively—of the firm and

SBU's vertical-integration strategy. The independent variables, x_{ij}, correspond to a coding scheme where i (equals 1, 2, . . ., 5) represents the structural equation's number, and j (equals 1, 2, . . ., 9) corresponds to the independent variables as numbered in tables A–15 and A–16.

Correlations

Table A–16 shows the correlations of the variables tested. In the interests of specification parsimony (and in keeping with the relationships outlined in chapter 4), the models are limited to one variable per category of force hypothesized to affect vertical-integration strategy (plus the pre-specified strategy dimensions, as shown earlier). Imprecise regression coefficients would have been produced by including multiple measures of each force per equation when the strategy dimensions are used for second-stage analyses; the sample possesses a high degree of multicollinearity.

Results

Results from the ordinary-least-squares (and two-stage OLS) models are presented in table A–17 in the appendix and are discussed in this section.

Number of Stages in the Integrated Chain

Positive sales growth and large synergies from shared facilities increased the number of stages firms were engaged in. Declining sales decreased the number of stages, and both variables were statistically significant (and their signs were as expected). The stages variable was positive and statistically significant (as expected) when used to generate second-stage estimators of the degree of SBUs' backward and forward internal transfers. This result suggests that firms are more likely to transfer goods and services internally if their SBUs operate in adjacent stages of processing. If this were the case, it would call into question the efficacy of some firms' SBU definitions as being the appropriate level for their resource-allocation and strategic-analysis activities. The intrafirm negotiation behavior which allegedly acts as a check on vertical integration would not seem to be in operation in these cases. Instead, corporate-level needs would seem to dominate the make-or-buy decision. If corporate-level attentions to market versus transfer prices are needed, perhaps resources should be allocated for the vertical chain of processing instead of by SBUs.

Degree of Backward Internal Transfers

Stable competitive conditions (proxied in this specification by the four-firm concentration ratio) encouraged higher degrees of purchases from in-house suppliers. Where the SBU possessed bargaining power over outsiders (by virtue of outsiders, dependence on the SBU), it did not purchase as much of its requirements from in-house sources. The stages variable (determined by industry sales growth and opportunities for synergies) is positive, suggesting that as industries develop and their markets stabilize (meaning demand is expected to be enduring), SBUs will increase their degree of backward integration.

The relationships found in table A–17 are as expected and are statistically significant, but knowledge of industry histories (and firms' performances within them) suggests caution in this relationship (Harrigan 1983c). Being highly backward-integrated over time cuts off firms from access to materials and processes that may prove to be less expensive substitutes. The more goods and services their SBUs transfer in house, the less firms are exposed to the stimulus of outsiders' innovations and the more they risk subsequent strategic inflexibility. Unlike the findings of MacMillan, Hambrick, and Pennings (1982) that demand and instability encourages backward integration, results suggest indirect evidence that demand instability *reduces* the degree of backward internal transfers, given the relationship between industry development and firms' stages of integration.

Thus results suggest that where SBUs possess relative bargaining power over outside suppliers and can wrangle better prices and terms from them, less backward integration will occur. The need to exploit synergies between SBUs is an example of a corporate intervention decision that results suggest will mitigate this force.

Degree of Forward Internal Transfers

Results in table A–17 suggest that high exit barriers at the SBU level (proxying an environment of volatile competition) discourage high degrees of internal transfers to the next stage downward. When competitors instigate rounds of price cutting, sales to sister SBUs are less likely to be assured if the downstream SBUs possess purchasing autonomy. The presence of high exit barriers increase the likelihood that marginal competitors who cannot exit will slash prices to fill their plants to break-even volumes. Again, the positive (and statistically significant) relationship with the stages variable suggests that corporate-level intervention to encourage sister SBUs to trade will mitigate these forces.

The positive sign (and statistical significance) of the relative-bargaining-power variable suggests that SBUs must rely more heavily on in-house conduits to their markets when they face strong outside distributors (or customers). This relationship is consistent with the resource-dependency framework, which argues that vertical integration is encouraged by high demand uncertainty. The relative lack of bargaining power such SBUs face would make them *price takers,* lacking bargaining power over sister units as well. SBUs that are dependent on in-house customers face another competitive disadvantage; if SBUs are heavily forward-integrated, they lack a good feeling for their markets. Field studies to validate industry histories indicated that when firms finally "bit the bullet" and dis-integrated their intrafirm stages of processing, those that uncoupled the downstream stages *first* obtained a better understanding of the true nature of demand for outputs produced by upstream stages and a clearer understanding of the superiority of competitors' offerings (Harrigan 1983c).

Firms often transfer large proportions of their outputs downstream through in-house units where there are cost advantages in doing so. The positive relationship obtained with the stages variable suggests that this corporate desire to capture more value-added may influence forward-integration decisions, but caution in interpreting this result is warranted. Investigations of *forward*-integration decisions are relatively novel in the literature treating vertical integration. In the past, vertical integration has meant primarily making one's own components (or obtaining raw-materials sources). Less attention has been devoted to downstream relationships, and this side of the vertical chain deserves more investigation in the future.

Breadth of SBUs' Activities

Results in table A–17 suggest that high demand uncertainty reduces the breadth of activities SBUs will undertake in house. Similarly, high exit barriers (proxying an environment of volatile competition) discourage SBUs from undertaking a broad range of activities in house. These results are as expected (although the demand-uncertainty variable is not statistically significant); firms will be unwilling to increase their strategic inflexibility if demand and competitive conditions appear to be adverse.

The negative (and statistically significant) relationships of SBUs' breadths of activities with their degrees of backward and forward integration is not surprising. The wider the boundaries defining an SBU—the greater the SBU's breadth and the broader the range of activities it performs in house—the less need it would have for purchases from (or sales to) adjacent SBUs.

Form (or Percentage) of Ownership of the Venture

Results in table A–17 suggest that the possession of high market share increases the likelihood that vertical business units will be wholly owned. This coefficient is not statistically significant, but its sign is consistent with the expected relationship. Low bargaining power also increases the likelihood that vertical units will be wholly owned. This relationship is statistically significant and suggests that when firms cannot use the market power of their SBUs to control outsiders, they will use ownership to control uncertainties, instead.

The relationship obtained with the degree of internal transfer variables indicate that firms are more likely to own fully their upstream business units than downstream ones. This result may be due to the larger capital requirements and scale economies associated with most upstream technologies. Furthermore, the greater strategic stakes associated with upstream business units may make full ownership attractive. Preliminary findings concerning the use of vertical joint ventures (described later) suggest that firms will often consent to partial ownership in order to gain market access and distribution channels. Finally, firms need not own distributors in order to influence their behaviors if their SBUs' market positions are strong enough.

Interpreting the Results

Validating the Framework

This study has expanded the operational meaning of *vertical integration* by developing its principal dimensions and testing them with field-interview data. The findings from this study offer substantial evidence that vertical-integration strategies differ across industries as well as within them. The findings also suggest that some combinations of vertical-integration strategy dimensions are more likely to be found within certain settings than within others. Firms must incorporate the forces of demand, competitive volatility, and the behaviors of outsiders into their schemes to meet resource needs through integration. Vertical integration is used differently when competitive conditions (and demand) are hospitable than when they are not. Since the bargaining power of outsiders can attenuate (or grow) with time, it will be helpful to use this knowledge of buyer-seller relationships to shift the burdens of risky investments where possible. Results suggest a contingency approach to the use of vertical integration in which firms make use of their inherent market power (when they possess such power) to spread risks and maintain strategic flexibility.

Volatile Competition

SBUs made less in house (and firms were engaged in fewer stages of processing) where demand was highly uncertain. More internal transfers occurred where SBUs lacked the bargaining power to urge outsiders to undertake risky ventures, and this condition may have exacerbated firms' strategic inflexibilities. Field studies (corroborated later) suggest that going against these patterns could prove disastrous. In particular, the findings regarding volatility of competition suggest that firms would be ill advised to embrace high degrees of vertical transfers when the structures of their industries are not conducive to vertical integration.

Although the empire-building tendencies of SBU managers may increase their desires to undertake a broad range of activities in house, high demand uncertainty and volatile competition often mitigate the advantage of doing so. SBU managers would be better advised to play off outsiders for the best terms and prices on some components and services, particularly if their bargaining power (as defined earlier) is high enough to exploit their advantage. (A similar argument is appropriate at the corporate level regarding the number of integrated stages undertaken.) Long chains of processing exacerbate firms' exposures to the volatility of demand in several industries and increase the risks of imbalances (and excess capacity) at one or more stages of processing.

Managing Vertical Integration

The choice of vertical integration strategies is the province of the CEO (the chief strategist). Policies to increase intrafirm cooperation often require the faith and perseverance of long-term vision that originates with the CEO. Intervention to exploit potential intelligence or economic advantages (or to dismantle inappropriate relationships) may be necessary, expecially where industries are characterized by increasingly brief product lives, accelerated rates of innovation, or rapid capacity expansion (and integration) by competitors. Critics of business performance might do well to give top management some acknowledgment for taking risks and shaping vertical strategies for the long-term benefit of shareholders.

Managing Synergies

Finally, the nature of synergies must be considered. No synergy between SBUs is created unless executives consciously enforce policies causing SBUs to (1) communicate; (2) share inputs, outputs, R&D or other useful attributes and capabilities; or (3) cooperate in some other useful manner. If firm's management systems are weak, they risk creating situations where vertical integration becomes a mobility barrier. If firms do not have internal mechanisms that trade off the needs of SBU autonomy and corporate strategy needs, they exacerbate their problems when using vertical integration. Although, as Williamson (1975) has suggested, firms may integrate to escape external costs associated with market transactions, there are costs to managing transfers across internal boundaries, as well. If firms are unwilling (or unable) to bear these management costs, they may as well go to the outside market.

Performance Differences

Harrigan (1987) found differences in the vertical integration strategies of firms that performed poorly when compared with the vertical integration strategies of firms that did not suffer losses or strategic inflexibility. Unsuccessful firms purchased less from in-house vendors when their products were complex. They missed opportunities to capture high value-added margins by using components supplied by insiders. The major exception to this pattern occurred where competition became so volatile that firms suffered strategic flexibility damage from too much backward integration.

Unsuccessful firms missed opportunities to capture high value-added margins by selling their complex or proprietary outputs to sister business units or through their sisters' distribution channels. The best use of forward integration is where customers (or sales representatives) can create a unique image for the product when sold to ultimate consumers. Forward integration offers less promise where products are treated as commodities. The best time for firms to invest in forward integration activities is when their industry is young and standards need to be created (or users need to be educated).

Unsuccessful firms did not read the opportunities of stable and concentrated environments astutely. Firms are least likely to be whipsawed by too much of the wrong kind of vertical integration in concentrated industries where a fringe of nonintegrated firms stand ready to fill in the gaps for larger competitors. Successful firms allowed their business units to perform high value-adding activities while using OEM vendors to make less lucrative products.

Unsuccessful firms missed opportunities to penetrate new, potentially profitable markets where they might later serve as vendors or distributors. They engaged in few stages of processing to tap promising new industries. Successful firms had their antennae extended to learn about (or influence) technological changes while they integrated downstream to influence customer expectations, as well. When they had achieved their strategic purpose, they often maintained a toehold for intelligence gathering while they backed away from unpromising activities. That is, successful firms varied the number of vertical stages of processing they engaged in as competitive conditions changed.

Successful firms did not have to own adjacent business units (or the target business unit) in order to influence their activities to their advantage. Many quasi-integration arrangements—including OEM vendor agreements, joint ventures, and franchising arrangements, among others—were used by effective firms to spread the risks encountered in environments where (1) profit margins were low; (2) technologies changed rapidly; and (3) bargaining power could be exerted to their advantage.

Harrigan (1987) also found differences in the vertical integration strategies of successful and unsuccessful firms when they were evaluated in light of environmental forces. Briefly, unsuccessful firms did not realize that it was possible to engage in several vertical stages of processing without necessarily transferring high percentages of goods and services to in-house business units. Caution was necessary in order to avoid exposing themselves when competition became volatile.

It was generally not advisable for firms to rely upon sister business units for more than 50 percent of their supplies (or to consume more than 50 percent of their outputs), unless these relationships could be secured by long-term contracts. Even in such situations, vertical agreements had to be reexamined as industry structures evolved. Pioneering strategies involving long vertical chains of processing offered *temporary* state-of-the-art technology advantages. In many cases these transitory advantages were easily overcome by stronger firms which integrated vertically later. Yet, pioneering with vertical integration was the only way for some firms to gain a toehold in new industries.

Finally, patterns of performance differences suggested that if there were no significant economic or strategic advantages to be gained through vertical integration, the burdens of such risky investments *should* be shifted to outsiders. When the advantages favoring particular vertical integration strategies have faded and the costs of emulating competitors' integrated strategies are unjustified, prudent firms should uncouple vertical integration linkages in a timely fashion—before other firms reach similar conclusions about the losing merits of integration—in order to dispose of their assets in a healthy market. But since competitors often evaluate the value of vertical integration differently or may not perceive the same dangers in being too integrated at the wrong time, a timing advantage can be gained by using this strategy preemptively—both in forging linkages and in dissolving them. Recognizing *when* outsiders can be entrusted with activities firms might otherwise perform internally is desirable when firms must ration investment funds and seek candidates for spin-off or liquidation.

Part III
Strategic Exit
(or Repositioning)

art III examines *exit barriers*—forces that prevent managers from making the frictionless repositionings assumed by economic theory. Exit barriers prevent (or delay) managers from taking actions to divest or reposition their business units. They impair firms' strategic flexibility.

The best setting for observing the dynamics of exit barriers is within environments where managers are most likely to encounter them—within declining businesses. When unit sales volumes fall for structural reasons that offer little hope of revitalized demand, the environment is termed an *endgame*. Strategic flexibility is lowest where exit barriers (or mobility barriers) are highest. The impact of such barriers seems to be greatest within the endgame.

Chapters 6, 7, and 8 describe the endgame—the half of an industry's life when excess capacity becomes a persistent problem as a result of declining demand. In a global context, endgame is merely a regional problem, because demand continues in some markets while endgames are played out in others. Exit barriers—both tangible and mental—prevent some firms from following demand into new markets. They also prevent managers from realizing the full profitability of playing the endgame well.

The topic of declining demand and exit barriers is presented as follows: First endgame strategies are sketched and a framework for their use is presented in chapter 6. Statistical tests for the determinants of exit barrier heights appear in chapter 7, but managers could skip that material and proceed to chapter 8—to a discussion of the management of the endgame—for a less robust understanding of the arguments concerning endgames and how to prosper within them.

Recommendations concerning the endgame are straightforward. Put in enough money so that the firm's competitive advantage will not erode if there is hope for future demand, but not so much money that the endgame gobbles up cash. Reward managers of endgame business units on a different basis than those of high-growth business units. Put the incentive on reducing cash requirements to run operations, rather than on profit margins or return on investment. Once the decision has been made to abandon the operation, make the transition orderly. Stop making the products; if necessary, buy them from a competitor to satisfy company and customer needs temporarily. Know when to exit.

6
Strategies for Declining Businesses

T his chapter examines declining demand and firms' responses to it. A normative model is developed based on strategies that may be pursued. Briefly, the appropriateness of particular endgame strategies for dealing with decline will be shown to depend on the characteristics of the industry in question, the firm's competitive posture within that industry, and the timing of competitors' repositioning or exit decisions.

Decline as a Strategy Problem

To date, very little attention has been given to the problem of declining industries and to the strategies appropriate for them. In general, the existing literature can be divided into four categories: (1) literature concerning declining brands of models of a product (Alexander 1964; Talley 1964; Kotler 1965; Hutchinson 1971; Hise and McGinnis 1975); (2) literature concerning divestitures (Bettauer 1967; Hayes 1972; Davis 1974); (3) product life-cycle literature (Buzzell 1966; Wasson 1974; Clifford 1976); and (4) strategic-portfolio literature (Tilles 1966; Boston Consulting Group 1972; Carter and Cohen 1972). None of these literatures made any attempt to sort out the factors that influence the strategic choices managers will face during such declines. Most of these writings looked at only one pattern of declining product or industry demand and espoused only one strategy alternative for coping with this problem. Unfortunately, such a simplified view of the strategies appropriate for declining industries is *inadequate* for the needs of managers running such businesses because differences in industry structures, in the reasons for such declines, in expectations regarding future demand, in

Adapted from articles that originally appeared in the *Academy of Management Review,* October 1980, by permission of the publisher, the Academy of Management; in the *Journal of Business Strategy,* Fall 1980, by permission of the publishers, Warren, Gorham & Lamont, Inc.; and in *Long Range Planning,* December 1982, by permission of the publisher, Pergamon Press, Ltd.

the strengths of different businesses, and so on, may substantially alter firms' performances.

No Single Success Pattern

About fifteen years ago, eight large U.S. firms committed an average of $10 million each to the construction of new plants that used an experimental technology to manufacture products for several customers who held long-term contracts. However, bugs in this technology cut these plants' maximum output to levels below their engineered capacity. Two years later, a rival technology relying on different raw materials was commercialized, and the firms' own raw materials prices quadrupled. As a result, industrywide consumption of the product dwindled.

Seeing this change, one firm wrote off its plant immediately and contracted for supplies consumed internally from a competitor. It broke even. Another firm was locked into production with customers who would not renegotiate their contracts. It suffered losses. A third firm managed to satisfy its contractual customers by retiring its own plant and leasing a competitor's plant that was of a smaller, more appropriate capacity for its customers' needs. It prospered.

About the same time, several even larger U.S. companies were heavily invested in a basic technology when a major technological breakthrough that could spawn several subsequent generations of product improvements was announced. The firms had been planning to erect highly automated plants for these basic products to lower the cost of their domestic labor forces. The new technology had not yet been commercialized and was quite expensive, but it would definitely make their basic product obsolete in the future.

One firm sold its patents and ideas to foreign producers who could import the product less expensively than it could be produced in the United States. It prospered. A second firm used the product internally; it made investments in automated plants and helped its competitors to exit. It prospered too.

Finally, less than ten years ago, over thirty U.S. firms were caught completely off guard when a new version of a consumer product was merchandised with great fanfare. Although the new version was quite expensive, it made their version obsolete overnight.

One firm, which produced inexpensive models of the older consumer product increased its output and prospered. Another firm, which produced high-quality models of the old consumer product slowly reduced its output as the newer product caught on, but continued to market the obsolete model. It prospered, too. A third firm's models looked very similar to those of the newer version. Unfortunately, retailers would not carry them because they seemed redundant. That firm lost money despite its low operating costs.

Strategy Alternatives

The structural environments of declining industries and the experiences of competitors described earlier differed. Thus it should not be surprising that many different strategies *could* be appropriate for coping with declining demand. What is somewhat surprising, however, is the successes some firms have achieved by *increasing* their investments in declining businesses.

Firms have renovated plants and machinery, acquired the assets of competitors, or otherwise increased their commitment to businesses where aggregate demand was falling as a result of obsolescence, demographics, or cultural changes, when structural circumstances have been favorable. They have accurately diagnosed the outlook for the various market segments of their business and analyzed where enduring demand might exist, despite a general Chicken Little attitude regarding the overall industry's fortunes.

Since firms prospered by using diverse strategies within declining industries, a key question is: What types of strategies are most appropriate for businesses that face endgame—environments of declining demand? Theoretically, it would seem there are alternatives.

Observation also suggests that there are different ways to respond to declining demand. Some firms, such as E.I. duPont de Nemours in rayon, exited quickly after recognizing demand for the product was deteriorating. Other firms milked their endgame businesses, as PPG Industries did in synthetic soda ash, and exited later when they were better prepared to do so. Still other firms, such as Regal Ware, Inc., in percolator coffeemakers, stuck it out to the end after most competitors had discontinued their products, and reaped the benefits of doing so. Since these firms had clearly devised more than one way of responding to declining demand, it seemed that additional research concerning strategies for declining demand was needed to improve understanding of this phenomenon.

Overall, five major types of strategic responses to declining environments can be identified, as follows:

1. Increasing the firm's investment (to dominate or get a good competitive position).
2. Holding the firm's investment level until uncertainties about its industry can be resolved.
3. Decreasing the firm's investment posture selectively, by sloughing

off the unpromising models of customer groups while simultaneously strengthening the firm's investment posture within the lucrative niches of enduring customer demand.

4. Harvesting (or milking) the firm's investment to recover cash quickly, regardless of the resulting investment posture.
5. Divesting the business quickly by disposing of its assets as advantageously as possible.

Early Exit. Firms may wish to exit from declining businesses quickly if competitors are cutting their prices or otherwise impairing the profitability of industries. Early exit may become imperative if the firm hopes to recover much of its assets' values. If industry structural traits do not appear to make the business hospitable for other strategies and if competitive vigor reduces the likelihood that later exits will not produce better performance in the business, it may be advantageous to cash in on a declining business early, before other firms reach the same conclusions, as Raytheon did in electronic receiving tubes or duPont in rayon acetate.

The objective of early exit is prudent timing. This could mean a sale of business assets or their abandonment. The firm may even sell its assets to competitors, if necessary, or junk them, as Diamond Shamrock did in acetylene, to avoid sustaining chronic losses and to release working capital to other uses yielding better returns.

Milk the Investment. A firm may try to increase its return on investment by surrendering market share, or may attempt to funnel as much cash as possible to other projects quickly. In such cases the firm tries to harvest its business. Milking strategies commonly occur when immediate exit is impossible (as a result of exit barriers). The risk in pursuing a milking strategy within a declining business is that if uncontrollable, adverse events force a firm to shut down early, it may be unable to extract all the value it may have invested. On the other hand, if attractive early exit had been available, the firm would have divested its interests rather than milk them. Examples of firms who milked their businesses before finally exiting include Spencer Products in its leather-tanning venture and Corning Glass Works in percolator coffeemakers.

Shrink Selectively. If demand within some market niches seems to be enduring, a firm pursuing a wide product-line posture could *reposition* itself to concentrate on serving the most desirable customer groups while retrieving the value of investments used formerly to serve less attractive customer groups within the now declining industry, as Celanese did in rayon. In order to do so, the firm must make additional investments in some aspects of the declining business. The objective of this strategy is to capture the most promising markets before competitors can identify them, as Mead Johnson did with infant formula when it abandoned Pablum and Bibb juices. The most desirable customers in a declining industry are those who are least likely to convert soon to a substitute product because of their high switching-cost barriers.

Holding Patterns. Holding strategies are pursued when the firm decides it is already in the best strategic posture to compete in the declining business or when the firm is waiting to take more dramatic actions until some key uncertainty is resolved. In this strategy of defensive reinvestment, the firm matches competitors' price changes and marketing expenditures and makes maintenance investments in its plants to compensate for losses of operating efficiency. The firm will probably not thin its product line or shut down plants to consolidate its position, because of expectations that demand will soon increase or that sacrificed market share would be difficult to recover if desired later when industry conditions improve. Courtaulds, for example, held its position in rayon and gained customers when other plants were forced to close.

Increased Investments. A firm might pursue market dominance by increasing its investment level in the declining business if it believed there were a longer-term advantage in doing so. Typically, such a firm will purchase the assets of competitors who wish to exit or will make other investments to ensure that the declining business does not become volatile when competitors experience difficulty in filling their plants' capacities. (Alternatively, the firm may use price cutting to encourage marginal competitors to exit earlier.) Dow Chemical increased its acetylene investment, and GTE Sylvania helped other receiving-tube competitors to exit from the declining industry by purchasing their assets. In synthetic soda ash, marginal competitors were squeezed out when prices did not rise in proportion with increasing energy costs.

Increased investment strategies usually occur where (1) there seem to be enduring pockets of demand for the declining product, (2) the cost of repositioning to serve these niches most advantageously seems likely to be recovered rapidly or is not substantial, and (3) few other competitors are capable of or positioned to serve the attractive customer niches advantageously. Thus a firm may choose to increase the level of its investment in a declining business if it is cost-efficient in manufacturing the endgame product or sells a patented or branded product to loyal customers. Increased investment strategies work best within declining industries that have relatively low exit barriers, few maverick competitors, high switching costs for customers, and other favorable character-istics (detailed later).

Increased investment strategies have been rewarding in declining in-dustries such as baby foods, replacement electronic receiving tubes, and acetylene production, among others. The attractiveness of these declining industries has been increased for remaining firms by their willingness to purchase competitors' assets, to act as a source for competitors who have discontinued production but continue to merchandise declining products, and to produce for private brand merchandisers.

Thus Gerber Products and Dow Chemical increased their invest-ments in baby food and acetylene, respectively—markets in which each firm faced excellent opportunities for profitability. On the other hand, Courtaulds and Havatampa Cigar held their respective investment pos-tures in rayon and cigars, where they were appropriately situated for the demand conditions they faced. However, Mead-Johnson and Sunbeam Appliance shrank their investment postures in baby foods and percolator coffeemakers when they could not compete profitably; and PPG Indus-tries and duPont milked their investments in synthetic soda ash and acetate when analyses suggested there would be little to be gained by staying in these businesses. Finally, Raytheon and duPont divested their electronic receiving-tube and acetylene business, respectively, when they saw an opportunity to cut their losses and recover a portion of their investments quickly.

Factors behind Firms' Strategy Choices

Observation suggests that product or industry demand may decline in many ways. It may deteriorate quickly, as was the case with rubber baby panties when disposable diapers were commercialized; or it may dimin-ish slowly, as with cigar consumption, which has been declining inter-mittently for half a century. Similarly, demand may plummet and then reach a plateau; this has occurred with baby food consumption, which has fallen with the declining U.S. birth rate, and with various other prod-ucts that are sustained by a core of replacement demand. Or demand may decline to zero without pausing. There may be substantial uncer-tainty regarding a product's revitalization, as in the case of millinery equipment for ladies' hats; or there may be relative certainty that the product is indeed obsolete, as in the case of electronic receiving tubes (vacuum tubes).

Types of Decline and Demand Traits

Overall, there were three major reasons for the declines that occurred: (1) technological obsolescence, (2) sociological or demographic changes, and (3) changing fashion. In general, declines induced by fashion or demographic changes produced great uncertainty about future industry prospects; declines created by technological change were far more predictable, especially when the firms involved understood the substitute technology.

Expectations. If there were relative certainty regarding (1) which pockets of demand would decline first, (2) how rapidly demand would decline for different market niches, and (3) whether demand would be likely to revitalize, then competition within the declining industry would be less likely to be volatile and the timing of exits would be more likely to be orderly. For instance, in these circumstances few firms suffered large write-off losses, and most of the firms that exited did so in a nondisruptive fashion about the time it was economically appropriate for them to do so. When there was substantial uncertainty concerning these three factors, however, chaos was more likely to ensue. Thus discontinuities in the rate and pattern of decline were especially disastrous since these demand conditions could trap some firms that were unable to sell their underutilized assets quickly. This condition increased the likelihood of price wars.

Enduring Niches of Demand. The presence of pockets of demand where customers' switching costs are financially high (or are perceived as being high as a result of the disadvantage of a degradation of quality) would determine whether the declining industry would be hospitable to a range of strategies that might include reinvestment. Favorable declining business environments contain at least one pocket of enduring product demand of viable size. Identification of market niches is desirable, but they do not exist in all declining businesses. The framework (presented later) identifies whether an industry offers hope for carving out an advantageous position with customers during decline. It counsels exit if the industry is not favorable for continued investments.

Demand could endure and remain at attractive levels where products appeal to customers who would switch products with great reluctance or only if use of the substitute product were clearly more desirable. Examples of such niches include: electronic receiving tubes for high-fidelity amplification uses or as replacement components in color television; leather goods and apparel designed and merchandised for the haute couture market; premium-branded cigars (retailing for $2.00 per cigar);

belted, nonradial tires merchandised through discount outlets; hypoallergenic infant formula; sterling silver electric percolator coffeemakers and plastic percolators; shiny acetate fabrics for disco wear and rayon filament fibers for high-quality menswear lining fabrics; and leather military boots.

Attractive Endgame Demand. Some declining environments were also more favorable than others in terms of long-term sales volumes and profitability, lack of asset losses, and price stability. Market attractiveness was increased whenever the niches of demand that the firms served were protected from incursions by displaced competitors whose primary markets had dried up; when the niches were not inhabited by maverick firms that frequently instigated price wars; and when the firms could enjoy some benefits from their well-established brand names or corporate reputations. Other traits that increased the attractiveness of these declining industries are shown in table A–18 in the appendix and discussed later.

Industry Structure Characteristics

Declining industry environments were relatively volatile when firms from significantly different (asymmetric) strategic groups were forced by shrinking demand to compete against each other for the same customers. Other factors that made the endgame volatile, expecially with respect to price levels, included the capital intensity (and excess capacity) of the industry, the presence of strong customer industries that controlled access to the ultimate consumers (usually shelf space), and/or a highly price-sensitive ultimate customer demand. On the other hand, high customer switching costs decreased the likelihood that competition would be volatile.

Product Traits. The market niche that protects the firm from potential entrants best in a declining demand context is established when the firm has effectively differentiated its product or holds patents that deter rival products from attaining a similar state of acceptability with the enduring customer group. If this niche is effectively fortified, competitors will be unable to hurdle the barrier using price-cutting alone.

Customer Traits. Continuing customer demand may be advantageous if customers can afford to bear the increased costs manufacturers will sustain in providing the declining product while underutilizing their assets. If the higher costs *cannot* be passed on to customers, there are fewer advantages to remaining in the industry. If customers would react unfavorably to a firm's discontinuation of a product by avoiding the firm's other products, their market power constitutes an exit barrier that should delay a firm's timely exit and may result in subnormal economic returns (or losses) for it.

Supplier Behavior. Suppliers could help firms weather competitive turbulence in decline, by financing their sales, advertising on their behalf, or extending discounts and other forms of assistance, if they believe that demand for the declining products will revitalize or that the firms in question serve promising customer niches that will endure.

Competitors' Traits. Decisions regarding strategies for declining businesses must be made with full consideration of the probable responses of the other industry members. Usually, during periods of industry growth, firms from different strategic groups compete on a nonprice basis because of their different approaches to and perceptions of the industry. During periods of decline, however, these same differences can often lead to severe price warfare as these firms fight for declining sales volumes.

Exit Barriers. Exit barriers are factors that dissuade firms from making smooth and timely exits from their various lines of business. They may assume a variety of forms, as table A–19 indicates. For example, the realizable liquidation value of the assets firms commit to the endgame shrinks as endgame progresses, especially if they cannot be easily converted to other productive uses, since the fact that demand is declining overall within the industry suggests that excess capacity will become endemic and many marginal competitors *should* be selling out.

Unfortunately, these competitors are locked into the declining business by one or more of several exit barriers. High exit barriers produce contorted maneuvers later, when rapid exit becomes imperative. (Suggestions concerning how to lower exit barriers are offered in a later section.)

When marginal competitors were locked into an adverse competitive situation by such exit barriers, stronger firms found they could remove these exit barriers and allow the marginal competitors to exit by purchasing the assets that constituted barriers. Such tactics must be predicated on an analysis of relative competitor strengths that suggest the *acquiring firm* will serve an enduring niche of demand more advantageously and hence is *justified* in increasing the level of its commitment to the industry by buying out the marginal firm.

Assessing Endgame Attractiveness

Thus the first step in endgame analysis is to assess an industry's attractiveness. In general, the less favorable declining industries had no niches of enduring demand, no mobility barriers to keep other competitors away, and little product differentiation. Other traits that *decreased* the attractiveness of declining industries included high reinvestment requirements, substantial diseconomies of scale, at least one maverick competitor who would cut prices below costs, the existence of customers who possessed and exerted strong bargaining power, and high exit barriers.

Within the more unfavorable declining industries examined, demand was highly price-sensitive and often plummeted abruptly, creating sizable write-off losses for firms that were forced to exit. Price cutting was rather severe, substantial reinvestment requirements often forced competitors to exit prematurely, and great uncertainty regarding the duration of demand frequently induced firms to reinvest in what was later revealed to be an unpromising industry. There was also substantial disorder in the patterns of firms' investments and exits, and quite often the need for major asset write-offs deterred some marginal competitors from making timely exits.

In favorable endgames, characterized by low demand uncertainty and low exit barriers, firms that possessed the appropriate strengths and commitments to do so increased the level of their investment in endgame by purchasing assets or improving their own operations. Guided by their analysis of the expected evolution of demand for the declining products, others repositioned their investment to eliminate unpromising portions of the investment while fortifying more promising products or campaigns to service more promising groups of customers.

Assessing Competitor Strengths

The next step is to assess which firms are best suited to serve the enduring pockets of demand. Factors such as (1) established relationships with customers who make up enduring (and lucrative) pockets of demand, (2) a highly valued brand name, (3) a plant that can operate efficiently when underutilized, (4) a large market share (if products are commoditylike), (5) strong and substantial distribution networks, (6) a favorable location or raw-materials contract, (7) flexible assets (or highly depreciated ones that could be removed without substantial costs), and (8) an advantageous posture of diversification are key strengths in declining industries. (Frequently they are also sources of exit barriers; see chapter 7.) Other traditional strengths, such as high vertical integration, shared facilities, and high scale economies in production, are frequently disadvantageous in endgame.

Finding the Right Strategy

From consideration of these and other industry and competitor factors, an assessment of appropriate endgame strategies may be made. If the firm's environment has undesirable conditions that mandate immediate exit, the firm should not consider the more aggressive approaches for coping with industry decline that are sketched in figure 6–1.

Table A–20 in the appendix presents the endgame strategy matrix. It summarizes the relationships between relative industry attractiveness (that is, favorability for continued investment), relative competitive strengths, and competitive investment strategies that would lead to the best economic results. These assertions are based on previous research and theory.

Comparing Expected with Actual

A study was made of patterns of strategies used to cope with declining demand. It sought patterns of responses to decline that were more (or

ENVIRONMENTAL TRAITS

• Demand-price insensitive.	Demand-price sensitive. •
• Replacement units likely to be needed by some customers for a long time.	Demand could deteriorate abruptly. •
• Loyal customer demand likely to endure.	Low customer switching costs. •
• Revitalization likely, albeit remote.	Competition usually volatile. •
• Firm serves protected (high entry barriers) market niche alone.	Competitors face high exit barriers. •
• Suppliers willing to help firm compete.	Customers likely to exert bargaining power. •

Aggressive ◄——————*The Strategic Continuum*——————► *Cut Losses*
(increased   (get-out-now
investment   strategy)
strategy)

Figure 6–1. Relating Strategy Alternatives to Environmental Conditions within a Declining Industry

less) successful than other responses. Several declining industries were studied to see whether certain strategies were always successful, or successful in only some situations. It compared the successes and failures of firms with the outcomes the matrix predicted.

Sample

The sample included sixty firms in eight industries chosen to cover the broadest range of situations and to contrast structural traits. In gathering data for this study, the strategic actions and plans of these firms were traced back to a common base year selected to contrast periods of relatively stable demand with the periods of decline. (Thus the base year in the study of cigars was 1964, a near-historic peak in U.S. cigar consumption and the year in which the surgeon-general announced that cigarette smoking was carcinogenic.) Sampling techniques were similar to those described in chapter 5. Strategies pursued in the years subsequent to declines in demand were compared.

Table A–21 presents the model's performance. The strategy matrix predicted successful endgame strategies well. Close matches between predicted and observed effective endgame strategies were found for the aggressive and successful firms. (The discrepancies were greater for unsuccessful firms.)

Overall, the endgame model was supported quite strongly as more than 92 percent of the firms that followed its directions were successful, while over 85 percent of those who violated its precepts failed. Although there were forty-two firms that were relatively successful and nineteen firms that were relatively unsuccessful, thirty-nine of the forty-two successful firms followed the prescriptions of the model, and sixteen of the nineteen unsuccessful firms violated its precepts. Stated somewhat differently, thirty-nine of the forty-two firms that followed the recommendations of the model were successful, while three failed. By contrast, sixteen of the nineteen firms that acted contrary to the recommendations of the model failed, and only three succeeded.

Outcomes

Overall, six of the sixty firms studied increased their investment levels in response to decline. Eleven held their investment positions near historic levels. Fifteen firms selectively repositioned their investments in their declining industries by shrinking selectively. Twenty-five firms milked their investments, and three divested quickly. For a detailed analysis of the outcomes and exceptions, see Harrigan (1980c).

The Exceptions

Two of the three firms that succeeded despite violating the prescriptions of the stategic matrix were ones that milked their investments in industries where a more aggressive strategy (such as holding their investment levels) was recommended. Both firms were pioneers in the technology of the declining industry and shut down their plants after milking them according to a depreciation schedule established in the 1950s. Both firms were out of time with the other competitors in their industry, who were still building plants when these firms had already decided to retire theirs. More important, both firms served only internal markets (that is, they were vertically integrated). Consequently, they did not really have a "hold" or "shrink selectively" choice open to them, since there were no excess customer groups to cast off. Instead, their real choice was between "divest" or "milk," and both chose the latter.

Firms did not always do what economic rationality would seem to indicate. In fact, in nineteen of the sixty-two cases, firms chose actions inconsistent with the hypotheses. There were a number of possible reasons for this inconsistent behavior, including limited or inaccurate information, lack of funds, and poor management. One of the most important factors seemed to be the strategic importance of the business to the company involved. Such importance—whether assessed in terms of corporate-image objectives, customer linkages, organizational reporting goals, or vertical-integration constraints—created *strategic* exit barriers that retarded the withdrawal of several firms that should have abandoned the declining industry in which they were competing much sooner than they did.

Two broad generalizations spring from this analysis. First, almost all firms either adopt the strategies they should (72 percent) or put *more* resources into declining business than they should (26 percent). *Almost none* (2 percent) withdraw more rapidly or more strongly than they should. Second, all the companies that invested more in their declining businesses than they should have had weak positions in unfavorable industries or intermediate (but not strong) positions in businesses of relatively high strategic importance to the firm. Taken together, these findings suggest that strategic exit barriers created by shared facilities, corporate identity, narrow diversification postures, and so on, are often significant deterrents to timely exits from volatile, declining industries. They are a major deterrent to flexibility that must be overcome.

Interpreting Results

Overall, six broad findings emerged from the research, as well as a number of particular findings. The broad findings were as follows:

1. There were a number of different types of decline. Some types were better than others because they represented superior opportunities to prosper during the decline or to exit successfully from the decline.
2. A number of different strategies were used during decline. There was no single road to success. Also, many innovative ways of retrieving the value of a firm's assets were found, and a variety of tactics for executing these different strategies proved effective.
3. A firm's relative success during decline was affected by its relative competitive strengths as well as by the structure of the industry it was in.
4. The appropriate strategies for coping with decline varied according to the firm's strengths and whether its industry environment was favorable for prolonged participation and relatively easy exit.
5. There were a few exceptions to the general patterns observed. Some firms discovered unique ways to beat the laws of the marketplace.
6. Firms did not always adopt the most economically appropriate strategies because competitors' actions sometimes shifted the balance in an industry seeming to be favorable or unfavorable, because they sometimes misread the signals that would have suggested an alternative action plan, and because they were sometimes willing to live with lower levels of performance as a result of the central importance of the business involved to their corporate portfolios.

Expectations

One of the more important findings regarding the determinants and effectiveness of declining industry strategies relates to the power of competitor and customer expectations regarding future demand. Thus some of the uncertainty that led to volatile price competition could have been reduced if better information about competitors and customers had been available. There seem also to be benefits to using scenario analysis and other qualitative forecasting tools that help managers to estimate:

1. How quickly competitors are likely to exit.
2. Which competitors would be most likely to remain.
3. What types of competitors would be potential entrants (by bringing a new technology to the industry, for example) when demand for a particular product declines.

Cost Advantages and Market Share

At the same time, the study indicated that if a firm is not the lowest-cost competitor in an industry where products are becoming commoditylike in nature, it will usually have to surrender market share during the decline. If the declining product is differentiated in some way, however, new investments in the business may be justified in order to secure a more favorable position. On the other hand, if the product does not service a demand that responds to differentiation—for example, if the product is developing commoditylike traits that make customers increasingly price-sensitive—such reinvestments may not be justified because no true customer niche is likely to exist. Without the protection of high mobility barriers, which product differentiation usually provides, such high-cost firms are vulnerable to market invasions by lower-cost competitors.

It would seem, therefore, that if a firm possesses a large share of the market but does not possess the lowest operating costs, a strong distribution system, or a loyal niche of customers, it should try to overcome its exit barriers early by selling the declining business to another competitor or even to a supplier. This is particularly true if it possesses a large proportion of undepreciated assets, since without these particular strengths it will be increasingly difficult to retrieve the value of the firm's investments as the decline progresses.

Rationalizing Excess Capacity

The execution of such maneuvers, however, requires that weaker competitors retire their plants in deference to more efficient competitors (or irrationally committed competitors)—a course of action they are sometimes reluctant to pursue because of the strategic exit barriers discussed earlier. One economic solution that the study suggests might work in such situations is the use of sourcing arrangements whereby the most efficient competitors (plants) would manufacture the declining product for several of their weaker competitors to sell under their own corporate or brand names.

Uncontrollable Events

Finally, the study indicated that certain external events could be particularly catastrophic for the vitality of a declining industry in the sense that investments might become necessary that were not likely to be recoverable. These events, which tended to encourage exits, included legislation concerning effluent standards, pollution controls, employee-health work rules, import tariffs, export quotas, and a variety of other public-policy decisions. In some instances, however, even these events can be used to the benefit of the firm. Thus, if a firm wished to ease others out of a declining industry, it might make such investments in anticipation of legislation and then actually encourage such laws to be enacted.

Since some types of uncontrollable external events can literally destroy entire industries, especially those facing decline already, and since many of these events are now of a governmental nature, it is essential that firms in such positions monitor government agencies closely. They should prepare factual forecasts of the likely economic impact of such legislation and regulations on communities where the firm is operating in order to draw attention to the loss of jobs, tax revenues, and other benefits that the demise of the business would cause. Such analyses should include forecasts of the cost of exit in order to facilitate informed decision making by management. In addition, it may not be out of order for the firms that have performed such analyses to provide copies of their findings to the salient public policymakers and affected residents of the community.

Implications for Management

Overall, the strategy matrix model suggests that firms with weak businesses in unattractive industries tend to hold on to these businesses *too long*. There is a need for better ways to accurately project the future prospects of declining industries, as well as to help weaker firms to overcome the strategic barriers that might keep them invested in these areas.

Competitors' staying power—that is, their ability or willingness to remain in the industry and fight for a shrinking number of customers— is determined by the exit barriers they face or inflict on themselves. An understanding of competitors' relative-operating-cost advantages is essential in order to estimate the relative break-even production-volume requirements of remaining competitors. If analysis suggests that, despite its efforts to avoid a price war, the firm will be drawn into a bloodbath by firms that will not yield market share despite their relative cost disadvantage and other competitive disadvantages, results suggest that the firm should contemplate an early exit. Moreover, if the industry offers promise of enduring demand from a customer group the firm *could* serve but cannot afford to (or is unwilling to) serve by purchasing the assets of disruptive competitors, the firm would be well advised to seek a means of exit, itself.

Exit Barriers

There was much evidence suggesting that firms will not necessarily exit when an economic analysis, such as an abandonment calculation, would suggest they should do so. It is useful to recognize that the stock market and other outsiders, who do not understand the complexities of managing declining businesses, will tend to overvalue companies that are willing to bite the bullet by divesting businesses when they first begin to sour. Consequently, although such early divestment behavior may actually shortchange the firm of possible returns on such businesses, it still may be preferable because of the increased P/E (price–earnings) ratio and bond ratings that outsiders give to such firms because they believe them to be well managed. This section suggests how to do so.

Lowering the Firm's Exit Barriers. If a firm's analysis suggests that it possesses no relative advantage to pursue by remaining within the endgame, the firm might lower its own exit barriers (as table A–22 indicates) by appealing to more staunchly committed competitors to purchase its assets in order to ensure retirement of excess capacity to improve their respective prospects for a nonvolatile endgame. In addition to making provisions early to facilitate the disposal of durable and specific assets, the firm might consider how to lease them to minimize their exposure to obsolescence.

Lowering Competitors' Exit Barriers. The endgame is particularly difficult to manage when many competitors face exit barriers that dissuade them from exiting. Table A–23 suggests ways to lower competitors' exit barriers. Theirs will be very similar to the firm's. For example, if several firms were unable to exit because they felt obliged or they were forced by militant unions to preserve the jobs of otherwise unskilled laborers, several excess plants would remain in operation, creating a particularly unpleasant endgame environment of low profit margins for the locked-in firms. Shutting them down can present a touchy situation.

The announcement of a firm's intended departure can precipitate (1) shifts by its former customers to alternative sources of supply and (2) price rises for the endgame products. Olin Corporation was left with brimming warehouses of soda ash when customers abruptly switched suppliers following a rumor that Olin planned to shut down its synthetic soda ash plants. By contrast, cigar makers have been able to raise the prices of their products as small cigar makers were forced out of the industry. Even if the capacity of the exiting firm will ultimately be operated by a successor firm, its exit provides an opportunity for the firm's competitors to reestablish wider profit margins for their endgame products and to exploit the confusion created during the lag time required by the successor firm to make the expenditures and adjustments necessary in order to regain some of these temporarily lost customers. Therefore, exits by competitors could provide short-term opportunities for remaining firms to influence the outcome of the endgame if these firms are poised to exploit this period of temporary confusion.

The Timing of Strategies for Declining Demand

The firm's strategy problem in endgame is one of timing. The firm's analysis of this problem must suggest not only *which* strategies are feasible, but also *when* to implement its decisions to buy a competitor's assets, to drop part of its product line, or to exit completely. All these tactics were executed with varying degrees of success by some of the firms in this study that were trapped within various declining businesses. The differences in their performances were largely differences in timing and in judgment, but the problems that confronted them were similar across industry boundaries.

Some of the strategy alternatives sketched here necessitate *early* execution if they are to succeed. Notably, where reinvestments or repositioning will be required in order to remain in the industry, the firm must commit its resources before competitors can maneuver into a more advantageous position. Similarly, exits should be executed before the asset resale market sours. Although it may seem desirable for the firm to wait for the situation to become less uncertain, waiting could be detrimental. The firm cuts off its strategy options (and their respective promises of profitable performance) by waiting.

As demand shrinks, only a few competitors' plants will be needed to satisfy remaining demand. If a firm could communicate its binding industry commitment to its rivals *early,* it may be able to prevent competitors from occupying the most desirable market niches and to signal unambiguously that it intends to fight bitterly to retain these niches, once occupied. The firm may even be able to avert bloodshed if an industry consensus is recognized among rivals and is considered important to maintain for the mutual profitability of the remaining participants.

Conclusions

It is possible to earn excellent returns on depreciated assets within declining businesses that do not need new infusions of cash to sustain the firm's momentum, but the endgame must provide a hospitable arena for doing so. Tennessee Eastman's acetate plant, General Electric's receiving-tube plant, and Monochem's acetylene plant provide examples of depreciated but lucrative operations within the endgame. The firm that cannot exit may initiate several aggressive policies (such as becoming private brand supplier to firms that will not abandon their branded products) in order to rationalize the potential disruptions of endgame competition; but even where the firm and its competitors do not face substantial exit barriers, results suggest that the prudent endgame participant will strive to attain an early recognition of other firms' commitments and asymmetries in order to formulate an appropriate schedule of exits to respond to them. Prudent timing and careful analysis of industry traits together can result in improved performance in decline.

Declining environments are not all alike, and there are a variety of strategies that may be used to cope with decline. Each of these strategies will have a different probability of success, depending on the nature of the decline and the relative competitive strength of the firm involved. Since the cost of erring in such decisions is quite high, managers need to anticipate the problems of decline earlier in order to have more options in their portfolio of strategies, and also to be able to divest sooner *if* that is their best strategic option.

7

Measures of Strategic-Inflexibility Exit Barriers

F irms face strategic inflexibility when they cannot redeploy their assets without friction. When exit (or mobility) barriers are high, firms cannot respond effectively to the innovations of new entrants (or ongoing competitors). They fall behind technologically and cannot respond adequately to changes in demand. Under unfavorable conditions, vertical integration may also impede firms' strategic flexibility.

Mobility barriers and exit barriers prevent firms from repositioning themselves to serve more attractive customers (Caves and Porter 1976) and from retrieving the value of their investments when they abandon markets they may have once served. High exit barriers can trap competitors within an industry, resulting in destructive competition and reduced profits (Porter 1976b; Harrigan 1980b, c, and d, 1981b, 1982, 1983a, 1985b). For the purposes of this chapter, the term *exit barriers* will be used to discuss *both* mobility and exit barriers. The effect of high barriers in either case will be to keep firms operating within an industry in a status quo fashion even when they earn subnormal returns on their investments.

Entry Barriers Become Exit Barriers

Managers have been cautioned recently to think carefully regarding the future flexibility of asset investments made when implementing their business strategies (Porter 1976b, 1979a; Harrigan 1980b, c, and d, 1981b, 1982, 1983a, 1985b). The substantial sums firms may have invested in automated manufacturing processes as well as in intensive brand-differentiation campaigns or captive distribution networks, to create en-

Adapted from articles that originally appeared in the *Strategic Management Journal*, April–June 1980, by permission of the copyright holder and publisher, John Wiley & Sons, Ltd.; and in the *Academy of Management Journal*, June 1981, by permission of the publisher, the Academy of Management.

try barriers (Bain 1956) could serve as millstones when firms try to reposition. They can become *exit barriers* that deter firms from making timely exits in the future.

Entry Barriers

As explained in chapter 1, *entry barriers* are a central concept in the study of industrial organization. They are circumstances within an industry that discourage entry by new competitors. Where entry barriers are high, prices can exceed costs by a proportion in excess of normal profits without attracting added entry (Bain 1956, 1972; Modigliani 1958; Gaskin 1971; Caves and Porter 1976).

Entry barriers can be circumstances that give an absolute cost advantage to established competitors, such as production techniques perfected through R&D expenditures or control of a scarce but necessary factor of production (Williamson 1963; Mueller and Tilton 1969; Stonebreaker 1976). Entry barriers can be competitive advantages that would be costly to overcome, such as the cumulative effect of advertising and distribution relationships, or of the learning curve (Comanor and Wilson 1967). Entry barriers may also be structural conditions indigenous to a particular industry's transformation processes, which permit significant scale economies to be enjoyed if substantial capital investments are made (Bain 1956; Stigler 1958, 1968; Weiss 1964; Shepherd 1967; Wenders 1971; Scherer 1980; Porter 1975; Caves, Khalizadeh-Shirazi, and Porter 1975).

Exit Barriers

Exit barriers, a concept in the study of industrial organization pioneered by Caves and Porter (1976), are circumstances within an industry that discourage the exit of competitors whose performances in that particular business may be marginal. Where exit barriers are high, prices may plunge below so-called normal profits, below variable costs, and conceivably below fixed costs as well, without encouraging certain inflexible competitors to exit. Intangible strategic barriers, such as the value of distribution networks, customer goodwill for the other products, or strong corporate identification with the product, are also significant deterrents to timely exits (Caves and Porter 1976; Porter 1976b).

The timely extrication of a firm's resources from a business that is failing can be a delicate maneuver. Studies by Caves and Porter (1976), Harrigan and Porter (1983), and Harrigan (1980c) have indicated that where a thin resale market exists for the assets of a business (or for the business unit itself), successful divestiture may be particularly difficult to attain.

The deterrent effect of these structural traits on a particular firm's business units will vary according to the types of competitive investments the firm has made. Differences in the ages of firms' assets and their specificity to one task (as well as in the nature of their distribution-network relationships) allow some firms to exit with greater ease than other firms, whose strategic postures may include more of the kinds of investments that evolve into exit barriers.

Firms that understand the pressures that exit barriers can exert on competitive behaviors could use this knowledge in shaping an industry's contours to their own advantage. If a firm believed adequate reasons to remain in a troubled business existed, early analysis of its competitors' barriers could suggest which might be most responsive to attempts to alleviate high exit barriers.

Economic Barriers. Economic exit barriers represent those factors that will influence firms to operate their assets even if they earn subnormal rates of return on them. These barriers can be the costs associated with eliminating a plant (such as the cost of dismantling a chemical plant and treating the land beneath the plant) or the deterrent effect created by the lack of a resale market for the plant and assets (Caves and Porter 1976). Their effect is to keep excess capacity in operation that should have been retired.

Physical assets such as plant, machinery, and inventory make up the major types of economic assets that could act as exit barriers, although (as is explained later) a plant that is shared with another business could also constitute such a barrier.

Porter (1976b) suggested that the factors influencing the "height" of economic exit barriers are predominantly characteristic relating to the product's manufacturing technology: (1) capital intensity, (2) asset specificity, (3) age of the assets (the extent to which their value has been depreciated), and (4) technological or operating reinvestment requirements. If the expenditures for other types of investments—advertising, R&D, or plant improvements—are not expensed, they too could constitute economic exit barriers in the sense that they might appear as an undesirable reported loss upon disposal when firms exit. (All assets that have been capitalized could act as exit barriers by virtue of the reporting loss they could create if firms exited before depreciating them.)

In the tests to follow, *high* manufacturing- or technology-related exit barriers were those for which the cost of disposal would exceed 10 percent of the firm's reported net income. If the value of the firms' fixed and working capital investments is difficult to retrieve except through continued operations, high economic barriers could lock them into prolonged competition at unattractive returns. Thus, if economic exit barriers are high, competition will be more volatile among trapped participants because their unfavorable cost structures would encourage them to use price cutting in order to fill their individual plant capacities.

Strategic Barriers. Exit barriers could also emanate from firms' reluctance to sacrifice the benefits of cumulative, intangible assets that they have created through previous investments. *Strategic* exit barriers such as these could be created by image-maintenance goals, customer-service obligations, potential loss of customers or distribution channels, internal synergies between related businesses, shared facilities, or a highly successful market position. Some forms of vertical integration (discussed later) may also act as strategic exit barriers. These benefits become exit barriers when a thin resale market for the business itself makes recovery of their past investments difficult. Exit becomes impossible to contemplate as a result of quasi-contractual and other strategic obligations that were once undertaken and cannot be discharged easily in an adverse market.

Caves and Porter (1977) established that the force of intangibles as exit barriers, which had not been recognized previously, could indeed be substantial. The effects they isolated included:

1. A high-quality image (created by previous R&D, production, or advertising expenditures), which could be damaged for other products in terminating the business.
2. Physical facilities shared with other healthy businesses that the firm preferred to retain.
3. Goodwill and loyalty in distribution channels and strong corporate recognition (created by previous marketing expenditures), which could be damaged for other businesses by abandoning the business in question.
4. Customer industries possessing strong bargaining positions that have relied on the products to be discontinued and that could potentially damage the firm's competitive position in other markets.
5. Businesses that are of high strategic importance to the firm.

Expectations Regarding Future Demand. Even if competitors experience declining demand for their industry's products, favorable expectations concerning demand for the products of an individual firm could induce firms to remain invested in the face of adversity. If a firm had served a lucrative subset of customers (for example, premium handmade cigars within the otherwise troubled cigar business, or rayon filament fibers used for suit linings within the otherwise beleaguered cellulosic-fibers business), it would not expect its customers to switch to other products. It would expect demand to endure and remain lucrative. Hence it would not divest the assets used to serve its market segment. In the following tests, exit-barrier heights were examined in light of individual firms' expectations that demand would endure for their products for a longer time into the future than for competitors' products because each firm acted *independently* of its rivals.

Estimates of Exit-Barrier Heights

The sections that follow examine the effects of barriers on firms' efforts to exit. The industries examined all experienced declining demand.

The Sample

As with the tests in chapter 6, the experiences of sixty-one firms that managed declining businesses from 1965 to 1978 were studied to determine which of them would exit from such industries.

Candidates for industry sites were selected according to screening criteria from the *1972 Census of Manufacturers*. The industries selected were electronic receiving tubes, rayon and acetate, cigars, synthetic soda ash, acetylene, percolator coffeemakers, U.S. leather tanning, and baby foods. A multistage research program, similar to that described in chapter 5, was employed to obtain scaled estimates of exit-barrier heights (for details, see Harrigan 1980b, 1981b).

Models

The relationship of the industry traits and strategic posture factors (sketched earlier) to the likelihood that a firm would face strategic inflexibility was specified in a model using a binary dependent variable, the decision whether to exit (where exit = 1). In an ordinary-least-squares (OLS) specification of this model, the coefficients of the independent variables (b_i) may be interpreted to represent the relative percentage contributions to the likelihood that exit would occur. The model was stated in the following form:

$$y = a + b_i x_i + e$$

where y = likelihood of exit, and the inducements and deterrents to exit (x_i) correspond to the following numbering scheme:

1. A high-quality product image.
2. The presence of a strong customer industry (whose patronage for other products might be lost by discontinuing the products of the business in question).
3. Facilities shared between businesses (where one of the businesses is a candidate for divestiture).
4. Good distribution-channel relationships and strong brand or corporate identification (created through previous expenditures for promotional activities and advertising).
5. Economic exit barriers (manufacturing technology and physical assets).
6. Favorable expectations that demand for the products of the business unit considered for divestiture will endure for a lengthy period into the future.
7. Substantial losses from operations.
8. Strategic importance to the firm.

Results

Table A–24 in the appendix shows several alternative specifications of the model. These were created by adding and deleting individual factors in order to demonstrate the *joint effects* of the factors as well as the relative magnitude of their influences on an exit decision. (This procedure yielded slightly different coefficient estimates for each specification.) The numbers in parentheses discussed in the text following represent *harmonic means* of the statistically significant coefficient values under discussion. These numbers, which may be interpreted as relative percentage contributions to the firm's propensity to exit, were calculated from the statistically significant coefficient values of the specifications in table A–24. For example, the harmonic means for "losses" (35 percent), which is referred to later in the text, was calculated from the statistically significant coefficient values for losses.

From these results, the following weights were obtained as a relative exit barrier heights:

1. An image of high product quality (−31 percent).
2. Strong customers (−25 percent).
3. Facilities shared with healthy business units (−27 percent).
4. Good distribution-channel relationships (−21 percent).
5. Economic barriers from the manufacturing assets (−38 percent).
6. Favorable expectations (−35 percent).

Losses increase the relative likelihood that firms will divest a declining business (+35 percent). Where losses were a significant factor, their relative weight frequently *equaled or exceeded* the deterrent effects of other factors.

Strategic Importance

Table A–25 summarizes the results of specifications tested for subsamples of firms whose declining business units had been of high strategic importance and for those whose business units were of relatively low strategic importance. (A business was judged to be of high strategic importance to the firm if it was the only (or major) business the firm is in, if the firm faced the possibility of significant negative repercussions to its other businesses by virtue of its strong and widely recognized former association and corporate identity with the divestiture candidate business, or if abandonment of this business could adversely affect an important core of the firm's customers.) Again, the figures in parenthesis are *harmonic means* computed from the coefficients of alternative model specifications.

For companies whose businesses were of high strategic importance, (1) an image of high product quality was a relatively strong deterrent (−36 percent) to exit, and (2) strong customers exerted significant pressures on the firm not to divest (−54 percent). Losses were a relatively low inducement to exit; moreover, they were not statistically significant in many of these specifications, indicating that if the firm perceived a business unit to be strategically important, exit barriers *further* deterred its exit, even if the firm suffered losses from continued competition.

For companies whose businesses were of relatively low strategic importance, table A–25 indicates that (1) the difficulty of disentangling shared facilities (with a harmonic mean of −42 percent), (2) the loss of a high quality reputation (−49 percent), and (3) the potential loss of distribution channel goodwill (−43 percent) acted as relatively strong deterrents to exit, each exerting a stronger negative deterrent than of losses from operations (41 percent).

Other Criterion Variables

The interactions of these structural factors were explored by subsetting the sample according to high- versus low-capital-intensity technologies, and high versus low product differentiability. Details of these tests are reported in Harrigan (1981b), and summarized in table A–26, which shows their relative importance (based on harmonic mean rankings).

Again, the dependent variable was interpreted as the relative likelihood that a firm would divest its declining business unit.

Table A–27 summarizes the differences in dependent variable values for exit in each of the subsets examined. Note that firms in the subsamples facing relatively low economic exit barriers or producing commoditylike products were most likely to exit. Business units that were judged to be of relatively low strategic importance were also relatively *more* likely to be divested. These results may be interpreted to support the likelihood that exit barriers do indeed exist and that these barriers could deter a firm that is floundering within a declining industry from making a timely exit.

The harmonic means of other variables tested (but not reported) included: (1) R&D-related barriers ($-.41$); (2) strong perceived differences between competitors' products (-37); (3) customer goodwill barriers ($-.32$); (4) high advertising expenditures ($-.32$); (5) high recognition of competitors' corporate logos ($-.30$); (6) image of technological leadership ($-.30$); and (7) relatively low operating costs ($-.30$). Other specifications were tested, such as weighted least-squares and the nonlinear cumulative logistic function, and agreed in sign and statistical significance with those of the predictors reported.

Interpreting Results

Tests of exit-barrier heights for businesses of high strategic importance revealed that such business units may seem difficult to divest as a result of the value created by *noncapital* investments. For example, a business that has developed an image of high product quality and that has loyal customers may become inextricably identified with the total firm, and hence its strategy may become less flexible with respect to divestiture. By contrast, a business unit offering less differentiated products, which might rely more heavily on the benefits of an effective distribution system or on operating economies for its success, would be less likely to balk at the loss of a quality image that it never possessed.

Among firms that attached low strategic importance to their declining business units, the statistically significant deterrents to timely exit included physical facilities which were shared with other, nondeclining business units; market advantages created by previous distribution relationships; and advertising and promotional campaign expenditures. The incurrence of losses, as indicated in table A–25, increased the likelihood that firms might exit; but that factor was less significant (statistically) and its regression coefficient's magnitude was lower than that of non-physical, structural barriers that deterred exit. The differences in results from those obtained for businesses of high strategic importance suggest that an image of product quality and quasi-contractual customer relationships may be the essence of desirable strategic posture dimensions that firms believe lead to successful performances.

In general, neither the strategically important nor the less important businesses were as likely to be divested if the particular customer niche serviced was expected to remain viable for a significant time into the future. (Expectations that industry demand would continue to be favorable for the business unit's products was a relatively stronger deterrent to exit where the unit in question was of lesser strategic importance.) This finding is consistent with observations that indicate some inertia within firms when determining the fate of declining business units of relatively low strategic importance.

Theoretical Extension: Vertical Integration as an Exit Barrier

The preceding section has established that the heights of exit barriers may be influenced by various economic, strategic, and managerial forces. In this section, vertical-integration dimensions are added to the model of strategic inflexibility. Some of the forces tested earlier are included as control variables in the model that follows.

For this portion of the analysis, the dependent variable is the economic factors hypothesized to create exit barriers *(economic exit barriers)*. Its value was estimated by using a scale-diseconomies measure, the magnitude of diseconomies incurred by operating 25 percent below engineered capacity, as shown in table A–28. When scale diseconomies are disproportionately large, economic exit barriers would be high.

Strategic exit barriers are represented by an estimate of relative product differentiation, reflecting the unwillingness of firms to give up the benefits created by their past image-building efforts. Average sales growth is used to represent the demand expectations that might encourage some firms to prolong their presence in unattractive industries.

Vertical-Integration Variables

The vertical-integration variables are the dimensions presented in chapter 4 and tested in chapter 5. *Stages* refer to the number and value of steps in the chain of processing—from ultraraw materials to final consumers—in which the firm's SBUs are engaged. *Degree* of integration indicates what percentage of a particular upstream or downstream need an SBU satisfies through product (or service) transfers from (or to) sister SBUs. *Form* refers to the firm's proportion of equity in an SBU.

Firms engaged in several stages of processing will face high exit barriers because vertical links represent larger investments to dispose of. High degrees of backward integration with sister SBUs will be more difficult to disrupt than high degrees of forward integration because of the dependency of upstream units on the SBU's purchases. (This effect is expected because most upstream stages of processing face higher minimum-efficient-scale (MES) plant sizes than do corresponding stages downstream. The throughput volumes involved in the deintegration decision will seem more substantial than when downstream linkages must be severed.) High degrees of forward integration need not raise exit barriers, however. This relationship is consistent with results (cited earlier) where strong customers (who could penalize the firm in other businesses if they were cut off) represented the strongest single contribution to exit-barrier heights. In vertical integration, outsiders' retaliations are removed.

Synergies

Access to information concerning firms' vertical linkages facilitated a test of whether *synergies* raise exit-barrier heights. Shared resources (one measure of synergies) increased exit-barrier heights in earlier studies (Caves and Porter 1976; Harrigan 1980b, 1981b). Resources shared with upstream SBUs were used to approximate the synergies in the following tests.

Models

The dependent variable, exit-barrier heights in 1981, indicates the judges' assessments of the difficulties firms would encounter in repositioning their strategic postures, closing plants, or exiting completely from the target industries. (The mean value of the exit barrier variable was .495, with a standard deviation of .245.) Independent variables (described in table A–28) were scaled using the procedure described earlier and in chapter 5.

The relationship of expectations, economic and strategic forces, and vertical-integration strategy dimensions upon exit barrier heights was tested in a regression model. This procedure is appropriate for hypothesis testing. In this ordinary-least-squares specification, the sign (and magnitude) of the coefficients (b_i) indicate contributions to the likelihood that exit barriers will be high, and the standardized coefficients represent relative contributions to the coefficient of multiple determination. The model is stated in the following form:

$$y = a + b_i x_i + e$$

where y equals the estimate of exit-barrier height, and b_i (where $i = 1, 2, . . .,8$) is the coefficient of each economic, strategic, expectations, or vertical-integration variable, corresponding to the numbering scheme of table A–28.

Results Concerning Control Variables

Economic Forces. Table A–29 indicates that the scale diseconomies variable is positively signed and statistically significant, as expected. This finding may be interpreted to suggest that keeping plants fully utilized and critically skilled laborers fully employed was substantially important for firms if they desired the flexibility to reposition or sell out with ease. Field interviews suggested that in the oil-refining industry—where minimum-efficient-scale plants processed large volumes of throughput (175,000 barrels per day)—high operating costs were incurred when refineries ran at low levels of capacity utilization, for example. Their unfavorable economics exacerbated the difficulties oil firms faced when they tried to rationalize their positions by disposing of their excess facilities.

Strategic Forces. Product differentiation was used as a proxy for the strategic forces that create exit barriers. As expected, it was positive and statistically significant. This finding may be interpreted to suggest that those firms that had the largest stakes invested in R&D and other intangible assets—those that differentiated their products effectively—would face the greatest impediments in repositioning their competitive postures, closing plants, or exiting completely. In brief, intangible sunk costs act as economic sunk costs when firms let them increase the heights of exit barriers.

Expectations. Table A–29 indicates that the sales growth variable was negatively signed and statistically significant, as expected. This result suggests that firm's exit barriers increase substantially when it becomes apparent that demand is declining. Expectations are important in SBU's abilities to change strategic postures in embryonic and emerging industries because they affect firms' abilities to raise capital or dispose of obsolete assets.

Stages per Integrated Activity. Table A–29 indicates that the number of vertical stages variable was positively signed and statistically significant, as expected. This result may be interpreted to suggest that being engaged in several stages of processing creates inflexibilities that could be avoided by using outsiders for some steps. In doing so, firms remain more flexible to changes in technology and demand.

Form of Ownership. The percentage of ownership variable was positive and statistically significant in table A–29, as expected. This result may be interpreted to suggest that firms with relatively low-equity investments in ventures (such as importers and bottlers in the whiskey-distilling business) could reposition themselves or exit with greater ease. As Harrigan (1985b) indicates, firms' experiences in the acetylene industry suggest that the relationship between percentage of ownership and height of exit barriers might be a curvilinear one.

Degree of Backward Integration. Table A–29 shows that the backward-integration variable is positively signed and statistically significant, as expected. High degrees of transfers from upstream sister SBUs exacerbate excess capacity in upstream plants, creating higher barriers than do relationships with downstream sister SBUs (discussed later) because of the larger MES plants involved in intrafirm transfers from upstream.

Degree of Forward Integration. Table A–29 indicates that the sign on the degree of forward integration internal-transfers variable was negative and statistically significant, as expected. This result may be interpreted to suggest that selling much of the SBU's outputs to in-house customers does not raise the height of exit barriers. It may also suggest that downstream intrafirm linkages are easier to overcome than upstream intrafirm linkages are.

High degrees of forward integration were not a significant exit barrier in the electronic-receiving-tubes industry, for example, because arrangements had been forged to protect crucial outside customer relationships without incurring high asset inflexibility. In other industries where firms contemplated exit (or strategic repositioning) from vertically integrated businesses, they often began implementation by terminating or divesting their low-margin, downstream operations *first,* in order to ease their ways out of unattractive investments.

Synergies with Adjacent Businesses. Table A–29 indicates that the synergies with *upstream* businesses variable was statistically significant and had a negative sign. This result was unexpected. Both Caves and Porter (1976) and Harrigan (1980b, 1981b) had found that shared facilities raised the heights of exit barriers. In this sample, chi-square tests showed no significant pattern of relationships between backward-integration synergies and the height of exit barriers. Explanations for this result appear in Harrigan (1985b).

Interpreting Results

Results may be interpreted to suggest that high degrees of internal transfers from upstream sister SBUs raise the heights of exit barriers. They may also be interpreted to suggest that exit barriers will be higher for firms engaged in many stages of vertically related processing, particularly where the business unit in question is fully owned. Thus these vertical-integration strategy dimensions can be added to the roster of forces that create high exit barriers. Since these barriers seem to be most destructive to profits when industries are mature, these results suggest that firms should take special care in using vertical integration within such settings. At the same time, however, the strategic inflexibility allegedly created by being engaged in several stages of processing should be reexamined in light of the experiences of Japanese competitors. In field studies of personal-computer competition, it became clear that Japanese firms were able to maintain strategic flexibility despite their high degrees of backward integration and many stages of vertically related activity. They did not act as though they felt the pressures of high exit barriers, and they were able to reposition themselves to maintain their competitive positions. More study of these apparent differences is needed. Perhaps there are cultural differences (originating in the value capital markets place on strategic flexibility) that could explain these differences in the use of vertical integration.

Implications for Managers

Customers are rarely homogeneous in their demands, and all firms face risks of strategic inflexibility when they invest in a particular set of assets to serve them. Their risks will be especially great if firms must forge their strategic postures while many uncertainties regarding demand and an industry's structure remain unresolved. Customers in another market segment may evolve to become more profitable to serve than those in the market segments chosen initially. Asset configurations, however, may make strategic repositioning difficult if firms' exit barriers are high. The implications of these findings are that firms should plan their exits at the time of entry into a business. Given the speed of technological changes and the resulting short life cycles for new products, it is not unreasonable for firms to make provisions for the efficient removal of excessive capital from low or negative growth businesses when contemplating their initial investments.

In order to attain strategic flexibility, it may be necessary to introduce duplicate assets (or service facilities) in order to sever units that were formerly linked. Conceptually distinct accounting entities may be created by redefining the boundaries of SBUs. Whether SBUs will wish to maintain their trading relationships after these changes depends in part on the economics of their relationships. It will also depend on corporate-level strategy objectives and the exit barriers firms must overcome. By recognizing the effects of these economic, strategic, and emotional barriers, managers can better prepare for the competitive adjustments that may be required as their industries change. They can better assess when they may be undertaking too much risk by being too highly integrated.

Exit barriers can be reduced early and consciously by reducing the degree, stages, and percentage of ownership in firms' vertical relationships. An orderly and incremental withdrawal of investments from SBUs that once served as suppliers or distributors for other SBUs may reduce the height of exit barriers, particularly if outsiders can be persuaded to undertake these less profitable tasks. Strategists must scan the effects of vertical integration on strategic flexibility just as they scan other forces that erect exit barriers.

Even in young industries, care must be taken to sustain strategic flexibility. When products must be modified frequently, or when technology changes rapidly, high degrees of backward integration (intrafirm transfers) could hamstring SBUs precisely the time when they need to change inputs and processes quickly. Vertical arrangements need updating just as other dimensions of competitive strategy do. If firms want their SBUs to supply (or buy from) each other, they should frequently reexamine their premises in forcing such arrangements, because the strategic window that may once have favored vertical integration can close.

8
Managing Declining Businesses

The endgame is the second half of the life of a business. Although there is no guarantee that a hundred-year-old business that has just reached a plateau in industrywide sales will have another hundred years for its endgame, it is true that some firms exit before others. The "last ice man" makes money. If a building's elevator system needs vacuum tubes, their price would have to be very high before the entire system would be replaced rather than pay for them.

How does a corporation prevent SBU performance from flagging in a declining business? The difference between running out a doggy business and easing down a declining one can be largely a difference in attitude and infrastructure. Assuming that managers have selected appropriate endgame strategies, how do they execute those strategies successfully while reducing some of the pain associated with this adjustment? Suggestions regarding organization problems offered in this chapter are based on observations gleaned while interviewing both the upper management of firms that owned declining businesses and the manager in charge of those units. The realities of the firm's strategic plans and financial condition rule out some of these suggestions. Necessarily, managers have differing perceptions at different administrative levels, which become involved in the endgame. Here is a report on what works.

Divestiture Is Clean, Repositioning Untidy

The factory was five years old and was already a strategic misfit. Although the plant operated efficiently enough, it could only process those particular grades of crude materials that were becoming increasingly scarce, hence expensive. Faced with insufficient long-term supplies of raw materials, management recognized that the plant—indeed, the entire

Adapted from an article that originally appeared in the *Journal of Business Strategy*, Winter 1984, by permission of the publisher, Warren, Gorham & Lamont, Inc.

business—was probably doomed to obsolescence within the next fifteen years, but it could not shut down the plant immediately. Management kept the obsolete factory operating, knowing it faced an uncomfortably near-term horizon date while they faced an unpleasant strategic choice regarding their firm's future as a competitor. While they deliberated, management tried to avoid losing many of their key workers and valued executives who might leave if they knew that exit or abandonment were being contemplated.

A frequent knee-jerk response to the news that a business is entering endgame is to sell the business. A more careful study of the business may reveal that no one could hope to operate the plant's assets as well as the present managers can and that even fewer knowledgeable buyers would pay the current value of the declining business's assets upon sale. The business unit is often worth more if it is retained and managed creatively instead of selling it, because the negative attitude of top management can quickly be sensed by the plant's managers and workers. An unhealthy cynicism regarding operations can develop, which will lessen the value of the business for a potential buyer.

In brief, top management cannot afford to dally in deciding the future of declining business units. If they will be sold, their value must be conserved until a buyer has been found and a sale has been consummated. If the firm is not willing (or able) to manage a declining business skillfully, it may be better for all parties involved to locate a buyer quickly and transfer ownership before significant damage has been incurred. Timely implementation is one important aspect of this management problem. Locating an outlet for disposal is another.

Field research concerning decline indicates that where divestiture was management's strategy choice, the most logical and appropriate candidates for a buyout were frequently right under their noses: customers, suppliers, offshore subsidiaries, *and* competitors. Employees are also fruitful avenues for the disposal of business units that the firm cannot manage profitably. In some cases, such as where plant assets are old but serviceable, employee groups assisted by local banks have acquired the spun-off business unit to save their jobs. Without the burdens allocated by corporate overhead charges, some companies have been able to survive and perform adequately for their new owners. If the divestiture is executed quickly (and following careful planning of the details of the sale), it can be a relatively bloodless activity. By contrast, strategies involving shrinking product lines, partial shutdowns, and eventual euthanasia can be quite messy. Unless they are managed thoughtfully, a variety of industry and organization factors can stymie the firm strategically.

Industry Exit Barriers

Managers who do not understand how industry factors influence profitability could be victimized by *cash traps*—conditions whereby the declining business unit consumes resources worth more than the cash it generates. Strategic and managerial exit barriers discourage managers from correcting this unprofitable situation quickly.

Customers that are sick can contaminate their suppliers, as in the leather tanning and man-made fibers industries where weak companies were carrying their customers—by financing their inventories, advertising on their behalf, and granting lenient return and credit terms—largely because they feared losing a customer, no matter the cost to the firm. As long as their sales volume was high, management excused the losses as a temporary industry aberration, rather than a fundamental, industry-wide decrease in demand for their products. Thus they obscured the true nature of their predicament from top management.

A panicking firm might backward-integrate to ensure a supply of necessary inputs at the very time when divestiture or abandonment would cost less than acquiring the supplying business affiliate. New investment redoubles the firm's commitment to the declining industry at a time when it should be investigating ways of easing down its exit barriers. Vertical relationships are a formidable deterrent to divestiture.

Finally, attitudes regarding old physical assets differ. Although old plants and equipment are nurtured and preserved in working condition in some countries, U.S. businesses seem to prefer new assets, believing perhaps that the next technological fix will solve their production problems. Thus managers upgrade assets or improve their current set needlessly. Although some plants, as in hydrocarbon cracking processes, do incur costly cleanup charges and require frequent recalibrations, many old plants could be run with only minor reinvestments. Human ingenuity could be substituted for new bricks and mortar to avoid the trap of new or undepreciated assets in declining businesses.

Suggestions: Capture the hearts of the workers. Get them to push hard for the firm. The whole shop works with more enthusiasm when it is lean than when there is too much fat—and the workers know there is fat. Be wary of counting on a quick fix through new equipment of technology. Most troubled businesses can not justify spending a lot of money on a new generation of equipment. Instead, the emphasis should be on finding better ways to use existing equipament and experienced workers.

Instead of buying new gear, make the company as pleasant a place to work as possible. Tie experienced workers (not just key executives) to the company with low-cost perks. Lease a small lake on the outskirts of town and parcel it out in small campsites. Let employees rent the sites for very little money and set up tents or campers. Now, when they are on a weekend trip, they talk shop with other workers. Purchase blocks of time at a local gym or health club where workers and their families can exercise together.

Organizational Exit Barriers

Declining businesses pose a vexing managerial puzzle. Tough but fair policies concerning endgame are needed because such "sick pussycat" businesses can absorb valuable (and unjustified) managerial attentions. Top management must guide the strategies of declining businesses by their choice of leadership and their overt attentions to the beleaguered unit's progress. Toughness strengthens the total fabric of the firm's organization by using the recognition that management must manage a slowly declining business just as they would perform any other professional task. Endgame represents an opportunity to introduce major changes in management policy throughout the company. But if management cannot overcome their prejudices concerning this phase of the life cycle, they will bungle their choices of (1) the right manager for the task; (2) how to motivate the managers who have been given this task; and (3) how to know when to exit.

Top management should keep a balanced perspective regarding the role of the declining unit. Managers should ensure that they understand the competitive dynamics of the troubled industry, of course, but they must also avoid being drawn into unrewarding efforts on the behalf of such businesses. Top management should use their visibility judiciously where declining businesses are involved because their official actions with respect to endgame businesses will be interpreted as precedents by groups beyond the managers, employees, and communities in which plants of the declining business operate.

Because managerial talent is one of the scarcest of corporate assets, the firm should design its systems and policies to retain the managers from declining businesses after milking has been completed. Performance measures should be forged that give operating managers maximum autonomy in managing declining businesses with dignity. Moreover, some indication of future operating responsibilities (within *non*declining businesses) should be sketched for managers or plant supervisors *if their service will be needed for the duration* of the endgame. Otherwise, their resumes may be circulating before the firm can reap its full benefits and satisfy its strategic obligations to customers.

Choosing a Manager

Decline requires a seasoned manager who can motivate the work force to remain competitive and can use the sophisticated market intelligence (suggested later on) effectively. In one of the most successful companies studied, division management was overtly fearful of the consequences of declining demand. They made these fears explicit to the business manager (in charge of four plants), who in turn communicated them to each plant manager. This company maintained a policy of moving its cadre of business managers to new assignments, but it had no such policies regarding its *hourly* workers. It did, however, encourage workers to propose methods of making operations more efficient, hence more profitable.

In this case, division management and the business manager had made a study of the cost of shutting down each respective plant and had estimated the timing of each closing based on milestones forcasted of cash flows. They were prepared to operate on this planned timetable of shutdowns. Both levels of management were surprised, therefore, when the workers at the very plant they had predicted to be least efficient took the initiative in tightening up their operations to become the *most* efficient plant. At the oldest plant, workers found ways to operate the aged equipment productively. (The workers' suggestions were more spartan than the managers'!) The shipping-dock workers suggested that the plant cut down the hundreds of colors it produced, because they had noticed only a few colors accounted for most of the shipments. News of their methods for improving productivity spread to one of the other plants, where the workers also devised methods to make the very assets divisional management had considered to be obsolete more lucrative than those they had planned to retain. The work force was fighting to preserve their jobs in the only manner they believed divisional management could value.

Based on the workers' suggestions, a way was found to eliminate redundant operations and low-volume products that preserved the jobs of over two-thirds of the work force. (Downsizing was achieved through retirements.) The newly streamlined business unit competed aggressively for those customers that its analysis said would offer the best promises of sustained profitability and need for their products. A less efficient competitor was forced to close its plants, instead. Divisional management credits this business's resurrection to the corporation's ongoing policy of horizon forecasting (explained later) and to the candidness of the work force within that business unit. (A postscript: When demand shrank to volumes that necessitated shutting down one of the business's plants, a newer plant was closed. The oldest and supposedly least efficient facility was one of the last two to close.)

This example suggests that a charismatic or entrepreneurial plant manager who can tap workers' ingenuity may be far more effective in managing a declining business than has generally been believed. The popular concept of a cost accountant's outlook for reducing expenses in troubled businesses must be challenged in endgame by a managerial style that builds a spirit of camaraderie to get useful ideas to percolate up to the managers who possess the power to implement any cost-saving suggestions that may be offered.

It seems that a *blend* of entrepreneur and cost accountant is needed to nurse old plants and machinery without incurring the new capital expenditures that can make a declining business uneconomic. However, managers who can motivate their work force to jury-rig equipment into running many years beyond its engineered life span and who can inspire confidence in their employees are often concerned with workers' future treatment at the hands of divisional management. Not only must these business managers be assured of new opportunities, but their workers should also be rewarded if they perform their tasks in endgame well.

In one of the less successful business units studied, the products were technologically obsolete and the substitute technology was quite unfamiliar to workers who had concentrated during their working lives on the old one. Apparently, no provisions were being made to retrain these obsolete workers; no alternative plants were prepared to take these laborers, either. They were being left high and dry by the corporation. The business manager was a gifted leader who struggled to retain those employees who knew the little tricks that made a particular machine more productive. One day the business manager discovered that no provisions would be made for the plants' workers. His guilt at this discovery was so immense that he jumped ship abruptly. The business's profits spiraled downward quickly without him.

Heroics and Endgame

There is no dishonor involved in managing a declining business unless top management treats it as a dumping place for burned-out executives. Rather, the endgame is simply a managerial task that must be done well. Supervising the controlled demise of a business unit in a declining market requires a very sophisticated, resourceful manager.

Sometimes a controversial management style is needed to manage a declining business. In one such industry, a business unit was spun off by a staid corporation that could not make a profit in the dismal environment of the endgame. A swashbuckling entrepreneur purchased the distressed unit and placed almost unattainable demands on the scientists and workers in his plants. Given the depressing alternative of no jobs, the work force responded to the charismatic leader's exhortations and, phoenixlike, the company revived. A competitor bit the dust instead. The endgame had been running twenty years. Another twenty were expected as a result of this victory.

It may not be necessary to sell the company to revitalize its work force. The examples given here suggest that workers can be motivated to surpass previous production quotas or exceed other day-to-day performance levels if they accept the need to do so. Caution should be exerted in applying this approach, however. In some cases the mere promise of keeping the plant operating is not sufficient reward to obtain this kind of performance from the work force. They can become cynical quickly if it seems to them that the corporation is sucking the plant dry. Again, the skills of the plant managers will determine the *interpretation* of corporate demands in the eyes of the work force.

How to Communicate the Endgame Mission

Do not let the managers entrusted with the details of managing the endgame become cynical either. Several managers interviewed for this study suggested that the most trying (and saddening) aspect of managing declining businesses is the inattention their unit received from its corporate parent. Endgame businesses are the cash generators of their firms, but sometimes upper management misses this point.

Indeed, when one diversified firm inherited a declining business as part of a package acquisition (including some supposedly attractive businesses), its managers were not very interested in the activities of the endgame unit. The managers of the endgame unit, by contrast, were very interested in performing well for their new parent. They were eager to play the endgame well. However, after months of inattention from the corporate level and no response to their action proposals, the eager cadre of managers grew disinterested and stopped submitting proposals. Ironically, these managers had identified the most profitable customer niche to serve (the one where high switching costs would have bound price-insensitive customers to them for an indefinite number of years to come), and their endgame strategy was good. Unfortunately, corporate management was so convinced that the unit was a loser, they would not fund repositioning activities and eventually killed the business. The second-strongest firm (the remaining competitor) stepped into the market niche and coined money on the first firm's mistake!

Use the Right Performance Measures

The managers of a declining business are usually expected to maximize the cash return on their investment base. Given the uncertainty of demand in such environments, few investments that do not offer short paybacks should be undertaken, unless required by law. Chapter 6 has suggested situations when investment in endgame is warranted. When evaluating such proposals, it may be appropriate to use other measures— such as return on cash utilized, cash contributions to corporate, or capacity utilization—in order to focus managers' attentions on the mission selected for the declining business (and to remind upper management that the endgame is a different game). If a dominance or niche strategy is chosen, for example, it may be appropriate to devise a reward system that measures how many of the targeted (preferred) customers the business unit has retained, as well as how profitable operations have been.

Top Management Should Set the Tone

Assuming that an effective management information system (MIS) is operative within the firm, upper-level management should use shorter review intervals to monitor the deterioration of declining businesses and frequent communications with their managers in order to evoke the desired responses. If the business must be operated for a specified period regardless of profitability or other performance measures as a result of term contracts that would be costly to abrogate), cost reductions and improved efficiency should be rewarded.

Whatever performance is rewarded, upper management must use the information it gathers to anticipate when to divest or shut down the declining business. This is a difficult suggestion to elicit from operating managers unless top management can foster trust in the corporation and pride in the task of running out the business. Doing so requires top management to pay special attention to the managers and workers within declining businesses in order to convey to the rest of the corporation that their task can be done with dignity. Include these managers in interdepartmental memos, seek their opinions, and share ideas with them. Put them in the limelight if they are doing well; talk to them about how to improve if they are not. Whatever happens, excluding them will hurt the viability of business units that need a longer-term outlook. By fostering an image of apparent inattention, management may be (1) forcing a valued manager to bail out prematurely, (2) killing a viable business too soon, and (3) generating labor problems that could have been avoided by not pulling any punches with operating managers in discussing corporate plans for the declining business unit.

If upper management takes pains to select appropriate business managers for declining business units and takes steps to focus their attentions on the desired behavior for managing in decline (through corporate policies, compensation, and other structural elements), the firm should be better enabled to confront the problem of declining demand squarely and to guide the endgame units' fortunes more precisely. The competitor intelligence system needed to build a horizon budget (to judge whether it is time to exit from the endgame) is based on information from endgame managers.

The Competitor Intelligence System

Competitor intelligence, unlike other forms of market intelligence, is used with declining industries to track the milestones of the plan leading to divestiture. Briefly, the market intelligence concerning competitors gathered from the sales force, clipping services, industry analysts, and other sources, which is routinely correlated in a heuristic program, can be used to create scenarios to forecast the conditions that would force the firm to exit. Adding horizon forecasts provides contingency plans that identify the competitive factors on which future profitability depends and the responses the firm is prepared to undertake.

Horizon forecasting is an explicit discussion of how the firm would look if it chose to divest the business in question tomorrow. It is a procedure that forces all managers—even those in charge of thriving businesses—to confront the interrelationships of their business units with others within the firm and to anticipate their customers' responses. (Narrowly deployed, the planning data are supplied by firms when sales volumes first begin to plateau.) Scenarios are analyzed to estimate the financial effect, asset-usage effect, and manpower effect of divestiture or shutdown.

Every manager is asked to make an annual assessment on whether operations should be continued or phased out. All managers are assured that there will be a place for them somewhere else in the company and that lower-level workers, too, will be retained and *retrained* for other jobs with the company.

In one company where such planning systems were employed, no plants were closed for as many as six years after business unit managers first began to be tracked using this planning format. When it was time to close a plant, however, the details and problems had been anticipated so well that few snags were encountered in implementing the endgame strategy. Top management was kept fully aware of anticipated cash flows, maintenance investment requirements, and manpower reassignments needed; middle management knew when these requirements exceeded their willingness to fund the declining business. The plan was communicated so well that the reoganization that followed the plant closing was easier as a result of this planning effort.

A horizon forecast can be developed easily by adding operating details to frequent demand updates from the firm's market research group. To these data, add analysis of industry structure factors that may deter exit in order to recognize when to divest or shut down.

Danger Signals in Planning Divestiture

A clean exit or closing is desirable, but the presence of certain factors can create a turbulent ending to the firm's participation in a declining business. Danger signals include vertical agreements to supply customers, activist community groups, and militant unions. Heavily unionized plants have provided access to corporate books (to justify proposed reductions in production) and invited union representatives to all corporate press conferences regarding the declining business. In cases where unexpected workers' compensation suits were filed following plant closings, management may wish they had been less secretive and had realized these substantial costs would have to be faced.

Potential Buyers

If exit does appear imminent, foreign investors should not be overlooked as a conduit for disposing of assets that cannot be redeployed in nondeclining operations. Suppliers have sometimes purchased declining businesses. (Customers usually prefer lifetime buyout sales instead of backward integration.) Also, it is not unusual for competitors to purchase the assets of a declining business to help clear the market of excess capacity. If the parent firm is contemplating the sale of obsolescent plants but will remain in the industry, it should consider removing the excess capacity itself because spinoffs and divestitures create new competitors. Finally, the employees and managers of the business to be divested may be interested in a purchasing arrangement that will enable them to retain their jobs and avoid corporate overhead assessments.

In conclusion, there are several ways to reap profits within declining business units by managing it intelligently. If the firm does not possess the planning infrastructure and managerial skills needed to obtain high performance levels (or if analysis in its horizon forecast indicates that the declining business's profitability potential is low as a result of an inferior strategic posture), management should do all concerned a favor by exiting in a timely and nondisruptive fashion, and handing over the reins to competent endgame managers.

Appendix

Table A–1
Regressions on Entry Behavior

	Expected Effect	Model 1		Model 2		Model 3		Model 4	
		Natural Coefficient	Standardized Coefficient	Natural Coefficient	Standardized Coefficient	Natural Coefficient	Standardized Coefficient	Natural Coefficient	Standardized Coefficient
Capital requirements$_{t-1}$	—	—	—	.00549	.02964	-.00202	-.00547	—	—
Changes in average scale economies$_{t-1}$	—	—	—	.00148	.05276	.00109	.03884	—	—
Percentage change in relative age of physical plant	—	—	—	-.35786[b]	-.13629	-.12741	-.04852	—	—
Labor to capital ratio$_{t-1}$	+	.17177[a]	.07017	.27475[b]	.11225	—	—	—	—
Variability of average R&D expenditures$_{t-1}$	—	—	—	—	—	—	—	-.04600	-.01868
Entries in previous periods$_{t-1}$	—	-.03409[b]	-.53784	—	—	-.03415[b]	-.53859	-.03679[b]	-.58033
Entries in previous periods$_{t-2}$								-.00879[b]	-.112133
Changes in dispersion of relative market shares$_{t-1}$	—	.19025	.02126	.26519	.02963	.21635	.02417	.30920	.03455
Average industry advertising outlays$_{t-1}$	—	-.00080[b]	-.25752	-.00085[b]	-.27475	-.00081[b]	-.26066	—	—

Excess capacity$_{t-1}$	−	—	—	-.00402[b]	-.14434	—	—	-.00539[b]	-.19353
Relative sales growth$_{t-1}$	+	-.00130	-.01625	-.00432	-.05402	-.17044	-.03262	-.00295	-.03690
Relative industry attractiveness$_{t-1}$	+	.01602	.05059	.00486	.01536	.01785[a]	.05638	—	—
Intercept		1.25329[b]	.00000	.38378[b]	.00000	1.28979[b]	.00000	.42207[b]	.00000
R_2 coefficient of multiple determination		.4151		.1727		.4142		.3989	
F-statistic test of significance		62.93[b]		12.27[b]		46.84[b]		58.83[b]	
Durbin-Watson d-statistic		2.2145		2.2629		2.6078		2.6467	

Notes: Average likelihood of entry = 50% (standard deviation = 45.94%).

Mean = 0.00 (standard deviation = 1) using standardized coefficients.

[a]Significant at the 5 percent confidence interval.
[b]Significant at the 1 percent confidence interval.

Table A–2
Regressions on Firms' Returns on Invested Capital at *t*

	Labor Intensity to Capital Intensity $t-1$	Percentage Change in GNP $t-1$	Industry Concentration $t-1$	Capacity Utilization $t-1$	Excess Capacity $t-1$	Firm's ROI $t-1$	Firm's ROI $t-2$	Firm's ROI $t-3$	Aggregate Failures $t-1$	Aggregate Incorporations $t-1$	Adjusted Price Index $t-1$
Equation 1 (corrected for heteroscedasticity and serial correlation)	−0.11655 (−1.89)a	0.38100 (4.60)c	−0.00301 (−0.03)	0.07640 (20.38)c	—	—	—	—	—	—	—
Equation 2 (corrected for heteroscedasticity and serial correlation)	—	—	0.22152 (10.09)c	—	−0.09226 (−5.38)c	0.53559 (5.74)c	0.97241 (5.34)c	0.00333 (0.02)	−0.03015 (−8.18)c	0.02118 (8.96)c	−0.01374 (−2.96)c

	Advertising to Sales (Lagged)	Research and Development to Sales (Lagged)	Capital Turnover Ratio $t-1$	Exits of Competitors $t-1$	Intercept	R^2 Coefficient of Multiple Determination
Equation 1 (corrected for heteroscedasticity and serial correlation)	3.33234 (2.26)b	−3.97386 (−2.72)c	−0.06244 (−42.44)c	−0.20087 (−4.69)c	0.02068 (11.75)c	0.9851 ($n = 530$)

$DW = 1.8974$
$A = 0.0459$

| Equation 2 (corrected for heteroscedastic- ity and serial correlation) | — | — | — | 0.05066 (5.41)c | 0.8103 (n = 528) | DW = 1.9050 A = 0.0413 |

Note: Figures in parentheses indicate the Student's *t*-statistic testing the null hypothesis that the parameter coefficient equals zero.

n = degrees of freedom in the error term.
a = significant at the 10 per cent confidence interval.
b = significant at the 5 per cent confidence interval.
c = significant at the 1 per cent confidence interval.
DW = Durbin-Watson *d*-statistic.
A = autocorrelation coefficient for residuals.

Table A–3
Construction and Discussion of Independent Variables' Expected Effects on the Entry of Fringe Competitors

Variable Name and Construction (Denomination)	Mean	Standard Deviation	Expected Effect on Entry	Explanation
1. *Capital Requirements*: $(1/M *$ total value of industry plant, property, and equipment$_{t-1})$ where M equals the number of establishments responsible for 50 percent of the industry's value of shipments [Dollars per plant, thousands]	67.21	133.83	Negative	If the capital requirements for effective competition are relatively high and if leading firms possess this requisite critical mass, fringe firms are less likely to attempt entry.
2. *Changes in Average Scale Economies*: $(1/$ LOG (capital turnover ratio)$_{t-1})$ less $(1/$ LOG (capital turnover ratio)$_{t-2})$ divided by the average industry scale measure [Dollars per plant, thousands]	4.22	17.71	Negative	If scale economies are rising (due to technological changes) entry at less than minimum efficient scale would result in substantial cost disadvantages which should discourage entrants not undertaking these changes.
3. *Percentage Change in Relative Age of Physical Plant*: (Net plant/gross plant)$_{t-1}$ less (Net plant/gross plant)$_{t-2}$ divided by the industry average change in age of physical plant measure [Relative percentage, decimal]	0.13	0.19	Negative	Increases in the net to gross physical plant ratio could indicate leading firms are making technological improvements or simply replacing their capital stock. Both explanations indicate that leading firms expect their particular market niches to become more attractive in spite of overall industry maturity. Expectations that a market opportunity exists would encourage some firms to attempt entry. However, the reinvestments leading firms made raises the height of entry barriers, reducing the likelihood that successful entry will occur.
4. *Labor to Capital Ratio*: Number of employees divided by gross book value of physical assets$_{t-1}$ [Percentage]	0.15	0.20	Positive	High proportions of labor to capital represent opportunities for technologies using high degrees of capital substitution. Fringe firms entering with technologies that obsolesce older processes might do so with greater likelihoods of success.

5. *Variability of Average R & D Expenditures:* (R&D expenditures/sales)$_{t-1}$ divided by average R&D sales measure $_{t-1}$ [Relative percentage, decimal]	0.05	0.20	Negative	High levels of R&D variability indicate some competitors are expending larger amounts to improve their products or processes. Although the existence of these expenditures indicates some differentiation, it also represents high R&D entry barriers, which few fringe firms could afford to overcome.
6. *Entries in Previous Periods:* Number of firms in industry$_{t-1}$ less number of firms $_{t-2}$ [Net change] This measure was also lagged for an additional period	−1.13 −2.31	7.83 6.34	Negative	Because each entering firm represents additional productive capacity, entries in previous periods should discourage entrants in the present period unless growth in demand is unusually rapid. (Exits in previous periods should relieve excess capacity and permit profit levels to rise, thereby encouraging new entrants unless growth in demand has been stagnant.)
7. *Changes in the Dispersion of Market Shares:* (Sales/industry sales)$_{t-1}$ less (sales/industry sales)$_{t-2}$ divided by industry average market share changes [Relative percentage, decimal]	.004	.056	Negative	A market structure characterized by high market shares among leading firms indicates they enjoy absolute cost and scale advantages, a condition fringe competitors would find difficult to overcome. Sizable changes in these market shares indicates aggressive growth strategies are pursued by these firms.
8. *Average (Industry) Advertising Outlays:* Advertising expenses divided by average expenses (Total advertising expenitures divided by number of firms$_{t-1}$) [Relative percentage]	111.94	15.96	Negative	High levels of advertising indicate some competitors are creating entry barriers through product differentiation activities. Although an entry by a differentiated product the market values could be successful, the high advertising barriers should discourage many fringe firms from entering.
9. *Excess Capacity:* MOS plant utilization less level of capacity that was employed$_{t-1}$ [Average percentage, decimal]	.08	.18	Negative	High levels of excess capacity represent unstable pressures on prices which could result in price cutting, a condition that is unattractive to fringe firms. Low levels of excess capacity represent the need for more plants, a condition that could be satisfied by fringe firms that enter.

Table A–3 continued

Variable Name and Construction (Denomination)	Mean	Standard Deviation	Expected Effect on Entry	Explanation
10. *Relative Sales Growth*: Changes in competitors sales$_{t-1}$ (deflated by GNP growth) divided by deflated industry sales growth [Percentage, decimal]	−0.0069	0.095	Positive	Mature industries where market segments are growing faster than GNP growth should appear to be more attractive to fringe competitors. Mature industries where no market segments are growing relatively faster than GNP would appear less attractive to such firms.
11. *Industry Attractiveness*: Relative returns on capital expenditures$_{t-1}$ capital turnover ratio divided by (industry average capital turnover ratio multiplied by the percentage of industry capital expenditures made by four largest competitors$_{t-1}$) [Relative percentage]	1.18	1.57	Positive	Industries where higher than average (1.00) returns were earned on additions to capital should encourage fringe competitors to attempt entry.

Table A–4
A Model of the Relationship of Traditional Static Economic Variables to the Likelihood of Entry

	Capital Requirements	Scale Economies	Relative Advertising Expenditures	Intercept	R^2 Coefficient of Multiple Determination	F-Statistic Test of Significance of the Multiple Determinant Coefficient
Parameter estimates	−.002 (−1.00)	−.002 (−1.86)	.000 (2.45)[a]	.494 (22.06)[b]	.0200	3.56[a]
Standardized coefficients	−.043	−.080	.106	.000	$n = 524$	

Notes: Figures in parentheses indicate students' *t*-statistic testing the null hypothesis that the parameter equals zero; average likelihood of entry = 50 percent; *n* = degrees of freedom.
[a]Significant at the 5 percent confidence interval.
[b]Significant at the 1 percent confidence interval.

Table A–5
Interdifference Matrixes from Clustering Analysis: (a) Full Retail Sample; (b) Department- and Discount-Store Sample

Full Retail Sample

	Cluster						
Cluster	1	2	3	4	5	6	7
1	0.52	18.51	26.37	25.27	22.80	10.10	14.78
2	18.51	0.48	59.78	59.96	58.41	35.49	41.45
3	26.37	59.78	0.27	3.71	8.08	14.03	6.16
4	25.27	59.96	3.71	0.50	4.78	12.73	6.86
5	22.80	58.42	8.08	4.78	0.38	11.39	9.22
6	10.10	35.49	14.03	12.73	11.39	0.72	6.30
7	14.78	41.45	6.16	6.86	9.22	6.29	0.50

Department- and Discount-Store Sample

	Cluster						
Cluster	1	2	3	4	5	6	7
1	0.18	3.67	3.51	5.78	6.59	5.51	11.06
2	3.67	0.18	2.23	5.96	4.35	1.39	10.17
3	3.51	2.23	0.25	2.18	2.33	1.99	5.62
4	5.78	5.96	2.18	0.21	1.44	3.44	2.73
5	6.59	4.35	2.33	1.44	0.19	1.19	2.49
6	5.52	1.40	1.99	3.44	1.19	0.10	4.95
7	11.06	10.17	5.62	2.73	2.49	4.95	0.24

Notes: The *tightness* of a cluster is represented by its average distance.

The *nearness* of clusters is represented by their maximum distances.

□ = Within-group distances.

Table A–6
Frequency of First Foreign Production within One and Five Years of U.S. Introduction by Period of U.S. Innovation

Period of U.S. Innovation	Number of Innovations	Percentage Produced in Foreign Markets	
		Within One Year of U.S. Introduction	Within Five Years of U.S. Introduction
1945–1950	161	5.6%	22.0%
1951–1955	115	2.6%	29.6%
1956–1960	134	10.4%	36.6%
1961–1965	133	24.1%	55.6%
1966–1970	115	37.4%	60.1%
1971–1975	75	38.7%	64.0%

A sample of forty-four large U.S. firms was on the criterion of broad representation across product sectors. On the basis of extensive library research and in-depth interviews with company executives, a list was developed of new products introduced by each company between 1945 and 1976. These products were then screened for commercial and technical significance. Only those with cumulative sales in excess of $10 million were included. In addition, knowledgeable persons were asked to categorize new products in terms of technical significance.

Each product was then traced from its initial introduction in the United States to all foreign markets in which the product had achieved sufficient sales volume to warrant the establishment of local manufacturng, assembly, packaging, or distribution operations through a licensing arrangement or direct investment.

Table A–7
Years to First Foreign Production by Organizational Stage of Innovator

Organizational Stage at the Time of Innovation[a]	Total Number of Innovations	Years to First Foreign Production					
		0	1	2	3–5	6–10	More than 10
Domestic function divisions	104	4	6	5	11	27	51
a. Without international division	79	1	3	1	7	21	46
b. With international division	25	3	3	4	4	6	5
Domestic product divisions	242	21	18	27	62	66	48
a. Without international division	95	5	3	9	26	27	25
b. With international division	147	16	15	18	36	39	23
Global product division	18	6	6	4	2	0	0
Global area divisions	6	2	1	1	2	0	0
Global matrix	19	5	7	2	5	0	0

[a]The sample used in this exhibit is limited to those parent firms for which historical data exist on successive organizational stages and years of organizational transition. Innovations are tabulated according to the organizational stage of the firm at the time the innovation was introduced in the United States. For definition of organizational stages, see J.M. Stopford and L.T. Wells, Jr., *Managing the Multinational Enterprise: Organization of the Firm and Ownership Subsidiaries* (New York: Basic Books, 1972).

Table A–8
Some Advantages and Disadvantages of Vertical Integration

Advantages	Disadvantages
Internal benefits	*Internal costs*
Integration economies reduce costs by eliminating steps, reducing duplicate overhead, and cutting costs (technology dependent).	Need for overhead to coordinate vertical integration increased costs.
Improved coordination of activities reduces inventorying and other costs.	Burden of excess capacity from unevenly balanced minimum-efficient-scale plants (technology-dependent).
Avoid time-consuming tasks, such as price shopping, communicating design details, or negotiating contracts.	Poorly organized vertically integrated firms do not enjoy synergies that compensate for higher costs.
Competitive benefits	*Competitive dangers*
Avoid foreclosure to inputs, services, or markets.	Obsolete processes may be perpetuated.
Improved marketing or technological intelligence.	Creates mobility (or exit) barriers.
	Links firm to sick adjacent businesses.
Opportunity to create product differentiation (increased value-added).	Lose access to information from suppliers or distributors.
Superior control of firm's economic environment (market power).	Synergies created through vertical integration may be overrated.
Create credibility for new products.	Managers integrated before thinking through the most appropriate way to do so.
Synergies could be created by coordinating vertical activities skillfully.	

Table A–5
An Illustration of the Strategic Framework

Strategy	Defining Characteristics	When Appropriate	Advantages	Risks
Degree of Integration				
Full integration	All of a particular input (or output) is transferred in-house to a sister business unit. Often adjacent, integrated stages are in balance in their throughput volumes.	• In mature and stable environments protect proprietary processes from espionage. • Maintain tight quality control at all stages. • Where firm seeks technological or quality leadership position. • Diseconomies from imbalance are not significant. • Technological changes occur slowly.	• Superior control of economic environment. • Avoid foreclosure to inputs or markets. • Guarantee quality is consistent with corporate image. • Capture integration economies (especially advantageous if market share leader).	• Decreases market power. • Technology does not provide many integration economies. • Asset inflexibility. • Price renegotiations difficult. • Minimum-efficient-scale plants are rarely the same upstream and downstream; thus some portion of linkage is likely to be out of balance.
Tapered integration	Some portion (but not all) of firm's requirements for an input are supplied in house or some portion of outputs are sold (consumed) in house.	• Physical interconnection unnecessary. • Diseconomies in minimum-efficient-scale plant that are underutilized are substantial. • Where firm seeks technological, quality, or market-share leadership in volatile competitive settings. • New products needing explanations or infrastructure no outsiders provide. • When firm desires to prod in-house units.	• Enables firm to monitor outside R&D and marketing practices. Could incorporate outsiders' innovations while gaining capability in house, as well. • Enables firm to understand suppliers' (or distributors') cost structures and profit margins. • Increases bargaining power (implied threat of full integration). • Same as full integration with less risk.	• Subcontractors will not be available to absorb fluctuations in production and demand. • Access to best suppliers (or distributors) will be cut off (competitive foreclosure). • Pay premiums for access to outsiders' goods and services. • Lower priority as a customer (or vendor) since outsiders are overflow outlets primarily. • Same as full integration but more advantageous.

Table A–9 continued

Strategy	Defining Characteristics	When Appropriate	Advantages	Risks
Degree of Integration				
Nonintegration	No internal transfers of inputs (or outputs) to in-house sister units.	• Better quality/prices available from outsiders. • Cost of investing to make components is too formidable or volume consumed is too low (and selling to outsiders would be difficult or a serious diversification from core businesses of firm). • Where technology is changing rapidly. • Where price competition (and other competitive tactics) cause market shares to fluctuate wildly. • Where demand is highly uncertain.	• No penalties from underutilized plants. • Avoids purchasing highly specific assets (avoids inflexibility). • Avoids purchasing large capacity when firm's needs are small. • Lowers overhead and break-even points. • Allows preplanned delivery schedules to reduce inventorying costs (*kanban*).	• Quality control may not be as high, and market power of firm may be unable to exert control over adjacent firms through contract. • Subcontractors will not be available to perform needed tasks. • Firm loses cost advantages of integration economies (where these exist).
Breadth of integration				
Broadly integrated	Many activities (inputs, services, or channels of distribution or consumption) related to the needs of a particular business unit are engaged in. (Broadly integrated strategies need not involve many vertical stages of processing.)	• Product differentiation is high. • No outsiders produce goods or services needed yet. • Industry structures becoming established and economies becoming approximate.	• Maintains intelligence concerning component costs and ways to streamline product design (experience curve). • Maintains product quality and design secrecy.	• No scale economies available at the small volumes needed for in-house (and market) consumption. • Costly setup costs associated with short production runs for disparate components.

Narrowly integrated	Few activities (inputs, services, or channels) are engaged in.	• When industry structure is embryonic, demand is highly uncertain, or industry is declining. • When firm's requirements for a particular good or service are low.	• No penalties from frequent setups or other production costs. • Access to the innovations of outside suppliers or distributors. • Lower mobility (or exit barriers).	• Loss of access to supplies or other scarce resources. • Less control over product specifications and quality (unless contracts can be used to control suppliers or distributors satisfactorily).

Stages of integrated activity

Many stages	Firm is engaged in many vertically related activities—from ultraraw materials to distribution to final consumers—in which buyer-seller relationships could occur.	• When product (or components) are state-of-the-art and firm seeks technological leadership. • When life of product is expected to be eight years or longer. • When firm is foreclosed by competitors. • When firm seeks quality leadership.	• Captures more of value-added in vertical chain of processing. • Firm can create substantial improvements in supplying technology or distribution practices. • Could create highly differentiated and high quality products. • Preempt nonintegrated competitors by forcing industry structures to evolve to firm's advantage. • Control proprietary advantages. • Reach ultimate consumers more effectively.	• Synergies foregone if communications systems do not exploit these linkages well. • Creates exit barriers due to obsolescence. • Risks of throughput imbalance magnified for each stage added to vertical chain. • Subcontractors needed to alleviate imbalances in throughput (due to technology or changing demand) will not be available. • Costly and inefficient if firms do not manage complexity well. • Involves firms in very diverse activities that may be far from its core strengths.

Table A–9 continued

Strategy	Defining Characteristics	When Appropriate	Advantages	Risks
Stages of integrated activity				
Few stages	Firm is engaged in few vertically related activities in the chain from ultraraw materials to distribution.	• When technological or customer scanning is less important. • When product lives are expected to be short or the new obsolescing technology will be very unlike past processes. • When product is very young or industry structure is embryonic. • When demand is declining. • When physical interconnections are few or not necessary.	• Outsiders' innovations can be harnessed to improve product quality or design. • Firm can piggyback on the marketing or brand image expenditures of outsiders.	• Firm's product perceived as a me-too entry. • Integrated competitors will enjoy superior cost structures and intelligence.
Form of ownership				
Wholly owned	Businesses are wholly owned by firm.	• When contracts or other quasi-integrated forms of control are inadequate. • When firm desires to protect technology or trade secrets from outsiders. • When demand is declining (except as a phase-out tactic).	• Proceeds from investment need not be shared with others. • Greater strategic flexibility since business units are fully owned and controlled.	• Same risks as being too integrated on other strategy dimensions above. Risk exposure is maximum.
Quasi-integration	Less than full ownership and control. Could include joint ventures, franchises, minority equity	• If risk of failure and investment costs are high. • Where economies of integration are insignifi-	• Reduces asset investments. • Allows firm to create spider's web of quasi-in-	• Could create mobility or exit barriers if partners are important to other businesses of the firm.

investments, loan guaran-
tees, or an "understand-
ing," regarding customary
relationships.

cant but need for
control is strong.
• Technology changes
rapidly.
• Industry structures are
still embryonic.
• To transfer ownership
of an undesirable busi-
ness unit to outsiders.
• Where corporate mission
does not require tight
control over quality.
• Where competition is
volatile.

tegrations to sample sev-
eral firm's approaches
to a technological or
marketing problem.
• Creates bargaining
power over adjacent
business units.
• Improves access to new
materials or processes.
• Scanning advantages of
taper integration with
less asset risk.
• Integration economies of
taper integration (pro-
vided firm manages
quasi-integrated rela-
tionship effectively).
• Lowers fixed costs while
providing access to adja-
cent firms' intelligence
and skills.

• Costs of managing
quasi-integrated rela-
tionship exceed benefits
of this control system.
• Contractual problems
could stymie strategic
flexibility and run up
administration costs.

Note: I am indebted to an anonymous reviewer for suggesting this tabular configuration.

Table A–10
Operationalization of Vertical-Integration Dimensions

Dimension	Measurement	Example 1	Example 2
Degree of backward integration	Percentage of requirements for a particular resource the business unit obtains from upstream sister business unit.	Sohio (Standard Oil of Ohio) produces more crude oil than it consumes in house. From the viewpoint of Sohio's refinery unit, it is fully integrated for crude oil.	Mobil is crude-short and must purchase much of its crude oil needs from outsiders. It is taper integrated and supplies a low percentage of crude oil needed to its refinery unit.
Degree of forward integration	Percentage of outputs business unit sold to (or through) downstream sister unit.	Upjohn sells ethical pharmaceuticals primarily through its own direct distribution organization. Since it does not sell *all* its output through this conduit, however (it uses some wholesalers), Upjohn is taper integrated to drug-distribution services unit.	Lilly uses wholesalers almost exclusively (except for government sales). It is taper integrated and sells a low percentage of its output through in-house sales unit.
Stages of integrated activity	Relative (index) number of steps in transformation process firm undertook times value-added per stage.	Texas Instruments produces silicon substrates, photo-masks, semiconductor chips, personal computers, and (for a few years) had its own retail stores for demonstrating and selling consumer electronics products. It was engaged in many stages of integrated activity and has a high index of integration.	Apple Computer makes no components and it has no retail outlets. It is engaged in only one stage of activity and its index of integration is low. Osborne Computer was merely an assembler; it had the lowest index value in that industry.
Breadth of activities undertaken	Number of activities (at one stage of processing) firm was engaged in divided by few number of activities it was possible to engage in.	Hiram Walker–Gooderham & Worts produced its own barrels, glass containers, and grain brokerage services (at one time) to supply the whiskey it distilled. In the whiskey business, Hiram Walker was broadly integrated.	Heublein did not bottle its own whiskey. It sold whiskey under its own labels that was bottled by outsiders. It engaged in activities and was very narrowly integrated.

Form of the venture	Percentage of ownership in the venture.
Royal Dutch–Shell proposed to build a coal gasificiation facility that would be jointly owned with Shell Oil (USA). This would be a wholly-owned venture from view-point of Royal Dutch–Shell, although Harrigan (1985c) would argue that it was an "internal joint venture."	The Great Plains Associates jointly owned the coal gasification project in Beulah, North Dakota. From the viewpoint of American Natural Resources, this was a joint venture.

Table A–11
Hypothesized Relationship with Dependent Variables—*Stages* of Integration, *Degree* of Backward and Forward Integration, *Breadth* of SBU's Activities, and *Form* of Integrated Relationship

Phase of industry development variables	Positive and rapid sales growth encourages more stages and breadth of activities. Positive changes in sales growth (demand uncertainty), particularly those associated with obsolescence from rapid technological change, discourage integration.
Corporate strategy variables	Large market shares and synergies created by shared facilities with upstream and downstream SBUs encourage firms to engage in more stages of activity and own greater percentages of vertical business units.
Volatility of competition variables	High exit barriers—which proxy other forces making industry competition volatile—discourage a broad range of SBU activities and high degrees of internal transfers because returns are unstable due to intensified competition. Highly concentrated industries, by contrast, are less likely to be volatile. Such industries encourage high degrees of internal transfers and a broad range of SBU activities.
Relative bargaining power variables	If the percentage of three largest outside suppliers' sales represented by SBU's purchases are large, high degrees of internal purchases need not occur. If many outside distributors (or customers) are available, SBUs do not possess relative bargaining power, and high internal sales are encouraged.

Table A–12
Industries Making Up Sample

Producer Goods Sold to Relatively Sophisticated Purchasing Agents		Mass Marketed Products Sold to Unsophisticated Buyers	
Acetylene	6.3%	Baby foods	3.1%
Coal gasification	4.2%	Cigars	3.6%
Genetic engineering	10.4%	Percolators	4.2%
Leather tanning	4.7%	Personal computers	7.8%
Petroleum refining	16.0%	Rayon and acetate	4.2%
Pharmaceuticals	10.4%	Solar heating	5.8%
Soda ash	3.1%	Tailored suits	6.3%
Receiving tubes	2.8%	Whiskey	6.3%
Totals	57.7%		42.3%

Table A–13
Distribution of Sample Firms by Various Dimensions of Vertical-Integration Strategies
(in percent)

Table A *Degree of Backward Integration*		*Table B* *Degree of Forward Integration*	
Nonintegrated (0 percent intra-firm transfers)	33	Nonintegrated (0 percent intra-firm transfers)	37
Taper integrated (0–80 percent intrafirm transfers)	52	Taper integrated (0–80 percent intrafirm transfers)	38
Fully integrated (greater than 80 percent intrafirm transfers)	15	Fully integrated (greater than 80 percent intrafirm transfers)	25

Table C *Breadth of Integrated Activities*		*Table D* *Stages of Integration*	
Not broad (less than 50 percent of all activities)	32	One stage (less than 75 percent)	29
Average breadth (50 to 75 percent of all activities)	34	Few stages (75–150 percent)	58
Broadly integrated (greater than 75 percent of all activities)	34	Many stages (greater than 150 percent index values)	13

Table E *Form of Venture*	
Contracts only (0 percent ownership)	39
Quasi-integration (less than 95 percent ownership)	23
Wholly owned (95 percent or greater ownership)	38

Table A–14
Description of Sample's Average Dimension Values

Acetylene: Some transfers of raw materials from upstream, substantial in-house consumption downstream, average breadth of business unit activities, short chains of owned processing activities, some joint ventures.

Coal Gasification: Few transfers of raw materials from upstream, substantial in-house consumption downstream, average breadth of business unit activities, long chains of owned processing activities, many joint ventures and other quasi-integration arrangements.

Genetic Engineering: Few transfers of raw materials from upstream, substantial in-house consumption downstream, narrow breadth of business unit activities, average-length chains of owned processing activities, many joint ventures and other quasi-integration arrangements.

Leather Tanning: Few transfers of raw materials from upstream, little in-house consumption downstream, narrow breadth of business unit activities, short chains of owned processing activities, high ownership equity.

Petroleum Refining: Most firms transferred raw materials from upstream, most firms consumed some outputs in-house, high breadth of business unit activities, long chains of owned processing activities, high ownership equity.

Ethical Pharmaceuticals: High transfers of raw materials from upstream, some in-house consumption downstream, medium breadth of business unit activities, short chains of owned processing activities, high ownership equity.

Synthetic Soda Ash: High transfers of raw materials from upstream, high in-house consumption downstream, wide breadth of business unit activities, long chains of owned processing activities, high ownership equity.

Receiving Tubes: Medium transfers of raw materials from upstream, high in-house consumption downstream, wide breadth of business unit activities, long chains of owned processing activities, high ownership equity.

Baby Foods: Few transfers of raw materials from upstream, low in-house consumption downstream, narrow breadth of business unit activities, short chains of owned processing activities, high ownership equity.

Cigars: Medium transfers of raw materials from upstream, low in-house consumption downstream, average breadth of business unit activities, medium-length chains of owned processing activities, high ownership equity.

Electric Percolator Coffeemakers: Few transfers of raw materials from upstream, low in-house consumption downstream, narrow breadth of business unit activities, short chains of owned processing activities, high ownership equity.

Personal Computers: Some firms transferred raw materials from upstream, low in-house consumption downstream, wide breadth of business unit activities, medium-length chains of owned processing activities, high ownership equity.

Rayon and Acetate: Some transfers of raw materials from upstream, low in-house consumption downstream, narrow breadth of business unit activities, short chains of owned processing activities, high ownership equity.

Residential Solar Heating: Some transfers of raw materials from upstream, low in-house consumption downstream, narrow breadth of business unit activities, short chains of owned processing activities, some quasi-integration arrangements.

Tailored Suits: Few transfers of raw materials from upstream, some in-house consumption downstream, wide breadth of business unit activities, medium-length chains of owned processing activities, high ownership equity.

Whiskey: High transfers of raw materials from upstream, little in-house consumption downstream, wide breadth of business unit activities, long chains of owned processing activities, several quasi-integration arrangements among vertical chains of processing.

Table A–15
Definition of Variables Hypothesized to Affect Vertical-Integration Strategies

Independent Variables	
Phase of industry development variables	
1. Sales growth	Percentage growth in SBU's industry sales.
2. Demand uncertainty	Average dispersion of SBU's sales growth over five years, 1976 to 1981.
Corporate strategy variables	
3. Synergy—upstream and downstream	Sum of percentage of resources shared with sister business units upstream and downstream.
4. Market share	Business unit's percentage of industry sales.
Volatility of competition variables	
5. Concentration ratio	Four-firm concentration ratio for target SBU's industry.
6. Height of exit barriers	Scale where exit barriers associate with plant and equipment were estimated for 1981 strategic posture.
Relative-bargaining-power variables	
7. Dependence on outside suppliers	Percentage of three largest outside suppliers' sales represented by the SBU's purchases.
8. Availability of alternative distributors (or customers)	Reciprocal of number of alternative distributors (or customers) where few distributors represent downstream bargaining power.
9. Competitors' degrees of backward and forward integration	An interactive variable created by multiplying the competitors' degrees of backward integration by their degree of forward integration to indicate the degree of integration in competitors' chains of activities.

Table A–16
Correlation Coefficients of Independent Variables Hypothesized to Affect Vertical-Integration Strategies

	Mean (Standard Deviation)	1	2	3	4	5	6	7	8	9
1. Sales growth	-.0031 (.0766)	1.00								
2. Demand (sales growth) uncertainty	.0631 (.0564)	-.18	1.00							
3. Synergy—upstream and downstream	.0880 (.1868)	.13	-.07	1.00						
4. Market share	.1371 (.1722)	-.11	-.04	-.05	1.00					
5. Concentration ratio	.3646 (.2106)	-.31[a]	.04	.06	.31[a]	1.00				
6. Height of economic exit barriers	.4950 (.2455)	-.02	-.06	-.08	.14	.17	1.00			
7. Dependency of outside suppliers	.1312 (.2133)	-.04	-.07	-.10	.07	.13	-.02	1.00		
8. Availability of outside customers	.1015 (.1663)	-.35[a]	.04	.08	-.14	-.17	-.12	-.11	1.00	
9. Competitors' degrees of vertical integration	1.0904 (.8693)	-.06	.07	.36[a]	.02	.08	.33[a]	-.03	.01	1.00

[a]Significance at 1 percent level.

Table A–17

Coefficients for Regression, Total Sample

	Dependent Variables				
	Firm's Number of Stages in Transformation Process	SBU's Degree of Backward Internal Transfers	SBU's Degree of Forward Internal Transfers	SBU's Breadth of Integrated Activities Undertaken	Firm's Form or Percentage Ownership of the Vertical Venture
Phase of Industry Development Variables					
1. Sales growth	1.12[a] (.19)	—	—	—	—
2. Demand uncertainty	—	—	—	−.15 (.03)	—
Corporate Strategy Variables					
3. Synergy—Upstream *and* downstream	.33[b] (.14)	—	—	—	—
4. Market share	—	—	—	—	.08 (.05)
Volatility of competition variables					
5. Concentration ratio	—	.19[b] (.12)	—	—	—
6. Height of economic exit barriers	—	—	−.33[b] (−.21)	−.16[c] (−.13)	—
Relative bargaining power variables					
7. Dependence of outside suppliers	—	−.46[a] (−.28)	—	—	—
8. Availability of outside customers	—	—	.92[a] (.41)	—	—
9. Competitors' degrees of backward and forward integration	—	—	—	—	.06[b] (.20)
Respecified vertical-integration strategy dimensions					
10. Firms' number of stages in transformation process	—	.38[b] (.18)	.61[a] (.31)	—	—
11. SBU's degree of backward internal transfers	—	—	—	−.66[a] (−.42)	.21[c] (.17)
SBU's degree of forward internal transfers	—	—	—	−.37[a] (−.27)	−.39[a] (−.29)
Intercept	.83	.01	−.09	.24	.86
Mean (standard deviation)	.86 (.36)	.35 (.34)	.69 (.27)	.88 (.27)	.86 (.26)

Table A–17 continued

	Dependent Variables				
	Firm's Number of Stages in Transformation Process	SBU's Degree of Backward Internal Transfers	SBU's Degree of Forward Internal Transfers	SBU's Breadth of Integrated Activities Undertaken	Firm's Form or Percentage Ownership of the Vertical Venture
Corrected coefficient of multiple determination R^2	.05	.16	.20	.35	.08
F-statistic (degrees of freedom)	4.72[a] (189)	11.88[a] (188)	15.37[a] (188)	25.13[a] (187)	4.14[a] (187)

Note: Figures in parentheses are standardized regression coefficients indicating their relative contributions to the coefficient of multiple determination, assuming inequal standard deviation.

[a]Significant at the .01 level using a student's t-test of the null hypothesis that the regression coefficient equals zero.

[b]Significant at the .05 level using a student's t-test of the null hypothesis that the regression coefficient equals zero.

[c]Significant at the .10 level using a student's t-test of the null hypothesis that the regression coefficient equals zero.

Table A–18
Structural Factors That Influence the Attractiveness of Declining Environments

Structural Factors	Environmental Attractiveness		
	Favorable	*Intermediate*	*Unfavorable*
Speed of decline	Very slow	Moderate	Rapid and/or erratic
Certainty of decline	100 percent certain predictable patterns	Fairly certain patterns	Great uncertainty, erratic patterns
Pockets of enduring demand	Several or major ones	Some niches	No niches
Price stability	Stable, price premiums attainable	Some volatility	Very unstable, pricing below costs
Reinvestment requirements	None	Some maintenance investments needed	High, often mandatory and involving capital assets
Diseconomies of scale	None	Slight	Substantial penalty
Excess capacity	Little	Some	Substantial
Asset age	Mostly old assets	Mostly undepreciated assets	Sizable new assets and old ones not retired
Resale markets for assets	Easy to convert or sell	Some outlets for disposal (overseas)	No markets available, substantial costs to retire
Product differentiability	Brand name loyalty	Corporate name recognition	Commoditylike products
Customer industries	Fragmented, weak	Long-term contracts	Strong bargaining power
Customer switching costs	High	Moderate	Minimal
Single-product competitors	None	Very few large ones	Several large firms
Height of exit barriers	Low	Moderate	High
Shared facilities	Few—free-standing plants	Few—connected with weak products	Substantial and connected with important businesses
Vertical integration	None	Little	Substantial
Dissimilar strategic groups	Few	Some	Several in same target markets

Table A–19
Forms of Exit Barriers

Accounting-loss treatments:
- Poor performance undermines confidence in management's capabilities.
- Valuation induces firms to prolong their presence in industry.

$$\text{BARR} = \frac{\text{EV (DCE of Future Operations)}}{\text{Immediate Salvage Value Realizable}}$$

Strategic exit barriers:
- Quality image, shared customers, shared physical facilities or other strategic facilities.
- Centerpiece of related strategies (corporate image).
- Customers may be cut off; may harm firm in other businesses.

Managerial exit barriers
- Emotional (prestige) investment.
- Turf battles (interdepartmental transfers or other integration).

Table A–20
Hypothesized Relationships between Relative Industry Attractiveness, Competitive Strengths, and Decline Strategies

Relative Industry Attractiveness[a]	Relative Competitive Strengths[a]		
	High	Medium	Low
Favorable	"Increase the investment" or "Hold investment"	"Hold investment" or "Shrink selectivity"	"Shrink selectivity" or "Milk the investment"
Intermediate	"Hold investment" or "Shrink selectivity"	"Shrink selectivity" or "Milk the investment"	"Milk the investment" or "Get out now!"
Unfavorable	"Shrink selectivity" or "Milk the investment"	"Milk the investment" or "Get out now!"	"Get out now!"

[a]It should be remembered that both the relative industry attractiveness and relative competitive strengths assessments are for declining industries and the firm within them. Thus, favorability is measured vis-à-vis the options of continuing to compete or withdrawing from the industry. This is different from the more typical situation in which a favorable environment is one in which the firm would normally want to invest substantially for growth.

Table A–21
Correlation between the Model and Success

	Number of Relatively Successful Outcomes	Number of Relatively Unsuccessful Outcomes	Totals
Number of firms that followed recommendations	39	3	42
Number of firms that did not follow recommendations	3	16	19
Totals	42	19	

Table A–22
How to Lower the Firm's Own Exit Barriers

Accounting:	Create reserves to offset the cost of write-off losses on disposal where allowed.
Technological:	Trade off highly specialized plant and equipment for more flexible assets.
Financial:	Lease, do not purchase.
Multinational:	Plan to move assets abroad on a scheduled basis, forcing jump-off points of reevaluation to fund new assets.
Planning:	Routinely evaluate whether to exit from a business when it falls below a prescribed level.

Table A–23
How to Lower Competitors' Exit Barriers

Acquire their physical plant or assets.

Offer to service and supply replacement parts to their customers.

If a supplier appears eager to help a competitor, offer to purchase more from the supplier.

Alert regulatory agencies to competitors' transgressions, particularly in pollution control.

Start a price war.

Go public in plea for their exit.

Table A–24
Regression Analysis on Exit[a]

Alternative Specifications of the Model of Exit Behavior	Coefficient of Multiple Determination (R²)	High Quality	Strong Customer Industry	Shared Facilities	Promotion/Advertising Barriers	Manufacturing/Technology Barriers	Favorable Industry Environment	Losses	High Strategic Importance	Constant
1	.555	-.2623 (.0107)	-.2374 (.0245)	-.3256 (.0015)		-.3833 (.0007)	-.3209 (.0017)	.3231 (.0022)		1.1629 (.0001)
2	.503	-.2841 (.0088)	-.1412 (.2019)	-.2501 (.0222)	-.1930 (.0620)	-.3736 (.0016)	-.4008 (.0002)			1.2744 (.0001)
3	.475	-.2905 (.0116)	-.2324 (.0451)	-.3109 (.0048)		-.2955 (.0139)		.3964 (.0005)	-.1101 (.3189)	.9883 (.0001)
4	.448	-.2541 (.0241)	-.3221 (.0050)	-.2262 (.0325)			-.2584 (.0175)	.3146 (.0063)		.8648 (.0001)
5	.401	-.2754 (.0188)	-.2246 (.0574)	-.1530 (.1741)	-.1957 (.0812)		-.3380 (.0024)			.9815 (.0001)
6	.367	-.2775 (.0200)	-.2685 (.0234)	-.2056 (.0647)			-.3352 (.0030)			.9624 (.0001)
7	.3421			-.3001 (.0113)		-.4350 (.0007)	-.4743 (.0001)			1.1063 (.0001)
8	.3127		-.2645 (.0259)		-.2428 (.0339)		-.3989 (.0005)			.8594 (.0001)
9	.2935	-.4256 (.0004)		-.2685 (.0274)		-.3359 (.0090)				.9618 (.0001)
10	.2679		-.3056 (.0144)		-.3809 (.0040)			.4045 (.0013)		.7299 (.0001)
11	.2542	-.4090 (.0010)		-.1153 (.3384)	-.2337 (.0524)					.7250 (.0001)
12	.2525	-.3875 (.0024)	-.1668 (.1957)			-.2058 (.1086)				.8007 (.0001)

[a]Parenthetical figures represent levels of significance, the probability indicated in using the student's *t* value for testing the null hypothesis that the parameter equals zero.

Table A–25

Exit Behavior in Businesses of High Strategic Importance to Firms Compared with Businesses of Low Strategic Importance

Alternative Specifications of the Model of Exit Behavior	High Product Quality	Strong Customer Industry	Shared Physical Facilities	Promotion/ Advertising Barrier	Manufacturing/ Technology Barrier	Favorable Industry Environment	Losses	Constant	Coefficient of Multiple Determination (R²)
1. Important	-.3882 (.0044)	-.6157 (.0010)	-.1804 (.2047)					1.0412 (.0001)	.4691
Not important	-.1078 (.6491)	.0309 (.8595)	-.4797 (.0150)					.8950 (.0001)	.2496
2. Important	-.3256 (.0149)	-.5000 (.0034)			-.1686 (.2954)			.9419 (.0001)	.4583
Not important	-.4913 (.0903)	.1391 (.5067)			-.2530 (.2567)			.7581 (.0002)	.1064
3. Important		-.5175 (.9949)		.2275 (.1085)		.1100 (.4354)		.6875 (.0005)	.3632
Not important		-.0507 (.7374)		.4819 (.0127)		-.4069 (.0132)		.8863 (.0001)	.3889
4. Important			-.1515 (.3873)		-.4242 (.0431)	-.3636 (.0265)		.8333 (.0044)	.2575
Not important			-.4196 (.0160)		-.2925 (.0735)	-.4236 (.0155)		1.1988 (.0001)	.4175
5. Important	-.3581 (.0271)		.0074 (.9642)	0.790 (.6246)				.3725 (.0375)	.1953
Not important	-.1869 (.3648)		-.3524 (.0503)	.4812 (.0143)				.9528 (.0001)	.4008
6. Important			-.3758 (.0149)	.3597 (.0417)			.3758 (.0149)	.7709 (.0001)	.0457
Not important			.0489 (.7882)	.1038 (.5595)			.1370 (.4630)	.1006 (.5160)	.5058
7. Important			-.4848 (.0034)		-.2001 (.1794)		.4514 (.0050)	.8494 (.0001)	.1455
Not important			-.0707 (.7001)		-.4040 (.0756)		.2121 (.2469)	.5353 (.0376)	.4601

Note: Figures in parentheses indicate levels of significance, the probability indicated in using the student's t value for testing the null hypothesis that the parameter equals zero. Average likelihood of exit where business is *low* = 58.06 percent (mean of dependent variable) average likelihood of exit where business is *high* = 23.33 percent (mean of dependent variable).

Table A–26
Harmonic Mean Rankings of Relative Influences on the Likelihood of Exit

	Reputation of High Product Quality	Strong Bargaining Position of Customer Industry	Physical Facilities Shared with Nondeclining Business	Barriers Created by Previous Promotion or Advertising Expenditures	Manufacturing or Technology Related Barriers	High Expectations of Favorable Industry Environment	Losses (Positive Sign)	Business of High Strategic Importance
Aggregate sample of 61 firms	4	6	5	7	1	3	2	(a)
Sample facing high capital intensity	1	(a)	5	3	—	2	6	4
Sample facing low capital intensity	(a)	(a)	(a)	(a)	—	2	1	(a)
Sample's product could be significantly differentiated	3	(a)	(a)	(a)	2	—	1	—
Sample's product was commoditylike in nature	1	(a)	2	(a)	(a)	—	(a)	—
Sample's business is of high strategic importance	4	1	(a)	(a)	2	3	(a)	—
Sample's business is of low strategic importance	1	(a)	3	2	6	4	5	—

(a) = not significant in this specification.

Table A–27
Comparisons of the Mean Values of Exit Likelihood for Various Partitioned Samples

	Average Likelihood of Exit (%)
Total sample	41.0
Relatively high economic exit barriers	33.3
Relatively low economic exit barriers	57.9
Differentiable product traits	28.9
Commoditylike product traits	60.9
High strategic importance	23.3
Low strategic importance	58.1

Table A–28
Definition of Independent Variables Associated with Exit Barriers

Variable Name	Mean	Standard Deviation	Explanation and Hypotheses
Economic Forces			
1. Diseconomies of scale	.1796	.1235	Percentage cost diseconomies incurred when operating 25 percent below engineered capacity. Manufacturing facilities subject to substantial cost diseconomies will be more difficult to divest.
2. Relative product differentiation	.3987	.2865	Scale of relative differentiation in which commodities were .01 and customized products were .99, and highly differentiated products represent an intangible asset that raises the height of exit barriers.
Expectations			
3. Sales growth	−.0031	.0766	Average sales growth over five years, 1976–1981, where rapid growth reduces exit barriers.
4. Number of integrated stages	.8604	.4486	Relative (index) number of steps in transformation process the firm undertook. Being involved in several stages of production increases the height of exit barriers.
5. Form of integrated venture	.8694	.2636	Percentage of ownership in the venture. Wholly owned vertical links represent larger investments to be recovered when divesting, hence higher exit barriers.
6. Degree of backward integration	.3471	.3421	Percentage of requirements the business unit obtains from upstream sister unit. High degrees of backward integration increase pressures to buy in house and difficult to disrupt.
7. Degree of forward integration	.3669	.3872	Percentage of outputs the business unit sold to (or through) downstream sister unit. High degrees of forward integration give firms greater control over exit because fewer important customers will be alienated by their departure.
8. Synergies with upstream businesses	.1756	.2701	Percentage of resources with sister business unit upstream, and high shared resources increase exit barriers unit in question.

Table A–29
Regressions on Height of Exit Barriers

Variable	Model specification
Economic forces	
1. Diseconomies of scale	1.0829[a]
	(.5449)
Strategic forces	
2. Relative product differentiation	.3640[a]
	(.4249)
Expectations	
3. Growth in sales	−.3472[c]
	(−.1083)
Vertical-integration variables	
4. Number of integrated stages	.1034[a]
	(.1890)
5. Form of integrated venture	.0884[c]
	(.0949)
6. Degree of backward integration	.1327[b]
	(.1849)
7. Degree of forward integration	−.0667[c]
	(−.1028)
8. Synergies with upstream business	−.1388[a]
	(−.1527)
Intercept	−.0087
Coefficient of multiple determination—R^2	.4550
F-statistic (degrees of freedom)	19.10[a]
	(183.0)

Note: Figures in parentheses are standardized regression coefficients indicating their relative contributions to the coefficient of multiple determination.

[a]Significant at the .01 level using a student's t-test of the null hypothesis that the coefficient equals zero.

[b]Significant at the .05 level using a student's t-test of the null hypothesis that the coefficient equals zero.

[c]Significant at the .10 level using a student's t-test of the null hypothesis that the coefficient equals zero.

References

Aaker, David A. 1971. "Cluster Analysis." In D.A. Aaker, ed., *Multivariate Analysis in Marketing: Theory and Application*. Belmont, Calif.: Wadsworth, pp. 299–350.

Abell, D.F. 1978. "Strategic Windows." *Journal of Marketing* 42(3):21–26.

———. 1980. *Defining the Business: The Starting Point of Strategic Planning*. Englewood Cliffs, N.J.: Prentice-Hall.

Abernathy, William J., and Wayne, Kenneth 1974. "Limits of the Learning Curve." *Harvard Business Review* 52(5):109–119.

Adams, W., and Dirlam, J. 1964. "Steel Imports and the Vertical Oligopoly Power." *American Economic Review* 54(5):640–655.

Adelman, M.A. 1955. "Concept and Statistical Measurement of Vertical Integration." In National Bureau of Economic Research (conference report), *Business Concentration and Price Policy*. Princeton, N.J.: Princeton University Press, pp. 281–330.

———. 1979. "Integration and Antitrust Policy." *Harvard Law Review* 63(1):27–77.

Aldrich, H.E. 1979. *Organizations and Environment*. Englewood Cliffs, N.J.: Prentice-Hall.

Alexander, R.S. 1964. "The Death and Burial of 'Sick' products." *Journal of Marketing* 28 (April):1–7.

Alloway, Robert M. 1976. "Executive Summary of Temporary Management Systems: Application of a Contingency Model for the Creation of Computer-Based Information Systems." Unpublished manuscript, Sloan School of Management, Massachusetts Institute of Technology, August.

Anderson, C., and Paine, T. 1978. "PIMS: A Reexamination." *Academy of Management Review* no. 3, pp. 602–612.

Anderson, C.R., and Zeithaml, C.P. 1984. "Stage of the Product Life Cycle, Business Performance." *Academy of Management Journal* 27(1):5–24.

Ansoff, H. Igor; Declerk, Robert P.; and Hayes, Robert L., eds. 1976. *From Strategic Planning to Strategic Management*. New York: Wiley.

Arnold, Stephan John. 1979. "A Test for Clusters." *Journal of Marketing* 16:545–551.

Arrow, K.J. 1975. "Vertical Integration and Communication." *Bell Journal of Economics,* 6:173–183.

Babcock, Guilford C. 1970. "The Concept of Sustainable Growth." *Financial Analysts Journal,* May–June, pp. 108–114.

Bachmann, Jules. 1965. "Joint Ventures in the Light of Recent Antitrust Developments: Joint Ventures in the Chemical Industry." *Antitrust Bulletin* 10 (January–April):7–23.

Bain, Joe S. 1956. *Barriers to New Competition*, Cambridge, Mass.: Harvard University Press.

———. 1968. *Industrial Organization*, 2nd ed., New York: Wiley.

———. 1972. *Essays on Price Theory*. Boston: Little, Brown.

Baker, H.K.; Miller, T.P.; and Ramsperger, B.J. 1981. "An Inside Look at Corporate Mergers and Acquisitions." *MSU Business Topics* 29(1):49–57.

Balestra, Pietro, and Nerlove, Marc. 1966. "Pooling Cross Section and Time Series Data in the Estimation of a Dynamic Model: The Demand for Natural Gas." *Econometrica* 34(July):585–612.

Baldridge, M. 1983. "Testimony: On Government Policies to Promote High Growth Industries Based on New Technologies and to Increase U.S. Competitiveness." Committee on Finance, U.S. Senate, January 19.

Ball, G.H., and Hall, D.J. 1967. "A Clustering Technique for Summarizing Multi-Variate Data." *Behavioral Science* 12:153–155.

Ballon, Robert J., ed. 1967. *Joint Ventures and Japan*. Tokyo: Sophia University.

Banks, H. 1981. "Partners of Necessity." *Europe*, November–December, pp. 31–33.

Barnard, Chester I. 1968. *The Functions of The Executive*. Cambridge, Mass.: Harvard University Press. (Originally published in 1938.)

Bartlett, C.A. 1983. "MNCs: Get Off the Reorganization Merry-Go-Round." *Harvard Business Review*, March–April, pp. 138–146.

Bass, Frank M.; Cattin, Phillippe; and Wittink, Dick. 1978. "Firm Effects and Industry Effects in the Analysis of Market Structure and Profitability." *Journal of Marketing Research* 15(February):3–10.

Bass, Frank, and Wittink, Dick R. 1965. "Pooling Issues and Methods in Regression Analysis with Examples in Marketing Research." *Journal of Marketing Research* 12(November):414–425.

Beamish, P., and Lane, H.W. 1982. "Need, Commitment and the Performance of Joint Ventures in Developing Countries." Working paper, University of Western Ontario, July.

Berg, Sanford V.; Jerome, Duncan, Jr.; and Friedmann, Philip. 1982. *Joint Strategies and Corporate Innovations*. Cambridge, Mass.: Oelgeschlager, Gunn & Hain.

Berg, Sanford V., and Friedmann, Philip. 1980. "Corporate Courtship and Successful Joint Ventures." *California Management Review* 22(2):85–91.

Bernhardt, I. 1977. "Vertical Integration and Demand Variability." *Journal of Industrial Economics* 25(3):213–229.

Bettauer, A. 1967. "Strategy for Divestment." *Harvard Business Review*, March–April.

Biggadike, Ralph. 1976. "Entry, Strategy and Performance." Ph.D. dissertation, Harvard Business School.

Bivens, Karen Kraus, and Lovell, Enid Baird. 1966. *Joint Venture with Foreign Partners*. New York, National Industrial Conference Board.

Blair, Roger, and Kaserman, David L. 1978a. "Uncertainty and the Incentive for Vertical Integration." *Southern Economic Journal* 26(July):266–272.

———. 1978b. "Vertical Integration, Tying and Antitrust Policy." *American Economic Review* 68(3):397–402.

Blair, Roger D., and Kraft, John. 1974. "Estimation of Elasticity of Substitution in American Manufacturing Industry from Pooled Cross-Section and Time-

Series Observations." *Review of Economics and Statistics* 56(August):343—347.

Blois, K.J. 1972. "Vertical Quasi-Integration." *Journal of Industrial Economics* 20(July):253–272.

———. 1980. "Quasi-Integration as Mechanism for Controlling External Dependencies." *Management Decision* (U.K.) 18(1):55–63.

Bork, R. 1954. "Vertical Integration and the Sherman Act: The Legal History of an Economic Misconception." *University of Chicago Law Review* 22(1):158–201.

Boston Consulting Group. 1972. *Perspectives on Experience.* Boston, Mass.: Boston Consulting Group.

Bourgeois, L.J., III, and Singh, Jitendra. 1982. "Organizational Slack and Political Behavior within Top Management Teams." Working paper, Stanford University, December 1982. (Presented at 1983 National Academy of Management Meetings, Dallas.)

Bower, J. 1970. *Managing the Resource Allocation Process.* Cambridge, Mass.: Division of Research, Harvard Graduate School of Business.

Bowman, E.H. 1978. "Strategy, Annual Reports, and Alchemy." *California Management Review* 20(3):64–71.

———. 1980. "A Risk-Return Paradox for Strategic Management." *Sloan Management Review,* Spring, pp. 17–32.

———. 1984. "Risk: A Strategy/Finance Connection." Paper presented at National Academy of Management meetings, Boston, August.

Boyle, S.E. 1968. "An Estimate of the Number and Size Distribution of Domestic Joint Subsidiaries." *Antitrust Law and Economics Review* 1:81–92.

Branch, Ben. 1984. "Linking Corporate Stock Price Performance to Strategy Formulation." In Robert Lamb, ed., *Competitive Strategic Management.* Englewood Cliffs, N.J.: Prentice-Hall.

Braybrooke, David, and Lindblom, C.E. 1973. *A Strategy of Decision.* New York: Free Press, 1973. (Originally published in 1970.)

Brodley, J.F. 1979. "Joint Ventures and the Justice Department's Antitrust Guide for International Operations." *Antitrust Bulletin* 24(Summer):337–356.

———. 1982. "Joint Ventures and Antitrust Policy." *Harvard Law Review,* pp. 1523–1590.

Buckley, Walter. 1967. *Sociology and Modern Systems Theory.* Englewood Cliffs, N.J.: Prentice-Hall.

Business International. 1971. *European Business Strategies in the United States: Meeting the Challenge of the World's Largest Market.* Geneva: Business International S.A.

Buzzell, Robert D. 1966. "Competitive Behavior and Product Life Cycles." In John S. Wright and Jac L. Goldstucker, eds. *New Ideas for Successful Marketing.* Chicago: American Marketing Association, pp. 46–48.

———. 1983. "Is Vertical Integration Profitable?" *Harvard Business Review* 61:92–102.

Buzzell, R.D.; Gale, T.; and Sultan, R. 1975. "Market Share—Key to Profitability." *Harvard Business Review* 53(1):97–106.

Carlton, D. 1979. "Vertical Integration in Competitive Markets under Uncertainty." *Journal of Industrial Economics* 27(March):189–209.

Carter, Eugene E., and Cohen, Kalman J. 1972. "Portfolio Aspects of Strategic Planning." *Journal of Business Policy,* Summer, pp. 8–30.

Caves, Richard E. 1979. "Industrial Organization, Corporate Strategy and Structure: A Survey." Working paper no. 79-706, Harvard Institute of Economic Research, May.

Caves, Richard E.; Khalizadeh-Shirazi, J.; and Porter, Michael E. 1975. "Scale Economies in Statistical Analyses of Market Power." *Review of Economics and Statistics,* May, pp. 133–140.

Caves, Richard E., and Porter, Michael E. 1976. "Barriers to Exit." In David P. Qualls and Robert E. Masson, eds, *Essays in Industrial Organization in Honor of Joe S. Bain.* Cambridge, Mass.: Ballinger, Chapter 3.

———. 1977. "From Entry Barriers to Mobility Barriers." *Quarterly Journal of Economics* 91(May):241–262.

Chamberlain, E.M. 1962. *The Theory of Monopolistic Competition,* 8th ed. Cambridge, Mass.: Harvard University Press.

Chandler, A.D. 1962. *Strategy and Structure: Chapters in the History of the American Industrial Enterprise.* Cambridge, Mass.: MIT Press.

———. 1977. *The Visible Hand: The Managerial Revolution in American Business.* Cambridge, Mass.: Harvard University Press.

Chang, Hui-Shyong, and Lee, Cheng F. 1977. "Using Pooled Time Series and Cross Section Data to Test the Firm and Time Effects in Financial Analyses." *Journal of Financial and Quantitative Analysis* 12(September):457–471.

Clevenger, T.C., and Campbell, G.R. 1977. "Vertical Organization: A Neglected Element in Market Structure-Performance Models." *Industrial Organizational Review* 5(1):259–262.

Clifford, Donald K., Jr. 1976. "Managing the Product Life Cycle." In Robert R. Rothberg, ed. *Corporate Strategy and Product Innovation.* New York: Free Press, pp. 349–369.

Coase, Ronald H. 1937. "The Nature of the Firm," *Economica* 4(November): 386–405.

Collins, N., and Preston, L. 1969. "Price-Cost Margins and Industry Structure." *Review of Economics and Statistics* 51(August):271–286.

Comanor, William S. 1967a. "Market Structure, Product Differentiation, and Industrial Research." *Quarterly Journal of Economics* 81(November):639–657.

———. 1967b. "Vertical Mergers, Market Power, and Antitrust Laws." *American Economic Review* 57(2):259–262.

Comanor, William S., and Wilson, Thomas A. 1967. "Advertising, Market Structure, and Performance." *Review of Economics and Statistics,* November 1967, pp. 423–440.

———. 1974. *Advertising and Market Power.* Cambridge, Mass.: Harvard University Press.

Crandall, R.W. 1968a. "Vertical Integration and the Market for Repair Parts in the United States Automobile Industry." *Journal of Industrial Economics* 16(July):212–234.

———. 1968b. "Vertical Integration in the United States Automobile Industry." Ph.D. dissertation, Northwestern University.

Cyert, R.M. and March, J.G. 1963. *A Behavioral Theory of the Firm.* Englewood Cliffs, N.J.: Prentice-Hall.

Daniels, John D. 1971. *Recent Foreign Direct Manufacturing Investment in the United States: An Interview Study of the Decision Process.* New York: Praeger.

Davidow, Joel. 1977. "International Joint Ventures and the U.S. Antitrust Laws." *Akron Law Review* 10(Spring).

Davidson, W.H., and Harrigan, R.S. 1977. "Key Decisions in International Marketing: Introducing New Products Abroad." *Columbia Journal of World Business,* Winter, pp. 19–23.

Davies, Howard. 1977. "Technology Transfer through Commercial Transactions." *Journal of Industrial Economics* 26(December):161–175.

Davies, S.M. 1976. "Trends in the Organization of Multinational Corporations." *Columbia Journal of World Business,* Summer, pp. 59–71.

Davis, J.W. 1974. "The Strategic Divestment Decision." *Long-Range Planning,* February.

Davis, Stanley M., and Lawrence, Paul. 1977. *Matrix.* Reading, Mass.: Addison-Wesley.

Delbecq, A.L.; Van de Ven, A.; and Gustafson, D.H. 1975. *Group Techniques for Program Planning.* Glenview, Ill.: Scott Foresman.

Demsetz, Harold. 1979. "Accounting for Advertising as a Barrier to Entry." *Journal of Business* 52(3):345–360.

Dennison, S.R. 1939. "Vertical Integration and the Iron and Steel Industry." *Economic Journal* 49:244–258.

Deutsch, Larry L. 1975. "Structure, Performance and the Net Rate of Entry into Manufacturing Industries." *Southern Economic Journal,* January, pp. 450–456.

Dixit, Avinash. 1980. "The Role of Investment in Entry-Deterrence." *The Economic Journal,* March, pp. 95–106.

Drucker, Peter. 1974. *Management: Tasks, Responsibilities, Promises.* New York: Harper & Row.

Duncan, J.L., Jr. 1980. "The Causes and Effects of Domestic Joint Venture Activity." Ph.D. dissertation, University of Florida.

Duncan, W.J. 1976. "Organizations as Political Coalitions: A Behavioral View of the Goal Formulation Process." *Journal of Behavioral Economics* 5(1):25–44.

Edstrom, Anders. 1975a. "Acquisition and Joint Venture Behavior of Swedish Manufacturing Firms." Working paper, University of Gothenberg.

———. 1975b. "The Stability of Joint Ventures." Working paper, University of Gothenberg.

Esposito, L., and Esposito, F.F. 1974. "Excess Capacity and Market Structure." *Review of Economics and Statistics* 56(May):188–194.

Everitt, Brian, 1974. *Cluster Analysis.* London: Heineman Educational Books.

Ewing, K.P., Jr. 1981. "Joint Research, Antitrust, and Innovation." *Research Management* 24(2):25–29.

Fayol, Henry. 1925. *Industrial and General Administration.* Paris: Dunod.

Fellner, W.J. 1949. *Competition among the Few: Oligopoly and Similar Structure.* New York: Knopf.

Ferguson, R.W., Jr. 1981. "The Nature of Joint Venture in the American Manufacturing Sector." Ph.D. dissertation, Harvard University.

Filley, A.C.; House, R.J.; and Kerr, S. 1976. *Managerial Process and Organizational Behavior*. Glenview, Ill.: Scott Foresman.

Flaim, T.A. 1977. "The Structure of the U.S. Petroleum Industry: Concentration, Vertical Integration and Joint Activities." Ph.D. dissertation, Cornell University.

Fouraker, Lawrence E., and Siegel, Sidney. 1963. *Bargaining Behavior*. New York: McGraw-Hill.

Frank, L.K. 1925. "The Significance of Industrial Integration." *Journal of Political Economy* 33(2):179–195.

Frank R.E., and Green, Paul E. 1968. "Numerical Taxonomy in Marketing Analysis: A Review Article." *Journal of Marketing Research* 5(February):83–98.

Franko, Lawrence G. 1971. *Joint Venture Survival in Multinational Corporations*. New York: Harper & Row.

———. 1976. *The European Multinationals*. London: Harper & Row.

Friedman, W.G., and Beguin, J.P. 1971. *Joint International Business Ventures in Developing Countries*. New York: Columbia University Press.

Friedman, W.G., and Kalmanoff, G. 1961. *Joint International Business Ventures*. New York: Columbia University Press.

Gabriel, Peter P. 1967. *The International Transfer of Corporate Skills*, Boston: Harvard Business School, Division of Research.

Gale, Bradley T. 1972. "Market Share and Rate of Return." *Review of Economics and Statistics* 54(November))412–423.

Gaskin, Darius W., Jr. 1971. "Dynamic Limit Pricing: Optimal Pricing under Threat of Entry." *Journal of Economic Theory* 3(3):306–322.

Gilpin, R. 1975. *Technology, Economic Growth, and International Competitiveness*. U.S. Congress, Joint Economic Committee, Subcommittee on Economic Growth, 94th Congress, 1st Session.

Gorecki, Paul K. 1976. "The Determinants of Entry by Domestic and Foreign Enterprises in Canadian Manufacturing Industries: Some Comments and Empirical Results." *Review of Economics and Statistics,* November, pp. 485–488.

Gort, M. 1962. *Diversification and Integration in American Industry*. Princeton, N.J.: Princeton University Press.

Green, Paul E.; Frank R.E.; and Robinson, P.J. 1967. "Cluster Analysis in Test Market Selection." *Management Science* 13:B387–B499.

Greenhut, M.L., and Ohta, H. 1979. "Vertical Integration of Successive Oligopolists." *American Economic Review* 69(1):137–141.

Gregory, Gene. 1976. "Japan's New Multinationalism: The Canon Giessen Experience." *Columbia Journal of World Business* 11(1):122–126.

Gulich, Luther, and Urwick, Lyndall F. eds. 1937. *Papers on the Science of Administration*. New York: Columbia University Press.

Gullander, Stefan O.O. 1975. "An Exploratory Study of Inter-Firm Cooperation of Swedish Firms." Ph.D. dissertation, Columbia University.

———. 1976. "Joint Ventures and Corporate Strategy." *Columbia Journal of World Business* 11(September):104–114.

Hall, M., and Weiss, L. 1967. "Firm Size and Profitability." *Review of Economics and Statistics* 49(August):319–331.

Hall, William K. 1980. "Survival Strategies in a Hostile Environment." *Harvard Business Review* 58(5):75–85.

Hambrick, Donald C. 1979. "Environmental Scanning, Organizational Strategy, and Executive Roles: A Study in Three Industries." Ph.D. dissertation, Pennsylvania State University.

———. 1980. "Operationalizing the Concept of Business-Level Strategy in Research." *Acadamy of Management Review* 5:567–575.

———. 1983a. "An Empirical Typology of Mature Industrial Product Environments." *Academy of Management Journal* 2(2):213––230.

———. 1983b. High Profit Strategies in Mature Capital Goods Industries: A Contingency Approach. *Academy of Management Journal* 26(4):687–707.

———. 1983c. "Strategies for Mature Industrial-Product Businesses: A Taxonomic Approach." Paper presented at the International Business Policy/Strategic Management Conference, Arlington, Texas, February 1983. In Grant, John (forthcoming). *Frontiers in Strategic Management*. Greenwich, Conn.: JAI Press.

Hambrick, D.D.; MacMillan, I.C.; and Day, D.L. 1982. "Strategic Attributes and Performance in the Four Cells of the BCG Matrix—A PIMS Analysis of Industrial Product Business. *Academy of Management Journal* 25:510–531.

Hambrick, Donald C., and Mason, Phyllis A. 1984. "Upper Echelons: The Organization as a Reflection of Its Top Managers." *Academy Management Review* 1(April):193–206.

Hambrick, Donald C., and Schecter, S.M. 1983. "Turnaround Strategies for Mature Industrial-Product Businesses." *Academy of Management Journal* (20):231–248.

Hamermesh, Richard G.; Anderson, M.G., Jr.; and Harris, J.E. 1978. "Strategies for Low Market Share Businesses." *Harvard Business Review* 56(3):95–102.

Hamermesh, Richard G., and Silk, Steven B. 1979. "How to Compete in Stagnant Industries." *Harvard Business Review* 57(5):161–168.

Hannan, M.T., and Freeman, J. 1977. "The Population Ecology of Organizations." *American Journal of Sociology* 82:929–964.

Harrigan, K.R. 1979. "Strategies for Declining Businesses," D.B.A. dissertation, Harvard University.

———. 1980a. "Clustering Competitors by Strategic Groups." *Proceedings, Southwest Academy of Management Conference*, San Antonio.

———. 1980b. "The Effect of Exit Barriers Upon Strategic Flexibility," *Strategic Management Journal* 1(2):165–176.

———. 1980c. *Strategies for Declining Businesses*. Lexington, Mass.: Lexington Books.

———. 1980d. "Strategy Formulation in Declining Industries," *Academy of Management Review* 5(4):599–604.

———. 1981a. "Barriers to Entry and Competitive Strategies," *Strategic Management Journal* 3:395–412.

———. 1981b. "Deterrents to Divestiture." *Academy of Management Journal* 24(2):306–323.

———. 1982. "Exit Decisions in Mature Industries." *Academy of Management Journal* 25(4):707–732.

——. 1983a. "Exit Barriers and Vertical Integration," in Chung, Kae, *Proceedings,* Academy of Management National Conference.

——. 1983b. "Research Methodologies for Contingency Approaches to Business Strategy." *Academy of Management Review* 8(3):398–405.

——. 1983c. *Strategies for Vertical Integration,* Lexington, Mass.: Lexington Books.

——. 1984a. "Formulating Vertical Integration Strategies." *Academy of Management Review* 9(4):638–652.

——. 1984b. "Innovations by Overseas Subsidiaries." *Journal of Business Strategy* 5:47–55.

——. 1984c. "Joint Ventures and Global Strategies." *Columbia Journal of World Business* 19(2):7–16.

——. 1984d. "Managing Declining Businesses." *Journal of Business Strategy* 4(3):774–78.

——. 1985a. "An Application of Clustering for Strategic Group Analysis." *Strategic Management Journal* 6(1):55–73.

——. 1985b. Exit Barriers and Vertical Integration. *Academy of Management Journal* 29(3):forthcoming.

——. 1985c. *Strategies for Joint Ventures,* Lexington, Mass.: *Lexington Books,* D.C. Heath & Co.

——. 1985d. "Vertical Integration and Corporate Strategy." *Academy of Management Journal* 28(2):forthcoming.

——. 1987. "Matching Vertical Integration Strategies to Competitive Conditions. *Strategic Management Journal* 7:forthcoming.

Harrigan, K.R. and Porter, M.E. 1983. "Endgame Strategies for Declining Industries." *Harvard Business Review.* 61(4):111–120.

Hartigan, J.A. 1975. *Clustering Algorithms,* New York: John Wiley & Sons, 1975.

Hatten, Kenneth J. 1974. "Strategic Models in the Brewing Industry." Ph.D. dissertation, Purdue University.

——. 1979. "Quantitative Research Methods in Strategic Management." In Dan E. Schendel and Charles W. Hofer, eds., *Strategic Management: A New View of Business Policy and Planning.* Boston: Little, Brown.

Hatten, Kenneth J., and Schendel, Dan E. 1977. "Heterogeneity within an Industry: Firm Conduct in the United States Brewing Industry, 1952–1971." *Journal of Industrial Economics,* December.

Hatten, Kenneth J.; Schendel, Dan E.; and Cooper, Arnold C. 1978. "A Strategic Model of the United States Brewing Industry, 1952–1971." *Academy of Management Journal* 21(4):529–610.

Hawks, E.T., Jr. 1984. "Strategic Diversification and Economic Performance: An Empirical Examination of Historical Costs, Current Costs and Security Market Performance." Ph.D. dissertation, University of Utah, Salt Lake City.

Hayes, R. 1972. "New Emphasis on Divestment Opportunities." *Harvard Business Review,* July–August.

Hayes, R., and Abernathy, W. 1980. "Managing Our Way to Economic Decline." *Harvard Business Review* 58(4):67–77.

Henderson, Bruce. 1974. "The Experience Curve . . . ." Boston Consulting Group.

Hines, Howard H. 1957. "Effectiveness of Entry by Already Established Firms." *Quarterly Journal of Economics,* February, pp. 132–150.

Hirsch, S. 1965. "Location of Industry and International Competitiveness." Ph.D. dissertation, Harvard Business School.

Hise, Richard T., and McGinnis, Michael A. 1975. "Product Elimination: Practice Policies and Ethics." *Business Horizons,* June, pp. 25–32.

Hlavacek, James D., and Thompson, Victor A. 1976. "The Joint Approach to Technology Utilization." *IEEE Transactions on Engineering Management* EM-23(1):35–41.

Hofer, Charles W. 1975. "Towards a Contingency Theory of Business Strategy." *Academy of Management Journal* 18:784–810.

———. 1980. "Turnaround Strategies." *Journal of Business Strategy* (1):19–31.

Holmer, O. 1967. *Analysis of the Future: The Delphi Method.* Santa Barbara, Calif.: Rand Corporation

Hotelling, Harold. 1929. "Stability in Competition." *Economic Journal* 39, March, pp. 41–57.

Hout, Thomas; Porter, Michael E., and Rudden, Eileen. "How Global Companies Win Out." *Harvard Business Review* 60(5):98–108.

Hsaio, Cheng. 1974. "Statistical Inference for a Model with Both Random Cross-Sectional and Time Effects." *International Economic Review* 15(1):12–30.

Hughey, A., and Kanabayashi, M. 1983. "More U.S. and Japanese Companies Decide to Operate Joint Ventures." *The Wall Street Journal,* May 10, p. 33.

Hunt, Michael S. 1972. "Competition in the Home Appliance Industry, 1960–1970." Ph.D. dissertation, Business Economics Committee, Harvard University.

Hustad, T.P., and Pessemier, E.A. 1973. "Will the Real Consumer Activist Please Stand Up: An Examination of Consumer's Opinions about Marketing Practice." *Journal of Marketing Research* 10(August):319–324.

Hutchinson, A.C. 1971. "Planned Euthanasia for Old Products." *Long-Range Planning,* December.

Hymer, Stephan, and Pashigian, Peter. 1962. "Firm Size and Rate of Growth." *Journal of Political Economy* 70(December):556–569.

Ijiri, Y., and Simon, H.A. 1964. "Business Growth and Firm Size." *American Economic Review* 54(March):77–89.

Jelinek, Marianne S. 1977. "Institutionalizing Innovation." Ph.D. dissertation, Harvard University.

Jewkes, J. 1930. "Factors in Industrial Integration." *Quarterly Journal of Economics* 44(3):621–638.

Johnson, Stephan C. 1967. "Hierarchical Clustering Schemes." *Psychometrika* 32:241–254.

Johnston J. 1972. *Econometric Methods.* New York: McGraw-Hill.

Johnston, K.H. and Lyon, H.L. 1973. "Experimental Evidence on Combining Cross-Section and Time Series Information. *Review of Economics and Statistics* 55(November):465–474.

Joyce, T., and Channon, C. 1966. "Classifying Market Survey Respondents." *Applied Statistics* 15:191–215.

Kamien, Morton J., and Schwartz, Nancy L. 1975. "Market Structure and Innovation: A Survey." *Journal of Economic Literature* 13(March):1–37.

Kaserman, D. 1978. "Theories of Vertical Integration: Implications for Antitrust Policy." *Antitrust Bulletin* 23(Fall):483–510.

Kaysen, C., and Turner, D.F. 1959. *Antitrust Policy*. Cambridge, Mass.: Harvard University Press.

Khandwalla, P.A. 1974. "Mass Output Orientation of Operations Technology and Organizational Structure." *Administrative Science Quarterly* 19(1):74–79.

Killing, J.P. 1980. "Technology Acquisition: License Agreement or Joint Venture." *Columbia Journal of World Business* 15(Fall):38–46.

———. 1982. "How to Make a Global Joint Venture Work." *Harvard Business Review* 61(3):120–127.

———. 1983. *Strategies for Joint Venture Success*. New York: Praeger.

Knickerbocker, F.T. 1973a. "Notes on the Watch Industries in Switzerland, Japan, and the United States." Intercollegiate Case Clearing House, Harvard University.

———. 1973b. *Oligopolistic Reaction and Multinational Enterprises*. Cambridge, Mass.: Division of Research, Harvard Graduate School of Business.

Kotler, Philip. 1965. "Phasing Out Weak Products." *Harvard Business Review*, March–April.

———. 1972. *Marketing Management: Analysis, Planning, and Control*, 2nd ed. Englewood Cliffs, N.J.: Prentice-Hall.

Laffer, A.B. 1969. "Vertical Integration by Corporations 1929–1965." *Review of Economics and Statistics* 51 (February):91–93.

Larson, D.A. 1978. "An Empirical Test of the Relationship between Market Concentration and Vertical Integration." *Industrial Organization Review* 6(1):71–74.

Lavington, F. 1925. "Technical Influence on Vertical Integration." *Economica* 7(March):27–36.

Lawrence, Paul R.; Beddows, Rodney C.; and Lane, Henry W. 1965. "A Study of the Research Administration Process in Selected Programs at NIH and Bell Laboratories." Unpublished manuscript.

Lawrence, Paul R., and Lorsch, Jay W. 1969. *Organization and Environment: Managing Differentiation and Integration*, Homewood, Ill.: Richard D. Irwin.

———, eds., 1972 *Organization in Planning: Cases and Concepts*. Homewood, Ill.: Richard D. Irwin.

Lehmann, Donald R. 1979. *Market Research and Analysis*. Homewood, Ill.: Richard D. Irwin.

Ling, R.F., 1973. "A Probability Theory of Cluster Analysis," *Journal of the American Statistical Association*, Vol. 68, 1973, pp. 159–164.

Livesay, H.C., and Porter, P.G. 1969. "Vertical Integration in American Manufacturing, 1899–1948." *Journal of Economic History* 29(September):494–500.

Lorsch, Jay W., and Morse, J.J. 1974. *Organizations and Their Members: A Contingency Approach*. New York: Harper & Row.

Lubatkin, M.H. 1982. "A Market Model Analysis of Diversification Strategies and Administrative Experience on the Performance of Merging Firms." Ph.D. dissertation, University of Tennessee, Knoxville.

Lustgarten, S.R. 1975. "The Impact of Buyer Concentration in Manufacturing Industries." *Review of Economics and Statistics* 57(May):125–132.

McGee, J.S., and Bassett, L.R. 1976. "Vertical Integration Revisited." *Journal of Law and Economics* 19(1):17–38.

McGuckin, Robert. 1972. "Entry, Concentration Change and Stability of Market Shares." *Southern Economic Journal,* January, pp. 363–370.

McKelvey, Bill. 1975. "Guidelines for Empirical Classification of Organizations." *Administrative Science Quarterly* 20:509–525.

———. 1978. "Organizational Systematics: Taxonomic Lessons from Biology." *Management Science* 24:1428–1440.

MacMillan, Ian C. 1980. "How Business Strategists Can Use Guerrilla Warfare Tactics." *Journal of Business Strategy* 1(2):63–65.

———. 1983. "Preemptive Strategies." *Journal of Business Strategy* 4(2):16–26.

MacMillan, Ian C., and Hambrick, Donald C. 1983. "Asset Parsimony: Strategic Imperatives for Rivalrous Industries." Working paper, Strategy Research Center, Columbia University.

MacMillan, I.C.; Hambrick, D.C.; and Pennings, J.H. 1982. "Backward Vertical Integration and Interorganizational Dependence—A PIMS-Based Analysis of Strategic Business Units." Working paper, Columbia University Business School.

Maddala, G.S. 1971. "The Use of Variance Components Models in Pooling Cross Section and Time Series Data." *Econometrica* 39(March):341–358.

Maddigan, R.J. 1979. "The Impact of Vertical Integration on Business Performance." Ph.D. dissertation, Indiana University, Graduate School of Business.

Magee, S.P. 1977. "Information and the Multinational Corporation: An Appropriability Theory of Direct Foreign Investment." In J.N. Bhagwati, ed., *The New International Economic Order.* Cambridge, Mass.: MIT Press, pp. 317–340.

Manke, R.B. 1972. "Irone Ore and Steel: A Case Study of the Economic Causes of Vertical Integration." *Journal of Industrial Economics* 20(3):220–229.

———. 1974. "Causes of Interfirm Profitability Differences: A New Interpretation of the Findings." *Quarterly Journal of Economics* 98(2):181–193.

Mann, H. Michael 1966. "Seller Concentration, Barriers to Entry, and Rates of Return in Thirty Industries, 1950–1960." *Review of Economics and Statistics* 48(August):296–307.

Mansfield, Edwin. 1962. "Entry, Gilbrat's Law, Innovation and Growth of Firms." *American Economic Review* 52(December):1031–1034.

Mao Tse-Tung. 1961. *On Guerrilla Warfare.* New York: Praeger.

———. 1966. *Selected Military Writings.* Peking: People's Press.

March, J.G. 1962. "The Business Firm as a Political Coalition." *Journal of Politics* 24:662–678.

March, J.G., and Simon, H.S. 1958. *Organizations.* New York: Wiley.

Marcus, M. 1969a. "A Note on the Determinants of the Growth of Firms and Gilbrat's Law." *Canadian Journal of Economics.* 3(November):580–589.

————. 1969b. "Profitability and Size of Firm." *Review of Economics and Statistics* 51(February):104–107.

Mariti, P., and Smiley, R.H. 1983. "Co-operative Agreements and the Organization of Industry." *Journal of Industrial Economics*, June, pp. 437–452.

Marquis, Harold L. 1963. "Compatibility of Industrial Joint Research Ventures and Antitrust Policy." *Temple Law Quarterly*, 38(1):1–37.

Mead, W.J. 1967. "The Competitive Significance of Joint Ventures." *Antitrust Bulletin* 12(Fall):819–849.

Meehan, James W. 1970. "Joint Venture Entry in Perspective." *Antitrust Bulletin* 15(Winter):693–711.

Meeker, Guy B. 1971. "Fade Out Joint Venture: Can It Work for Latin America?" *Inter-American Economic Affairs* 24:25–42.

Menge, John A. 1962. "Style Change Costs as a Market Weapon." *Quarterly Journal of Economics* 76(November):632–647/

Merrifield, D.B. 1983. "Forces of Change Affecting High Technology Industries." *National Journal*, January 29, pp. 253–256.

Miles, R.E. and Snow C.C. 1978. *Organizational Strategy, Structure and Processes*. New York: McGraw-Hill.

Miller, Danny. 1978. "The Role of Multivariate 'Q-Techniques' in the Study of Organizations." *Academy of Management Review* 3:515–533.

Miller, Danny, and Friesen, Peter H. 1977. "Strategy-Making in Context: Ten Empirical Archetypes." *Journal of Management Studies* 14:254–280.

————. 1980. "Archetypes of Organizational Transition." *Administrative Science Quarterly* 25(June):268–299.

Miller, E.J., and Rice, A.K. 1967. *Systems of Organization: The Control of Task and Sentient Boundaries*. New York: Tavistock.

Miller, Richard D. 1981. "Strategic Pathways to Growth in Retailing." *Journal of Business Strategy* 1(3):16–29.

Miller, Richard D., and Springate, David J. 1979. "Modelling Strategic Behavior within an Industry." Paper presented at Joint National Meeting, TIMS/ORSA, New Orleans.

Mintzberg, H. 1973. *The Nature of Managerial Work*. New York: Harper & Row.

————. 1978. "Patterns of Strategy Formation." *Management Science* 24:934–948.

Mintzberg, H.; Raisinghani, D.; and Théorêt, A. 1976. "The Structure of 'Unstructured' Decision Processes." *Administrative Science Quarterly* 21:246–275.

Modigliani, Franco. 1958. "New Developments on the Oligopoly Front." *Journal of Political Economy* 66(3):215–232.

Montgomery, Cynthia. 1984. "Strategy Appraisal from a Value Perspective." Paper presented at National Academy of Management Meetings, Boston, August.

Morrison, Donald G. 1967. "Measurement Problems in Cluster Analysis." *Management Science* 13(12):B775–B780.

Mueller, D.C., and Tilton, J.E. 1969. "Research and Development Costs as a

Barrier to Entry." *Canadian Journal of Economics,* November, pp. 570–579.

Mueller, W.F., and Rogers, Richard T. 1980. "The Role of Advertising in Changing Concentration of Manufacturing Industries." *Review of Economics and Statistics* 62(February):89–96.

Mundlak, Yair. 1978. "On the Pooling of Time Series and Cross Section Data." *Econometrica* 46(January):69–85.

Needham, Douglas. 1975. "Market Structure and Firms' R & D Behavior." *Journal of Industrial Economics* 23(4):241–255.

———. 1976. "Entry Barriers and Non-Price Aspects of Firms' Behavior." *Journal of Industrial Economics* 25(1):29–43.

Nelson, R.L. 1963. *Concentration in the Manufacturing Industries of the United States.* New Haven: Yale University Press.

Nerlove, Marc. 1971. "Further Evidence on the Estimation of Dynamic Economic Relations from a Time Series of Cross Sections." *Econometrica* 39(March):359–382.

Newman, H.H. 1973. "Strategic Groups and the Structure-Performance Relationship: A Study with Respect to the Chemical Process Industry." Ph.D. dissertation, Business Economics Committee, Harvard University.

———. 1978. "Strategic Groups and the Structure-Performance Relationship." *Review of Economics and Statistics* 50(August):417–723.

Ohmae, K. 1982. *The Mind of the Strategist.* New York: McGraw-Hill.

Ornstein, S.I.; Weston, J.F.; and Intriligator, M.D. 1973. "Determinants of Market Structure." *Southern Economic Journal,* April, pp. 612–625.

Orr, Dale. 1974. "The Determinants of Entry: A Study of the Canadian Manufacturing Industries." *Review of Economics and Statistics* 56(February):58–60.

Orski, C. Kenneth. 1980. "The World Automotive Industry at a Crossroads: Cooperative Alliances." *Vital Speeches* 47(3):89–93.

Pate, J.L. 1969. "Joint Venture Activity, 1960–1968." *Economic Review,* Federal Reserve Bank of Cleveland, pp. 16–23.

Pearce, J.A. 1984. "The Relationship of Internal vs. External Orientation to Financial Measures of Strategy." *Strategic Management Journal* (4):297–306.

Pearce, J.A., and DeNisi, A.S. 1983. "Attribution Theory and Strategic Decision Making: An Application to Coalition Formation." *Academy of Management Journal* 26(1):119–128.

Pennings, Johannes H.; Hambrick, Donald C.; and MacMillan, Ian C. 1982. "Interorganizational Dependence and Forward Integration." Columbia University Working Paper, January.

Perry, Martin K. 1978. "Vertical Integration: The Monopsony Case." *American Economic Review,* 69(September):561–570.

———. 1980. "Forward Integration by ALCOA: 1888–1930." *Journal of Industrial Economics* 29(1):37–53.

Pfeffer, Jeffrey. 1972. "Merger as a Response to Organizational Interdependence." *Administrative Science Quarterly* 17:382–394.

Pfeffer, Jeffrey, and Nowak, P. 1976. "Joint Ventures and International Interdependence." *Administrative Science Quarterly* 21(3):398–418.

Pfeffer, Jeffrey, and Salancik, G.R. 1978. *The External Control of Organizations: A Resource Dependence Perspective.* New York: Harper & Row.

Picard, Jacques. 1977. "How European Companies Control Marketing Decisions Abroad." *Columbia Journal of Business,* Spring, pp. 113–121.

Pinder, Craig C., and Moore, Larry F. 1979. "The Resurrection of the Taxonomy to Aid the Development of Middle Range Theories of Organizational Behavior." *Administrative Science Quarterly* 24:99–118.

Pindyck, Robert S., and Rubinfeld, Daniel L. 1976. *Econometric Models and Economic Forecasts.* New York: McGraw-Hill.

Porter, Michael E. 1975. *Note on the Structural Analysis of Industries.* Intercollegiate Case Clearing House #9-376-054. Boston: ICCH.

———. 1976a. *Interbrand Choice, Strategy, and Bilateral Market Power.* Cambridge, Mass.: Harvard University Press.

———. 1976b. "Please Note Location of Nearest Exit: Exit Barriers and Strategic and Organizational Planning." *California Management Review,* Winter, pp. 21–33.

———. 1979a. "How Competitive Forces Shape Strategy." *Harvard Business Review* 57(2):137–145.

———. 1979b. "The Structure within Industries and Companies' Performance." *Review of Economics and Statistics* 60(May):214–227.

———. 1980. *Competitive Strategy: Techniques for Analyzing Industries and Competitors.* New York: Free Press.

Posner, R.A. 1981. "The Next Step in the Antitrust Treatment of Restricted Distribution: Per Se Legality." *University of Chicago Law Review* 48(1):6–26.

Qualls, David. 1972. "Concentration, Barriers to Entry, and Long Run Economic Profit Margins." *Journal of Industrial Economics,* April, pp. 146–158.

Quinn, J.B. 1980. *Strategies for Change: Logical Incrementalism.* Homewood, Ill.: Richard D. Irwin.

Rao, Ram, and Rutenberg, David P. 1980. "Preempting an Alert Rival: Strategic Timing of the First Plant by Analysis of Sophisticated Rivalry." *Bell Journal of Economics* 11(2):412–428.

Ray, Edward John. 1977. "Foreign Direct Investment in Manufacturing." *Journal of Political Economy* 85(2):283–297.

Reddy, J. 1980. "Incorporating Quality in Competitive Strategies. *Sloan Management Review,* Spring, pp. 53–60.

Riker, W.H. 1962. *The Theory of Political Coalitions.* New Haven, Conn.: Yale University Press.

Rogers, E., and Shoemaker, F.F. 1971. *Communications of Innovations.* New York: Free Press.

Rosenbluth, G. 1957. *Concentration in Canadian Manufacturing Industries.* Princeton, N.J.: Princeton University Press.

Rostow, W.W. 1977. *World Economy: History of Prospects.* Austin: University of Texas Press.

Rowe, F.W. 1980. "Antitrust Aspects of European Acquisitions and Joint Ventures in the United States." *Law and Policy in International Business* 12(2):335–368.

Rumelt, R.P. 1974. *Strategy, Structure and Economic Performance.* Boston: Division of Research, Graduate School of Business Administration, Harvard University.

Rumelt, Richard P., and Wensley, Robin. 1980. "In Search of the Market Share Effect." Working paper MGL-61, Graduate School of Management, University of California at Los Angeles, November 7.

Salter, M.S., and Weinhold, W.A. 1979. *Diversification through Acquisition: Strategies for Creating Economic Value.* New York: Free Press.

Schelling, Thomas C. 1960. *The Strategy of Conflict.* Cambridge, Mass.: Harvard University Press.

———. 1980. *Industrial Market Structure and Economic Performance.* Chicago: Rand McNally.

Schermerhorn, John R., Jr. 1975. "Determinants of Interorganizational Cooperation." *Academy of Management Journal* 18(December):846–956.

———. 1976. "Openness to Interorganizational Cooperation: A Study of Hospital Administrators." *Academy of Management Journal* 19(June):225–236.

———. 1977. Information Sharing as an Interorganizational Activity. *Academy of Management Journal* 20(3):148–153.

Schmalensee, Richard. 1976. "Advertising and Profitability: Further Implications of the Null Hypothesis." *Journal of Industrial Economics* 25(1):45–53.

———. 1978. "Entry Deterrence in the Ready-to-Eat Breakfast Cereal Industry." *Bell Journal of Economics* 8(2):305–327.

Schoeffler, S.; Buzzell, R.D.; and Heany, D.F. 1974. "Impact of Strategic Planning on Profit Performance. *Harvard Business Review* 52(2):137–145.

Selznick, Phillip. 1957. *Leadership in Administration: A Sociological Interpretation.* New York: Harper & Row.

Shepherd, William G. 1967. "What Does the Survivor Technique Show about Economies of Scale?" *Southern Economic Journal,* July, pp. 113–122.

———. 1972. "The Elements of Market Structure." *Review of Economics and Statistics,* February, pp. 25–37.

———. 1979. *The Economics of Industrial Organization.* Englewood Cliffs, N.J.: Prentice-Hall.

Shubik, Martin. 1959. *Strategy and Market Structure.* New York: Wiley.

Sichel, W. 1973. "Vertical Integration as a Dynamic Industry Concept." *Antitrust Bulletin* 18(2):463–482.

Simon, H.A., and Bonini, C.P. 1958. "The Size Distribution of Business Firms." *American Economic Review,* September, pp, 607–617.

Snow, C.C., and Hambrick, D.C. 1980. "Measuring Organizational Strategies: Some Theoretical and Methodological Problems." *Academy of Management Review* 5:527–533.

Spence, A. Michael. 1977. "Entry, Investment and Oligopolistic Pricing." *Bell Journal of Economics* 8(2):534–544.

———. 1979. "Investment Strategy and Growth in a New Market." *Bell Journal of Economics* 10(1):1–19.

Spengler, J.J. 1950. "Integration and Antitrust Policy." *Journal of Political Economy* 68(August):347–352.

Steiner, George A. 1969. *Top Management Planning.* New York: Collier-Macmillan.

Stigler, G.J. 1951. "The Division of Labor Is Limited by the Extent of the Market." *Journal of Political Economy* 59(3):185–193.

———. 1958. "The Economies of Scale." *Journal of Law and Economics,* October, pp. 54–71.

———. 1968. *The Organization of Industry.* Homewood, Ill.: Richard D. Irwin.

Stonebreaker, R.J. 1976. "Corporate Profits and the Risk of Entry." *Review of Economics and Statistics,* February, pp. 33–39.

Stopford, J.M., and Wells, L.T. 1972. *Managing the Multinational Enterprise.* New York: Basic Books.

Strategic Planning Associates. 1984. "Strategy and Shareholder Value: The Value Curve." In R. Lamb, *Competitive Strategic Management.* Englewood Cliffs, N.J.: Prentice-Hall, pp. 571–596.

Strebel, P.J. 1983. "The Stock Market and Competitive Analysis." *Strategic Management Journal* 4(3):279–292.

Sun Tzu. *The Book of War* (approx. 450 B.C.). Cited by Samuel B. Griffith, translater, in Mao Tse-Tung. 1961. *On Guerrilla Warfare.* New York: Praeger.

Suzman, C.L. 1969. "The Changing Export Activities of U.S. Firms with Foreign Manufacturing Affiliates. DBA thesis, Harvard Business School.

Talley, Walter J. 1964. "Profiting from Declining Products." *Business Horizons* 7(Spring):77–84.

Telser, L.G. 1972. *Competition, Collusion, and Game Theory.* New York: Aldine-Atherton.

Thompson, James D. 1967. *Organization in Action: Social Science Bases of Administrative Theory.* New York: McGraw-Hill.

Tilles, Seymour. 1966. "Strategies for Allocating Funds." *Harvard Business Review,* January–February.

Tractenberg, Paul. 1963. "Joint Ventures on the Domestic Front: A Study in Uncertainty." *The Antitrust Bulletin,* November–December,, pp. 797–841.

Treeck, Joachim. 1970. "Joint Research Ventures and Antitrust Law in the United States, Germany and the European Economic Community." *Journal of International Law and Politics* 3(1):18–55.

Tsurumi, Y. 1976. *The Japanese Are Coming.* Cambridge, Mass.: Ballinger.

Tucker, I.B., and Wilder, Ronald P. 1977. "Trends in Vertical Integration in the U.S. Manufacturing Sector." *Journal of Industrial Economics* 26 (September): 81–94.

U.S. Bureau of the Census. *Census of Manufacturers, 1973, 1977,* Washington, D.C.: U.S. Government Printing Office.

U.S. Department of Justice, Antitrust Division. 1981. "Antitrust Guide for Joint Research Programs." *Research Management* 24(20):30–37.

Utterback, James M., and Abernathy, William J. 1975. "A Dynamic Model of Product and Process Innovation." *Omega* 3(2).

Uyterhoeven, H.E.R.; Ackerman, R.W.; and Rosenblum, J.W. 1973. *Strategy and Organization: Text and Cases in General Management.* Homewood, Ill.: Richard D. Irwin.

Van de Ven, A.H. 1976. "On the Nature, Formation and Maintenance of Relations among Organizations." *Academy of Management Review* 1:24–36.

Vernon, John M. 1972. *Market Structure and Industrial Performance: A Review of Statistical Findings.* Boston: Allyn & Bacon.

Vernon, R. 1966. "International Investment and International Trade in the Product Cycle." *Quarterly Journal of Economics* 53(2):191–207.

———. 1971. *Sovereignty at Bay: The Multinational Spread of U.S. Enterprise.* New York: Basic Books.

———. 1977. *Storm over the Multinationals.* Cambridge, Mass.: Harvard University Press.

Vernon, Raymond, and Wells, Louis T., Jr. 1976. *Manager in the International Economy.* Englewood Cliffs, N.J.: Prentice-Hall.

Vitorovich, N. 1983. "How Companies Learn to Love Their Competitors." *The Wall Street Journal* (Europe), March 15, p. 23.

Von Neumann, J., and Morgenstern, O. 1944. *Theory of Games and Economics Behavior.* Princeton, N.J.: Princeton University Press.

Warren-Boulton, Frederick R. 1974. "Vertical Control with Variable Proportions." *Journal of Political Economy* 82(July–August):783–802.

Wasson, Chester R. 1974. *Dynamic Competitive Strategy and Product Life Cycles.* St. Charles, Ill.: Challenge Books.

Weiss, Leonard W. 1963. "Factors in Changing Concentration." *Review of Economics and Statistics* 45(February):70–77.

———. 1964. "The Survival Technique and the Extent of Suboptimal Capacity." *Journal of Political Economy,* June, pp. 246–261.

Wells, W.D. 1975. "Psychographics: A Critical Review." *Journal of Marketing Research* 12(May):196–213.

Wenders, J.T. 1971. "Collusion and Entry." *Journal of Political Economy,* November–December, pp. 1258–1277.

Wernerfelt, B., and Balakrishnan, S. 1984. "Competition, Technical Change and Vertical Integration." Paper presented at the Forty-fourth National Academy of Management Meetings, Dallas, August 15.

Wheelwright, S.C. 1981. "Japan—Where Operations Really Are Strategic." *Harvard Business Review* 59(4):67–74.

Wiek, J.L. 1969. "An Analysis of The Relation of Vertical Integration and Selected Attitudes and Behavioral Relationships in Competing Channel Systems." Ph.D. dissertation, Michigan State University.

Wilson, J.W. 1975. "Market Structure and Interfirm Integration in the Petroleum Industry." *Journal of Economic Issues* 9(2):319–336.

Wilson, T.A. 1975. "To Maintain the Aerospace Industry's Economic Health: Foreign Procurement, Technological Transfers and Joint Ventures." *Vital Speeches* 41(22):685–689.

Williamson, Oliver E. 1963. "Selling Expenses as a Barrier to Entry." *Quarterly Journal of Economics,* February, pp. 112–138.

———. 1969. "Allocation Efficiency and the Limits of Antitrust." *American Economic Review: Papers and Proceedings* 59:105–123.

———. 1971. "The Vertical Integration of Production: Market Failure Considerations." *American Economic Review* 61(May):112–123.

———. 1975. *Markets and Hierarchies.* New York: Free Press.

Woo, Carolyn, Y.Y. 1979. "Strategies of Effective Low Share Businesses." Ph.D. dissertation, Purdue University.

————. 1984. "Goals, Strategies and Financial Policies." Paper presented at Academy of Management Conference, Boston, August.

Woo, C.Y.Y., and Cooper, A.C. 1980. "Strategies of Effective Low Market Share Businesses." In R.C. Huseman, ed., *Proceedings*. Academy of Management National Conference.

————. 1982. "The Surprising Case for Low Market Share." *Harvard Business Review* 60(6):106–113.

Woodward, J. 1965. *Industrial Organization: Theory and Practice*. London, Oxford University Press.

Wright, Neil R. 1978. "Product Differentiation, Concentration and Changes in Concentration." *Review of Economics and Statistics* 60(November):628–631.

Wright, Richard W. 1977. "Canadian Joint Ventures in Japan," *Business Quarterly*, Autumn, pp. 42–53.

Wright, Richard W., and Russel, Colin S. 1975. "Joint Ventures in Developing Countries: Realities and Responses." *Columbia Journal of World Business* 10(Summer):74–80.

Yip, George S. 1982. *Barriers to Entry: A Corporate-Strategy Perspective*. Lexington, Mass.: Lexington Books, 1982.

Yoshino, M.Y. 1976. *Japan's Multinational Enterprise*. Cambridge, Mass.: Harvard University Press.

Young, G. Richard, and Bradford, Standish, Jr. 1976. "Joint Ventures in Europe—Determinants of Entry." *International Studies of Management and Organizations* 1–2(6):85–111.

Index

About the Author

Kathryn Rudie Harrigan (D.B.A., Harvard; M.B.A., Texas; B.A., Macalester) is an associate professor of strategic management at the Columbia Business School in New York City. Her research interests include industry and competitor analysis, strategic management, turnaround management, competitive dynamics, global strategies, and business-government relationships. Her books, *Strategies for Declining Businesses* (1980), *Strategies for Vertical Integration* (1983), and *Strategies for Joint Ventures* (1985), are published by Lexington Books.

Professor Harrigan received the General Electric Award for Outstanding Research in Strategic Management, presented by the Business Policy and Planning Division of the National Academy of Management, for her research on declining businesses, and their Best Paper Award in 1983 for her research on vertical integration (or make-or-buy decisions). She also won an IBM Research Fellowship in Business Administration and a Division of Research Fellowship at Harvard Business School.

Professor Harrigan has started and sold four businesses. Her consulting experience includes work on competitive strategy and strategic management for both private and public organizations. She has acted as consultant to strategic consulting firms, as well. She is a founding member of the Strategic Management Society and appears each autumn on their international programs.

Professor Harrigan writes for and serves on the boards of editors of the *Academy of Management Journal,* the *Strategic Management Journal,* and the *Journal of Business Strategy.* She is an ad hoc reviewer for and frequent contributor to the *Academy of Management Review.* Her articles have also appeared in the *Harvard Business Review, Long Range Planning, Boardroom Reports, Executive Woman,* and the *Proceedings* of the National and Regional Meetings of the Academy of Management.